CONTRACEPTION:
AUTHORITY AND DISSENT

CONTRACEPTION:
Authority and Dissent

Edited by Charles E. Curran

HERDER AND HERDER

1969
HERDER AND HERDER NEW YORK
232 Madison Avenue, New York, N.Y. 10016

Library of Congress Catalog Card Number: 69–18902

1492637

Contents

Contributors

ROBERT MCAFEE BROWN is professor of religion at Stanford University, Palo Alto, California. He is the author of *The Ecumenical Revolution*.

JOHN COULSON is a member of the faculty at Downside Abbey, Stratton on the Fosse, Bath, England, and the author of *The Common Tradition*.

CHARLES E. CURRAN is associate professor of moral theology at the School of Theology of The Catholic University of America, Washington, D.C., and the author of *A New Look at Christian Morality*.

BERNARD HÄRING is professor of moral theology at Academia Alfonsiana, Rome, Italy. He is the author of *Shalom, Peace: The Sacrament of Reconciliation*.

ANDRÉ E. HELLEGERS is professor of obstetrics and gynecology at Georgetown University Medical School, Washington, D.C.

JOSEPH A. KOMONCHAK is professor of dogmatic theology at St. Joseph's Seminary, Dunwoodie, Yonkers, New York.

DANIEL C. MAGUIRE is assistant professor of moral theology in the department of religious education at The Catholic University of America. He has contributed articles to *Commonweal*, *Cross Currents*, and *The Living Light*.

JOHN T. NOONAN, JR., is professor of law at the Law School of the University of California, Berkeley. He is the author of *Contraception*.

BRIAN TIERNEY is professor of medieval history at Cornell University, Ithaca, New York, and the author of *Foundations of the Conciliar Theory: Contribution of the Medieval Canonists*.

Introduction

The encyclical *Humanae Vitae* of Pope Paul has touched off many different reactions throughout the Roman Catholic world. Some bishops and theologians have adopted a position which excludes the possibility of dissenting from its practical conclusions. Other bishops and theologians alike have admitted that Catholics in full hierarchical and eucharistic communion with the Roman Church can disagree with the practical conclusions of the encyclical which absolutely condemns any form of artificial contraception as being illicit. All acknowledge that the encyclical and its aftermath have created a crisis in the Roman Catholic Church.

The contributors to this volume in general are arguing for the position that Roman Catholics may be loyal Catholics and still dissent from the practical conclusion of the encyclical that artificial contraception is always illicit. There is some difficulty with the word "dissent." A number of contributors did not want to employ the term in the title of the volume. "Dissent" tends to connote rebellion and disloyalty. The positions taken in this book in no way constitute disloyalty or revolt against the Roman Catholic Church. All the Roman Catholic contributors accept the office and function of the papacy and the hierarchical magisterium in the Church. The main purpose in publishing this volume is to show that disagreement with authoritative, non-infallible, papal teaching is itself a commonly accepted theological position.

Such dissent does not merely reduce the role of the papal teaching office to that of another theologian in the Church. Such dissent does not involve disrespect for the papal teaching office. No Catholic faithful or theologian can lightly dismiss the authoritative teaching of the papal or hierarchical teaching office in the Church. Great respect is due to such teaching. However, this does not mean that the teaching itself is always correct. The papal and hierarchical teaching offices must be seen in the whole context of a theology of the Church. A good theological analysis will avoid the two simplistic extremes: either saying that a loyal Catholic can never dissent from the authoritative, non-infallible magisterium or maintaining that the Pope is just another theologian in the Church.

The first part of the volume treats in an historical and theological perspective the question of the assent to be given by Catholics to the authoritative, non-infallible teachings of the hierarchical magisterium. The term "authentic, non-infallible magisterium" is of comparatively recent origin in the history of theology. However, the first three essays illustrate the fact that dissent from authoritative papal statements has a long and honorable tradition in Catholic theology and practice. The particular areas of disagreement illustrated in these three essays also cast light on the more important question of the theological reasoning behind such dissent. They also point up much of the tragedy and suffering which eventually occurs in such situations. The fourth essay, from an ecclesiological perspective, cites approved and accepted Catholic theologians of the past who have admitted the possibility of dissent in such circumstances; also the understanding of the Church in the documents of Vatican II indicates there are many other ways in addition to the hierarchical magisterium in which the Church teaches and learns. A final chapter indicates some of the elements that have contributed to an unbalanced understanding of the magisterium and of the way in which it functions. Thus the first part proves the assertion that it is common teaching in the Church that Catholics may dissent from authoritative, non-infallible teachings of the papal magisterium when sufficient reasons for so doing exist.

The second part of the volume examines the encyclical and its teaching from the various scientific viewpoints of moral theology, Protestant ecumenical theology, and medical science. The essays criticize the teachings of the encyclical in the light of these particular sciences. In recent years there have been many books and articles on the subject of contraception. A conscious effort was made to avoid repeating many of the arguments that have appeared earlier. For this reason many aspects of the question of contraception (for example, demographic, psychological, experiential) have not been included. We have also assumed that the reader is familiar with the historical development of the teaching on contraception in the Roman Catholic Church, the debates in Vatican II about responsible parenthood, and the majority and minority reports of the papal commission on responsible parenthood. The inadequacies and insufficiences of the reasoning employed in *Humanae Vitae* furnish sufficient reasons for the theologian to conclude that spouses may responsibly decide that artificial contraception in some circumstances is permissible and indeed necessary to preserve and foster the values and sacredness of marriage.

Note that nowhere in these pages is an appeal made to an argument based on the general principle of the freedom of conscience. Very frequently the terms "freedom of conscience" and "rights of conscience" have been employed in the debate about the encyclical. A lack of precision in the use of these terms can create unnecessary confusion in the theological order. In fact, it appears as if some have purposely invoked the rights of conscience in order to permit pastoral disagreement from the conclusions of the encyclical while not contradicting in theory the conclusions of the encyclical.

Scholastic theologians have traditionally distinguished various types of conscience although not all have agreed on the terminology. The problem arises from the tension between the subjective pole of morality and the objective pole; or the

11

tension between freedom and truth. (Theologians today are trying to overcome the dichotomies inherent in these terms.) Conscience is true (*vera*) if it corresponds to the objective order; conscience is erroneous (*erronea*) if it does not correspond to the objective order. A sincere conscience (*conscientia recta*) is a conscience which is subjectively formed in the proper way, but which may be erroneous. Again note that I am using conscience here in the restricted sense of the scholastics as the judgment of practical reason. There is no problem about the case of the true and sincere conscience. The problem arose in Catholic theology about the sincere but erroneous conscience. Theologians generally admit that the sincere but invincibly erroneous conscience (sometimes called the erroneous conscience in good faith) must be followed by the individual. However, a conscience which is vincibly erroneous cannot be followed as a legitimate subjective norm of action without some guilt on the part of the subject.

Properly to appraise statements about the rights of conscience by people speaking in the context of the scholastic idiom, it is necessary to be familiar with the above distinctions. My personal viewpoint as expressed in these categories is that the conscientious decision to use contraception can come from a true and sincere conscience. Statements by some bishops and theologians indicate that a Catholic's decision to use contraception can only come from a sincere but erroneous conscience. In that case, the error on the part of the person might be invincible. Others would maintain that now that the Pope has spoken such a conscientious decision would be vincibly erroneous and could not be followed without incurring moral guilt.

My conclusion that contraception in some circumstances may be good and even necessary for married couples is not based on a universal moral principle of the rights and freedom of conscience. Moral theology or Christian ethics knows no such universal principle expressed without any nuances and qualifications. In fact, such an unnuanced universal principle would destroy the possibility of moral theology which among other things tries to point out what is the good, right, or fitting thing to do.

Students of theology are familiar with other attempts in history to explain away papal teaching. The most famous instance is the introduction of the distinction between thesis and hypothesis by Bishop Dupanloup to explain away the rigoristic condemnations in the "Syllabus of Errors" of Pius IX. Dupanloup employed the distinction between thesis and hypothesis to say that the Pope was speaking in terms of the thesis or the ideal and not in terms of the hypothesis which is based on the present historical circumstances. There seem to be some similar approaches being used today concerning *Humanae Vitae*. The attitude which accepts the teaching of the encyclical but also insists on the inviolability of conscience can easily be such an approach. However, in the scholastic terminology, this is a case of a sincere and invincibly erroneous conscience. There would still exist the obligation on the part of all in the Church to lead that person to the truth and overcome such an erroneous conscience.

Another attempt to soften the encyclical on the pastoral level is based on the distinction between the objective order and the subjective order. Although contraception is always gravely illicit, artificial contraception does not always involve subjectively grave sin on the part of the person. The distinction between the two orders does have a foundation in Catholic theology. However, it appears that some statements on the encyclical are extending such a distinction beyond its intent. Simply to say that couples should not refrain from eucharistic participation and communion if they are using artificial contraception is not to do full justice to all that is involved in the traditional distinction between the objective order and the subjective order.

Such attempts to soften the conclusions of the encyclical

13

are admirable from the viewpoint of pastoral concern. However, like many practical solutions to difficult problems, they seem to involve some inconsistencies in trying to maintain the truth of the papal teaching and allow some room for the individual in practice to use artificial contraception. Such pastoral solutions might help solve the perplexed conscience of the individual person, but they do nothing to alleviate, and in fact ultimately perpetuate, the social problems connected with overpopulation in many parts of the globe. For the sake of truth and the best interests of the Church and all mankind, I have concluded that it is necessary to take the more radical solution which maintains that the papal teaching on this point is in error.

The crisis caused by such public dissent from the papal teaching has undoubtedly caused much tension in the Church. There is no doubt that the authority of the papal teaching office has suffered because of *Humanae Vitae* and the ensuing discussion. However, a proper understanding of the possibility of such dissent in the Church should ultimately enhance the claim of the Church as the pillar of truth as well as make the teaching of the Church more credible in the future. If people realize that such authoritative papal teachings do not demand absolute assent and that Catholics have a responsibility to respond to such teachings, truth and the credibility of the Church's teaching are better served.

The present crisis in the Church obviously shows the need for a better understanding of what some theologians claim to be a common teaching in the Church. Also there is an urgent need for the teaching authority of the Church to be exercised in a different manner. Even the canon law of the Middle Ages taught that the pope cannot be considered apart from the Church itself, and he is even limited by the Church. Vatican II has already admitted in theory that there are many ways in which the Church teaches and learns—the experience of all men of good will, the lives and teachings of other Christians

14

as well as non-Christians, the prophetic office in the Church, the Holy Spirit dwelling in the hearts of all men of good will. There are other magisteria or teaching offices in the Church in addition to the hierarchical and papal magisterium. The Church today needs to restructure its ways of teaching and learning so that teaching proclaimed in the name of the Church truly speaks for the Church. Such a restructuring cannot aim at a mere majority consensus but rather at a discernment of the Spirit through the many ways in which the Spirit can teach the Church. I hope that these essays and their loyal dissent will contribute to such a better understanding, in theory, and a restructuring, in practice, of the ways in which the Roman Catholic Church, in hierarchical and eucharistic communion with the Roman pontiff, teaches and learns.

CHARLES E. CURRAN

PART ONE

PAPAL MAGISTERIUM
AND THE INDIVIDUAL CATHOLIC

JOHN COULSON LIVING WITH AUTHORITY—
THE NINETEENTH CENTURY

The very conception of the Catholic Church as a world-wide and self-determining body is a political one. You cannot claim to exercise a universal witness and to determine that what you say is in conformity both with your past decisions and with the sense of the Church at present throughout the world without finding yourself in the midst of a problem about authority. But although Catholics have, by virtue of such a conception of the Church, to live with authority this does not imply that they must indiscriminately tolerate all its actions.

The polarities of potential conflict have been crudely defined as between clergy and laity, because the Church has always conceived the world as being, in the words of the fifth-century Pope Gelasius I, ruled over by two powers or authorities—the pontiffs and the kings. As temporal society became based upon an explicit Christian confession, this distinction was used to justify the submission of one authority to the other—the spiritual order succeeded in confiscating the temporal—and early struggles to hold a due discrimination between clerical and lay were stigmatized by Pope Boniface VIII, for example, as "wickedness" and "disobedience." In his bull *Unam Sanctam*, of 1302, he refers to the distinction between the two authorities in order to claim that both are "in the power of the Church: the one, indeed, to be wielded for the Church, the other by the Church: the one by the hand of the priest, the other by the hand of kings and knights, but at the will and sufferance of the priest."

It is this claim—that clerical and lay, Church and state,

theology and philosophy must be held in an integral synthesis —which is at the heart of the medieval vision and of its order. It was the norm to which the nineteenth-century papacy struggled to return and by which its hostile reaction to the counter-claim made by the Liberal Catholics was determined. This was that the world we were moving into was one of distinctions and discriminations, of plurality rather than uniformity, and that its moral order was based not upon simple obedience but upon the rights and duties of a free conscience.

This counter-claim, that conscience is free, and its resistance particularly by the higher clergy, will be found at the root of many early crises in the Church. St. Joan, for example, asserts that her obedience to the Church was not absolute but conditional upon "Our Lord being first served"—a phrase and a condition she repeats simply and firmly throughout her trial. When she was accused of refusing to listen to the voice of God by refusing to conform "to the words and opinions of the university of Paris and other doctors," she replied that the ultimate court of appeal was not the Church on earth, but the Church in heaven. But at the heart of the contemporary misunderstanding of St. Joan was her insistence that civil peace and justice were rights which the Church must not only tolerate but strive for. The medieval Church could understand such a political struggle only if it were for the rights of the papacy—the Crusaders had no difficulty in securing a papal blessing. What it did not understand was how a political mission for a purely secular end—the ejecting of a corrupt, occupying power from France—could be said to emanate from God.

The question which is provoked by the struggle for liberty of conscience is to what extent the lay world may develop independently of detailed ecclesiastical control. This is the source of many celebrated and still unsettled disputes such as that, for example, about usury. Medieval capitalists employed theologians to lobby support in the universities for the proposal that to charge interest on transactions between merchants was lawful; and Bellarmine complained that even in the seventeenth-century, pious merchants were still propounding complex economic problems in the confessional. It took even longer to question the assumption that details of economic conduct belong to the province of the ecclesiastical jurist; and a similar kind of claim still affects the stability of political life in Catholic countries. Leo XIII, for example, condemned what nowadays we know as nationalization as contrary to natural law. With usury, as with other similar matters, positions which the facts have made untenable are no longer manned; ineffective clerical condemnation is silently eroded; but the claim is never retracted—"He who takes usury goes to hell; and he who does not goes to the workhouse." The paradox is unresolved.

It is not until the nineteenth century that we find the suggestion that when the Church is obliged to modify its position in the face of the facts, this should be explicitly recognized for what it is—a development of doctrine—rather than passed over in silence. And even in the nineteenth century it took nerve to shatter the silence. The first to do so had been Galileo; and from his trial emerges a principle with a much wider application than to the matter which occasioned it—whether a scientific theory may be permitted to contradict existing interpretations of Scripture. What is sometimes overlooked is how serious the implications of Galileo's theory seemed for "the simple faithful"; since, if the earth were not the center of the universe, it was no longer favored beyond other planets; and to threaten the status of his planet was to threaten the status of man. Galileo's argument, as put forward in his *Letter to the Grand Duchess Christina*, is still unfortunately highly relevant. It rests upon distinguishing between ecclesiastical competence to pronounce on those truths necessary to salvation, and that unlimited claim to pronounce which is as if "an absolute despot, being neither a physician nor

21

an architect but knowing himself free to command should undertake to administer medicines and erect buildings according to his whim." If a layman produces a theory or explanation of the natural order, the only ground for condemnation is if it can be shown "to be not rigorously demonstrated"—that is, if it is contradictory or otherwise inconsistent with its criteria. Thus, although Galileo concedes that the supreme pontiff has the power "to admit or condemn" propositions which are not "directly *de fide*," "it is in the power of no creature whatever to make them true or false, otherwise than they are *de facto*." Galileo's claim was interpreted correctly (and condemned) by his judges as limiting clerical authority to general principles which have to do with faith and morals, and as freeing the layman's investigation of the physical universe from detailed theological guidance *a priori*.

This claim is still at issue; and nowhere has the alternative —acquiescence in a process of silent erosion—been more thoroughly practiced than in attitudes to marriage. Early writers treat marriage as one of the consequences of original sin and distinguish between pure and mixed love—the former never terminating in carnal union and therefore less offensive to God and less damaging to husband and wife. Not only is there no place for pure love in marriage, but in the pleasure which married people take in each other there is the risk of concupiscence. So wrote Andreas Capellanus in the twelfth century. The wife of the Chevalier de la Tour Landry says that it is better for a girl not to fall in love, even with her betrothed, otherwise piety will suffer. Where marriage is solely for procreation, wives are expendable; and a pure love which is—in theory—reserved for God may be reserved in practice for an idealized and courtly lover—the rise of courtly love (and adultery) may be an inevitable byproduct of such teaching. What is more important is to realize that an adequate consideration of marriage has to wait for the *political* emancipation of women.

Medieval people were robust, and did not allow their natural instincts to be much inhibited by theology. There is no treatise on the Church in its modern sense as the body of all believers before 1300—there was little need for it as long as there were men like Robert Grosseteste who claimed the right to disobey the pope *filialiter* and *obedienter* ("*Filialiter et obedienter non obedio, contradico, et rebello*"). But in a less robust and more submissive age, obedience is readier, provided authority is prepared to present its credentials for rational inspection. The claim to hold all details of life now and hereafter in an ordered synthesis could not survive the pressure of intellectual investigation to free itself from *a priori* control; and the breakup of the medieval order was both inevitable and desirable. But it is only when a political separation of lay from clerical authority occurs that it becomes possible to work out how the authority of the Church may be justly imposed without abuse. For as long as the political and ecclesiastical structures were interdependent, freedom of conscience was for the few who were prepared to be martyred for it; and the temporal remained confiscated by the spiritual.

It is thus the *political* separation of Church and State wrought by the French Revolution which lays the foundation for all subsequent attempts to discriminate theologically between "the two orders or authorities," and to determine the appropriate range of each. From it arises that general tendency known as Liberal Catholicism, whose birth certificate was the publication by de Lamennais (in association with Lacordaire and Montalambert) of the periodical *L'Avenir*, which first appeared in October, 1830. It had for its motto "God and Liberty."

De Lamennais, who has been compared to Karl Marx for his prophetic power to read the signs of the times, wrote the

23

agenda for Liberal Catholicism: the end of the temporal power of the papacy, and the consequent issue of the extent and nature of the pope's spiritual authority culminating in the decree on infallibility of 1870; the rise of representative democracy, its recognition as an inalienable right, and the effect of this upon the traditional pattern of Church and state relations. But the dominating issue remained that of liberty of conscience. The authority of the pope was conceived as being intended to help not the rulers, but the emerging people against the tyranny of their oppressors. Leo XII was so impressed by de Lamennais's ultramontane assertion of papal prerogatives that he almost decided to make him a cardinal; but his successor, Gregory XVI, preferred to let his authority rest upon temporal alliances with princes; and he condemned de Lamennais in the encyclicals *Mirari Vos* (1832) and *Singulari Nos* (1834), speaking of the wild license of opinion and speech and the lack of a due submission to authority which such teachings encouraged. With particular emphasis he condemned "an absolute liberty of conscience." De Lamennais reviewed his position, and left the Church, never to return.

Thus collapsed the first attempt to bring the Church into relation with modern or post-Revolutionary society. The second and more critical encounter, which involved Newman and Acton, was to take place during the pontificate of Pius IX. The issues are the same—the legitimate range and extent of ecclesiastical authority and of papal authority in particular, and the rights of conscience and therefore of the laity in relation to these institutional forms and claims.

Acton's development of de Lamennais's position constitutes a major contribution to the philosophy of political liberty, its best known expression being his Inaugural Lecture as Regius Professor of History at Cambridge; but it also took the form of an attempt to establish freedom of speech within the Church, particularly during the years 1858–1864 which mark the period of his association with *The Rambler* and the *Home and Foreign Review*.

For Acton, as for de Lamennais, the idea of freedom is the ultimate consequence of the acceptance of the Christian faith by the ancient world. Pre-Christian society, since it was both Church and State in one, tended to absolutism; and it lacked, therefore, representative government and liberty of conscience. But when Christ said, "Render unto Caesar the things which are Caesar's and to God the things which are God's," the civil power was both divinely sanctioned and circumscribed; and with the repudiation of absolutism comes the inauguration of freedom, since not only does our Lord deliver the precept, but he creates in the Catholic Church the force to execute it. "To reduce all political authority within defined limits," wrote Acton, "ceased to be an aspiration of patient reasoners, and was made the perpetual charge and care of the most energetic institution and the most universal association in the world."

Although such freedom may not be the deliberate aim of Church and State, it arises out of their collision as when, for example, the only power capable of resisting the feudal hierarchy was the ecclesiastical. But the germs of the doctrine may be seen at work as the idea grows that man has a right to the unhindered fulfilment of his duty to God; but it is not, significantly, until after the Reformation and under the aegis of Protestant thinkers such as Milton, Taylor, Baxter, and Locke that it is recognized that religious liberty is the generating principle of civil liberty, which is in turn the necessary condition of religious liberty.

The associated principle is that of the freedom of conscience. Since directly it is accepted that the knowledge of good and evil derives from something more than the laws and customs of a particular society, then the sovereign voice within is heard above the expressed will and settled custom of surrounding men: conscience limits power. Whereas medieval men were taught to distrust conscience when it was their own and trust it only in others, by the mid-seventeenth century it could be asserted that the greatest of all sins was to go against conscience, and that liberty of conscience was England's greatest good. Since, for Acton, the crucial factors in contemporary experience were liberty of conscience and the political freedom of the individual, he spoke of himself as being preoccupied with those problems which lie "on the wavy line" between Church and State. Perpetually and inevitably in conflict, they could only remain true to their respective roles if they were permanently separated. A union of Church and State would produce that most dangerous of absolutisms—a State whose demands possess a perpetual religious sanction, or a Church whose temporal connections cause it to interfere perpetually in those matters which are within the competence of the laity. The principle of the separation of Church and State admits that a man's allegiance can never be completely absorbed by one institution; and it is this which makes possible the emergence of his sense of individual identity and liberty of conscience.

Such views obliged Acton to distinguish his ideal of the Catholic Church from its reality not only in the past but, what was even more dangerous for the editor of a Catholic review, in the present. He was especially critical of the temporal claims of the papacy, and it is towards these that his celebrated maxim about power is directed. In trying to maintain their spiritual independence by developing their temporal power, the early popes had created and extended the papal states, and formed the complicated network of temporal alliances. Acton believed that the Reformation was precipitated by the higher view of the papal monarchy in spirituals that grew with the papal monarchy in temporals; and he saw the papal claim to temporal power as responsible for the absolute nature of its claim to spiritual power. The continuing exercise of temporal power produced a moral insensitivity and degeneration which could be seen at work in papal policy in spiritual matters: power tends to corrupt, absolute power corrupts absolutely. The particular form taken by such corruptions was that the end justifies the means; and Acton isolated the medieval Inquisition and the popes who fostered it as "the breaking point, the article in their system by which they stand or fall." To accept any extenuation for such offenders and offenses was, as he puts in his Inaugural, to debase the moral currency. It is to imply that Christianity is "a mere system of metaphysics which borrowed some ethics from elsewhere."

As society comes to understand that there is a fuller justice than that which is embodied and administered through the existing legal system, so it chooses to protect the right to pursue this justice: and that is the basis for granting the rights to freedom of conscience, thought, and speech. Acton's position and its bearing upon the problems of authority within the Church might be summarised thus: The religious consequences of the idea of freedom oblige the Catholic layman to understand that he has not only the right but the duty in conscience to speak out on all matters of Church policy which appear to be ones of moral principle. Thus free speech in the Church is not only a right but a duty, since it is part of the general process by which the moral refinement of the Church's authority from its origins historically in temporal power is achieved.

These were the attitudes which informed Acton's conduct as editor of *The Rambler* and *Home and Foreign Review*, and they account for the uncompromising tone which his fellow Catholics found so objectionable. It was tragically inevitable that a fatal collision with authority would occur, since the issues of the moment were ones as fundamental as mixed education, the temporal power of the papacy and papal infallibility—issues which an editor less conscientious than Acton could not have avoided. In the ten years from 1860–1870, the

27

papal states were invaded (1860), the Vatican Council was assembled and promulgated the dogma of papal infallibility (1870), and the Pope withdrew under protest into the Vatican to become, in the language of his supporters, its prisoner.

By the 1870's Acton was a defeated man. His efforts to establish freedom of speech within the Church had suffered three defeats, each of deepening catastrophe. In 1859 he had been obliged to hand over the conduct of *The Rambler* to Newman after publishing articles on Catholic education which the English bishops threatened to condemn; but a more serious threat arose in 1864.

In 1863 the historian Döllinger had called a Congress in Munich to make yet another attempt to bring the Church into relation to modern thought, particularly in the historical field. A telegram of good wishes had been sent to Pius IX, but the papal reply, when it arrived six months later, took the form of a Brief Addressed to the Archbishop of Munich, and re-emphasised the need for an entire obedience to the decrees of the Roman congregations. Although not denying the distinctions between dogma and opinion, it reduced them almost to nothing; and it asserted that the common opinions of Catholic theologians ought not to yield to the progress of the secular sciences but ought at all times to be controlled by the decrees of the Index and the doctrinal decisions of the Roman congregations. Newman thought it to be the Galileo case all over again, since in his opinion the Brief insisted that Catholic scholars and scientists must keep theological conclusions before them while treating of their respective sciences.

Believing that such a policy made it impossible to conduct a scholarly periodical of any integrity, Acton brought the *Home and Foreign Review* to an end in a final article entitled "Conflicts with Rome." The measure of the general loss may best be gauged from Matthew Arnold's valedictory notice: "Perhaps in no organ of criticism in this country was there so much knowledge, so much play of mind; but these could not save it: the *Dublin Review* subordinates play of mind to the practical business of English and Irish Catholicism, and lives."

The climax was reached in 1870 at the Vatican Council when the pope's infallibility was declared. Acton had been one of the leading "inopportunists"; and he even spoke of himself as fearing assassination by the Jesuits. That he was not excommunicated, as he expected, was because he was a layman, a peer, and Gladstone's intimate friend. He survived his collisions with ecclesiastical authority because he was protected by political freedoms gained and maintained by Protestants; but he died believing the papacy, in its temporal and curial form, to be "the fiend skulking behind the crucifix." The issues he raised remained theologically unresolved; but his achievement is to place de Lamennais's prophetic vision into a thorough historical perspective, by showing how the political emancipation of the laity must be the precondition for their spiritual emancipation, and for bringing the Church into relationship with modern society.

It is Newman's achievement to give theological form to issues thus resolved, and by doing so, to anticipate the agenda and acts of the Second Vatican Council. Newman's life, like Acton's, was a series of mounting conflicts with authority. The first occurred in 1859 after he had taken over, at the request of his bishop, the editorship of *The Rambler* from Acton and his collaborator Simpson in order to preserve what he regarded as an essential means of raising the level of Catholic thought and education. He conducted it in such a way as to make his own downfall inevitable, because he made two assumptions: that Catholics believed the Church to be a developing organism rather than a static system; and that, therefore, in order to determine the nature and correctness of its developing life, the authorities of the Church were anxious to consult the plentitude of its witness among the faithful. If the mind of the Church were to be accurately and adequately gauged, then it was right and proper that the faithful

29

witness of priests and laity should be consulted by authority, especially "in the case of doctrines which bear directly upon devotional sentiments." This was because such consultation adds a dimension to authority's understanding of the mind of the Church, since "there is something in the pastorum et fidelium *conspiratio* which is not in the pastors alone." Furthermore the association of the laity with the pastorate or ecclesia docens is better for the Church, which "is more happy when she has such enthusiastic partisans about her . . . , than when she cuts off the faithful from the study of her divine doctrines . . . and requires from them a fides implicita in her word, which in the educated classes will terminate in indifference and in the poorer in superstition."

Directly Newman printed such remarks in his *Rambler* article, "On Consulting the Faithful in Matters of Doctrine," [1] he discovered himself violently opposed and delated to Rome on a charge of heresy. His conception of the mind of the Church was far too wide for current tastes, which preferred to keep authority narrowed down upon the papacy and the higher clergy.

This "creeping infallibility" or tightening up of authority at the top increased relentlessly until 1914, and the Vatican Council was called in 1870 to strengthen that authority by defining it. For Newman this was "the climax of tyranny" and "thunder out of a clear sky." Unnecessary and potentially harmful, it was likely to increase difficulties rather than resolve them, by giving rise to inevitable misrepresentations. These were brought to a head by Gladstone's challenge that papal infallibility was incompatible with political freedom. Newman's reply, in the teeth of those who wished to *maximalize* the pope's authority, insisted that such authority was best met "with a wise and gentle *minimism*"; and in his "Letter to the

1. *On Consulting the Faithful in Matters of Doctrine,* John Henry Newman, edited with an introduction by John Coulson (New York, 1961), pp. 104, 106.

Duke of Norfolk" he grasped the nettle firmly by asking whether it could be our right in conscience to deny an *ex cathedra* pronouncement by the pope. He quotes Bellarimine to the effect that the pope's authority may be lawfully resisted if he assaults a man's person, or his soul, or "troubles the state," or "tries to destroy the Church"; and he notes that some theologians have held that a pope, should he teach heresy, ceases *ipso facto* to be pope. When theologians claim that to say what has been infallibly defined requires skilful interpretation, they are not compromising the authority of the pope, since "this is a real exercise of private judgement and an allowable one." Nor do the rights of conscience have to be reasserted, since they are assumed from the start; and Newman answers Gladstone by saying that he gives an absolute obedience neither to the queen nor the pope. If he has to drink a toast, it will be to conscience first, and to the pope afterwards.

Such sentiments were not well received in Rome; and before he died Newman made a final effort to define and distinguish the modes and functions of authority within the Church. He does so by drawing out the consequences of that ancient tradition which speaks of the Church as fulfilling the offices of Christ as prophet, priest, and king. "Christianity is at once a philosophy, a political power and a religious rite. . . . As a religion its special centre of action is pastor and flock, as a philosophy the schools, as a rule the papacy and its curia." The originality of Newman's insight lies in the extent to which he accepts the tendency of each office naturally to encroach upon the other. The abuse of authority is therefore an inevitable condition of the structure of Catholic Christianity. The prophetical office exercised through theologians will tend to degenerate into rationalism; the priestly office through the abuses of devotion into superstition; and the kingly office through the abuse of power into ambition and tyranny. If such abuses are inevitable, then by which office is the life of the Church regulated? The answer given by Newman's contemporaries and not seriously questioned until Vatican II was that the Church is regulated by papal authority imposed upon an obedient clergy and laity. Newman's answer is that in the end it is the prophetical office, as it is exercised by theology, which is "the fundamental and regulating principle of the whole Church system." It is "commensurate with Revelation, and Revelation is the essential idea of Christianity. It is the subject matter, the formal cause, the expression of the Prophetical office and as being such has created both the Regal office and the sacerdotal. And it has in a certain sense a power of jurisdiction over those offices, as being its own creations." It is the task of the theologians to keep within bounds the political and popular elements of the Church's constitution which, because they are far more congenial than theology to the human mind, are always attempting to liberate themselves from its restraints, which are, however, "necessary for their well being."

For Newman, therefore, although living with authority is a necessary condition of Catholic Christianity, it does not supersede conscience, but assumes it as its foundation. And obedience to the Church is not the automatic response exacted by a totalitarian principality, but an ever anxious, and complex affirmation—a prayerful, reverent, but reflective waiting upon the Spirit which is the ultimate regulating factor of the Church.

In the next crisis in the relations of the Church to the modern world it is von Hügel who is Newman's spiritual inheritor. This, the so-called Modernist movement, was more an ethos or the slow dawning of a general critical tendency than an organized movement. Among its pioneers were the French biblical scholar, Alfred Loisy, the English convert Jesuit George Tyrrell, and Baron Friedrich von Hügel. Not only did it arise from within theology, but it adopted a specifically Catholic standpoint: the spirit of Christ dwelt and could be known only within the community which had arisen from his teachings; and the language of Scripture and religion could be understood and verified only within that collective memory and continuing experience. Such was the standpoint from which these scholars prepared a Catholic reply to the new, liberal Protestant biblical criticism. It was soon realized that the theory of the development of doctrine advanced by Möhler in Germany and Newman in England was crucial to this position; but, from the start, the factor in Modernist thinking which was to lead Loisy to abandon the Church and Tyrrell to believe that it was irreformable was, by our standards, an uncritical progressivism. Leaning somewhat too naïvely upon Darwin, the Modernists came to believe that "whereas formerly religious men had thought that truth in its most perfect form had lain in the past, they were now led to think that the more perfect form lay in the future." [2] The future seemed in this sense more knowable than the past; and it is but a step to Loisy's dangerously circular definition of the Church: that it has become what it has become in order to live. The Church is true because it works; if it works, then it is true; but what if it fails to work, to adapt and to reform?

The movement, such as it was, raised difficulties of verification, the status of symbolic language, the relationship between the Jesus of history and the Jesus of the Church, which in other disciplines are no more than part of the give and take of university life. But in a Church whose ways of thinking and devotion had become dangerously removed from their primary sources in Scripture, such questions broke with the same force as those raised by Galileo; and it was inevitable that the Modernists would be condemned. What is important for an understanding of our present position is the manner of their condemnation. Passages were taken out of context, reduced to propositional form, and in scholastic manner fitted together to form an heretical counter-system. This was pub-

2. *Baron Friedrich von Hügel, Selected Letters 1896–1924* (London, 1928), p. 15.

lished as a syllabus of errors in a decree, *Lamentabili sane exitu*, in July, 1907, to be followed up in September by the encyclical *Pascendi Dominici Gregis*. Questions or speculative deliberations had been reduced to assertions so crude that they answered themselves, such as that "the Christ of History is far inferior to the Christ who is the object of faith," or "dogmas, sacraments and hierarchy, both their notion and reality, are only interpretations and evolutions of the Christian intelligence," and "Modern Catholicism can be reconciled with true science only if it is transformed into a non-dogmatic Christianity; that is to say, into a broad and liberal Protestantism."

Because argument had been answered not by counter-argument, but by oversimplified counter-assertions, the encyclical was obliged to treat the actual form of Modernist writing—"without order and systematic arrangement in a scattered and dis-jointed manner"—as evidence of bad faith and "a clever device" to conceal the "fixed and steadfast" nature of a plot against the Church.

In bringing theological discussion to an end in this way, the Pope had acted, so Tyrrell-considered, as if he were above rather than within the Church. *L'église, c'est moi* seems to be his attitude, he wrote. "The pope is the steam engine; the episcopate is the carriages; the faithful are the passengers"; and all that remains to the layman (or, it appears, the theologian) is "to pay his fare and take his seat as so much ballast in the bark of Peter, while the clergy pull him across the ferry."

The condemnation was reinforced by attempts to revive the Inquisition, a total obedience from the clergy being exacted by test oaths, espionage, and secret delation. Loisy abandoned the Church. Tyrrell stuck it out—to be excommunicated and refused Catholic burial. The laity—in the person of von Hügel —were protected as Acton had been previously by the political liberties gained and maintained by their separated brethren.

34

But there was more to von Hügel's survival than this. Although he describes the Church as having become a prison for the intellect, and of himself as being held within an iron vice, von Hügel also affirms its authority, speaking of it as his hair-shirt. When the Cross is planted right into our intellectual life, if we accept it, we grow; since our knowledge of God is always circumscribed by "what he is to us and in us." Von Hügel pleads with Tyrrell, therefore, to fight indifference as well as bigotry, by not taking his own good faith or the integrity of his motives in searching for the light too much as a matter of course. Just before the condemnation he wrote that survival lay in dampening down "cleverness as distinct from wisdom, clearness as distinct from depth, logic as distinct from operativeness, simplicity as distinct from life."

These are the authentic accents of that Catholic humanism which went underground at the Reformation; but they are also the accents of Newman, as Von Hügel admitted. "It was he who first taught me to glory in my appurtenance to the Catholic and Roman Church"; and it was Newman who taught him to conceive religion in its three dimensions, of which what von Hügel called "the institutional element" was fundamental. Without it religion evaporated into a baseless mysticism or into arid and refutable rationalism. It became less vivid, less concentrated. "The history of religion," he wrote, "teaches us that it needs to be developed socially . . . a simple mental cultus is too brainy for mere man." He conceived the Church to be a mystery we cannot penetrate but only respond to, a slow growth across the centuries in which all the good and true were mixed up with error and with evil in a never-ending process of self-determination, whose ultimate purpose was to hold "the greatest possible multiplicity in the deepest possible unity." Yet the "costingness" and pain of bringing this to birth within the confines of an institutional Church Von Hügel spoke of as his "greatest teacher." His writings are full of images of what to do when confronted by this mystery of the Church's double aspect, when authority seems tyranny, and worship, superstition: we must be like the mountaineer caught in a thick mist—sit quietly, smoke a pipe, and wait for the mist to lift.

It is this prayerful detachment which distinguishes von Hügel from those who were broken in the Modernist crisis and its aftermath. Many had been so conditioned to a simple submissive obedience that when a more mature conception of membership was demanded of them they panicked and thought themselves to be no longer Christians.

The idiosyncrasies of the Modernists arose as much from their situation as from conviction: they were a handful of men who came before their time. As such they could be isolated, pinned down, and condemned. The general effect of the condemnations was further to narrow the magisterium upon the papacy at the expense of the bishops, who became little more than papal delegates or, in the words of one contemporary, mitred sacristans. As shepherds they seemed more afraid of their own sheep dogs than of the wolves outside the fold.

The authority of the Church became marginal to the general concerns of society; and it was once again upheavals and revolutions external to the Church which forced this recognition by increasing those pressures to which the Modernists had testified. The outbreak of the First World War, the apocalyptic nature of its destruction, and the unparalleled number of casualties cut the disputes between ecclesiastics down to size. In 1914 the liturgical scholar Edmund Bishop wrote of the futile, dead, self-centered spirit and atmosphere of religious life which the War now revealed. It showed how much "futility and make-believe are of the essence of the 'mind' that dominates in our 'Church.'" And he wrote of the War, "One needs to go to the Apocalypse to find imagery in which to express the truths of the fight we are in the midst of."

The war exposed the optimistic naïveté of the Modernists more ruthlessly and finally than had ecclesiastical authority, but equally it exposed the pretensions of that authority to impose effective solutions. "What passing-bells for those who die as cattle?" cried the war poet Wilfrid Owen; and out of the battle came a moral priority in which genocide and total warfare seemed issues of a different order from arguments about the nature of the conjugal act or whether modernism was a conspiracy. In Catholic countries an even sharper *crise de conscience* occurred in the second world war when that distinction for which St. Joan was martyred—between an acquiescent piety and the duty to resist corruption—was learned upon the pulse of the resistance to Nazi Occupation. Pius XII was as unable to halt the slaughter of the Jews as Benedict XV had been able to bring the earlier holocaust to an end by negotiation; but an authority which claims submissive obedience yet has to allow expedience to determine when it will speak and when it will remain silent cannot survive unchanged; and the wars, with their promises of increased political liberty, made the holding of another Vatican Council both necessary and inevitable. The laity, in the form of the world's press, broke in upon the council; and popular concern thwarted those who had expected to manage, by confining, its deliberations in the manner of 1870. And it was the mass media of communication—the fruits of yet another revolution external to the Church—which kept the council open.

It was inevitable that the balance of authority within the Church would be reappraised; and the papal style of John XXIII, together with the pre-eminence subsequently given to the *Constitution on the Church*, were taken as confirming this expectation. The consequences for papal authority were thought to be that the pope could no longer act as if outside the Church, but only as participating in the infallibility of the whole people of God: "There are not three infallibilities, of the *sensus fidei* in the body of the faithful, of the episcopal college, and of the pope. There is the single infallible Church, exercising its infallibility, according to circumstances and the guidance of the Holy Spirit, in three different modes." [3]

The assumption was thus encouraged that condemnation or rule by papal encyclical in the manner of Pius IX had been superseded, such assumptions being further strengthened by the abolition of the Index. The hopes of Newman and von Hügel had at last been realized: open theological discussion —no longer subjected to secret delation—had been restored to its rightful place in the economy of the Church. Arguments would be answered not with counter-assertions but by counter-arguments. The principle of doctrinal development, honored more in the breach than in the observance, was at last to be accepted explicitly and in practice; and the mind of the Church in all its diversity and width was to be sought for and consulted as a matter of course.

These expectations were reinforced by the council's formally conceding the principle for which the early Liberal Catholics were condemned—liberty of conscience—and it was confidently assumed that, especially on matters touching them intimately, the laity would now be brought fully into the life and councils of the Church. At last the Church seemed prepared to move off the margins and into the modern world.

Humanae Vitae has brought such expectations to an immediate test, both in its subject matter and form. Matters which affect the laity so intimately must raise the question of consultation. If the Pontifical Commission was not thought to be a due organ for expressing the *sensus fidelium*, then what alternatives are proposed? In the light of the *Constitution on the Church* what is now the status of papal rulings: do they require, for example, to be completed by the bishops acting collegially? And what is the force of an appeal to "rulers" and "their peoples" in a liberal democracy where the "rulers"

3. B. C. Butler, *The Theology of Vatican II*, p. 112.

hold office only for as long as they represent the common consciences of their electors? This uncovers the most fundamental question of all—on what grounds do the intimate details of personal relations continue to be a matter for ecclesiastical legislation?

Questions of this kind have always been asked of papal rulings but, in the past, by scholars only. Newman asked them in 1870, and von Hügel in 1907. The difference now is that such questions are pressed in front of television cameras, and there exists in the documents of Vatican II a series of written constitutions in popular paperback form to which, like Scriptures newly translated into the vernacular, an appeal can be made.

The present encyclical also raises difficulties of a formal kind, since as the London *Times* pointed out, its exercise of the papal prerogative appears "pre-conciliar in its individuality." For the reasons already stated, we have been led to expect a more thorough explanation than what is provided. The grounds for rejecting the findings of the Papal Commission are, for example, asserted but not argued; nor have the findings been officially published, but merely "leaked" to the press. Changes which have taken place between *Casti Connubii* and the present encyclical are left to be inferred rather than explicitly justified as developments; in the former document wives were held, on scriptural authority, to be subject to their husbands; and the conjugal act was considered as intended primarily for the begetting of children, no contraceptive intention (rhythmical or otherwise) being considered permissible.

That the Church is divided on these matters has never been questioned, and in the lawful exercise of his office the Pope has thought it necessary to bring these divisions to a head. He has spoken out; the bishops and the faithful have started to speak back; and the unfinished business of Vatican II becomes of a more serious and urgent nature than we had supposed.

Yet, as von Hügel saw, it is out of such "costingness" and painful tension that the Church has grown and has been enabled to determine the development of Christian doctrine. Living with authority is the Catholic tradition; what is still in question is how to live with it in the modern world.

JOHN T. NOONAN, JR. THE AMENDMENT OF PAPAL TEACHING BY THEOLOGIANS

In the current controversy over the force of the encyclical *Humanae Vitae* it has been sometimes stated or assumed that it is unheard-of arrogance for theologians to criticize or to correct a solemn authentic statement of Catholic moral teaching as to the requirements of divine and natural law issued after investigation, reflection, and prayer by a pope. *Humanae Vitae* is a document in which the pope "in virtue of the mandate given to us by Christ" replies to questions on conjugal life with a "teaching founded on the natural law illuminated and enriched by divine revelation," articulates a theory of God's will or plan for married life, and conclusively holds that certain acts preventing procreation must be "condemned." It may be helpful in understanding the nature of this document and the nature of teaching authority in the Church if there is greater familiarity with other instances of similar papal documents criticized by the theologians where the view advocated by the theologians prevailed as the teaching of the Church.

I propose to explore the theologians' response to papal teaching on a single subject at a single point of time. I choose this instance because the papal teaching was set out in order to change the behavior of a mass of Catholics and to end a theological controversy, because the teaching was given after mature examination of the issues, because it was based on a foundation of natural law enriched by divine revelation, because it was given in solemn discharge of the pope's teaching office, and because it was substantially reshaped by the response of the theologians a few years after it was uttered.

41

1. A Commission is Formed

In 1565 Charles Borromeo became archbishop of Milan. He found prevalent in his diocese the practice of deposit-banking, exchange banking, and business investments where the investor was guaranteed his capital and a return. He viewed these practices in the light of the Church's teaching on usury which had been the common teaching of theologians, bishops, and popes for more than 1000 years. This teaching was succinctly stated in the Roman Catechism of which Borromeo was the principal editor:

"Whatever is received beyond the principal and that capital which is given, whether it be money or whether it be any other thing which can be purchased or estimated in money, is usury; for it is written in Ezekiel, 'He has not lent at usury nor received an increase,' and in Luke the Lord says, 'Lend, hoping nothing thereby.' This was always a most grave crime, even among the gentiles, and especially odious. Hence the question, 'What is usury?', is answered, 'What is it to kill a man?' Those who commit usury sell the same thing twice or sell what is not." [1]

The rule on usury proclaimed by three general councils of the Churches and a dozen popes rested on the belief that by divine law (Luke 6, 35) profit on a loan was mortal sin,[2] and that by natural law it was intrinsically unjust to sell money in a loan at a price higher than its face value, for the law fixed its value, and the value of the use of money could not be separated from the value of the principal.[3] This view of divine law, this theory of money, and the existing rule forbidding

1. *Catechismus Romanus* (Rome, 1871 ed.), "De septimo pracepto," 8, 11.
2. Urban III, *Consuluit, Decretales Gregoiri IX*, ed. E. Friedberg (1879–1881), V, 19, 10.
3. St. Thomas Aquinas, *Summa theologica*, II–II, q. 78, a. 1.

usury were challenged by the financial practices of the people of Borromeo's diocese.

In the first provincial synod held under his presidency to reform the morals of the diocese, these customs were noted and characteized. They were "the more frequent" species of the genus usury in the province and therefore serious sin (*crimina*). The plea "widows and orphans" as a defense for investment practices is an old slogan. The synod solemnly reminded the faithful that nothing beyond the principal might be taken on loans or on deposits, even if the depositors were widows or wards.[4]

To a reforming archbishop the question looked simple. But the practice of extending credit at a profit was inveterate, and much of the practice was justified by theories of some of the more recent theologians. In particular, three types of transaction had their defenders. One was the so-called triple contract. The classical medieval theologians had always accepted the principle that profit might be made by an investor in a partnership. Here the investor ran the risk of losing his capital, and his return depended on the success of the venture; he was not a lender with principal and a profit owed to him whatever happened to the enterprise. The classical theologians also admitted the lawfulness of charging for insurance. The innovators proposed combining contracts of partnership and insurance. Suppose that the probable return from investment in a partnership was 12%; deduct 2% for insurance that the principal would be repaid; deduct 5% for insurance that a

---

4. Synod of Milan (1565), Part 2, "De usuris," *Constitutiones et decreta in provinciali synodo Mediolanensi, Actorum S. Mediolanensis Ecclesiae,* vol. II, ed. Achille Ratti (1890).

Borromeo in his book for pastors also urged the necessity of preaching against the various contracts used to disguise usury. Under the heading "Sins which are more frequently committed against the commandments of the divine law and which are to be taken away by the zeal of the preacher," Borromeo enumerated "so many classes of contracts which have been devised in fraud of the law prohibiting all usury." *Pastorum instructiones* (Ghen, 1824 ed.), Part I, c. 12.

regular return of 5% would be made—by the threefold contract of partnership and guarantees the effect is achieved of a loan at 5%; each step has been analytically defensible as lawful. The case had been first defended in 1485 by the Franciscan Angelo Carleto de Clavasio; it had been adopted by the liberal German theologians at the new University of Tübingen, Gabriel Biel and Conrad Summenhart; it had been popularized in Germany by John Eck; and it had been vigorously attacked as usurious by the Spanish Dominican professor at Salamanca, Domingo de Soto. By 1565 the triple contract was a way of justifying profit on a business loan—a way which subverted the postulates of the usury prohibition for it implicitly treated money as fertile, a way contrary to the old prohibition, and a way debated by modern theologians.[5]

A second approach was in terms of annuities or contracts of *census*. The classical medieval theologians admitted the lawfulness of making of profit on a purchase. They also admitted that one could buy the right to an annual return from some fruitful property like a farm. The purchaser of an annuity was, of course, extending credit because he put up a lump sum of cash in exchange for the right to an annual payment, but an annuity was not identical with a loan if it had to be related to the expected returns from a fruitful base, if the annuity ceased should the base be destroyed, and if there was no obligation on the seller's part ever to refund the principal. A contract in the form of an annuity could, however, be virtually identical with a loan if it were personal—that is, based on the labor of the seller; if it were guaranteed— that is, the seller agreed to pay whatever happened to the base; and if it were redeemable at the buyer's option—that is, the buyer could call for the return of the principal. In the

5. For a classic exposition of the triple contract, see Navarrus, *Enchiridion seu Manuale Confessariorum*, 17, n. 252, *Opera Omnia* (vol. I; Lyons, 1589); for the history, see John T. Noonan, Jr., *The Scholastic Analysis of Usury* (1957), pp. 202–230.

sixteenth century the Tübingen liberals began to champion the contracts by which an annuity was made indistinguishable from a loan, and Summenhart made a comprehensive defense of the personal, guaranteed, redeemable annuity. These German novelties were welcomed in Spain, with only slight reservations, by Soto. But they were warmly attacked by Soto's colleague at Salamanca, Navarrus. By 1565 there was here, too, a development of medieval theological principles which, contrary to their restrained use by the medieval theologians, subverted the usury theory, and where a controversy between modern theologians needed decision.[6]

A third controverted approach to profit in credit transactions involved the purchase of foreign exchange. Where foreign currency was bought for cash across a counter, there was no problem at all—the exchange banker extended no credit and made a profit on his service; the foreign currency was properly treated not at its legal face value but as a commodity. The difficulty occurred when the banker paid for foreign currency to be delivered later. Then a purchase of money as a commodity was made, but credit was also extended. Was the profit on this transaction lawful or was it usury? The masters of medieval moral theology had judged the transaction usurious! [7]

There was, however, a minority current of medieval moral opinions that defended the exchange bankers, and in the sixteenth century, this minority opinion had become dominant, so that by 1565 there was no substantial controversy over the lawfulness of the banker's profit when he bought a bill of foreign exchange.[8]

6. For a full defense of personal annuities as known in Germany, see Conrad Summenhart, *Tractatus de contractibus licitis atque illicitis*, q. 79–84 (Venice, 1580); for the history, see Noonan, pp. 230–248.

7. The classic condemnation is St. Antoninus, *Summa sacral theologiae*, 3, 8, 3 (Venice, 1581–1582).

8. For the sixteenth-century defense, see Cajetan, *De cambiis, Scripta philosophica: Opuscula oeconomica-socialia*, ed. P. Zammit (Rome, 1934); for the history, see Noonan, pp. 171–192, 310–335.

Controversy on exchange banking centered on two points. One was the theoretical ground on which the banker's profit rested. A theory of some theologians was that the profit depended on his "virtual transportation" of money from one city to another.[9] Taken literally this theory meant in practice that the price of foreign money ought to depend on the distance of the foreign places from the place of purchase of the exchange and on the difficulty of transporting species from there. The advantage of this theory was that it distinguished the purchase of foreign exchange from a loan by saying that money absent in space was different from money absent in time: there were "intrinsic" difficulties in transporting money in space, while there were no "intrinsic" difficulties to which money distant in time was subject. But it was generally recognized that "the foundation" of the exchange market was the supply and demand for money, and that profit depended on accurately gauging changes in this market. The transportation change was not the basis for money-making in the exchanges. A different theory therefore justified the banker's profit as lawful because it was made in the purchase of money as a commodity. Yet if money could be purchased at a profit in foreign exchange transactions, why could it not be purchased at a profit in loans? This question, posed by the alternative justification of exchange banking, wrecked the usury prohibition completely unless a distinction could be sustained.

A second controversy concerned the technical operations of the exchange bankers. In a typical transaction, the Medici bank in Florence bought from a customer a bill on Bruges. When the bill arrived for payment in Bruges, the Medici branch there acted for the customer and drew a new bill on him in Florence. When this bill reached Florence, the customer paid the Medici there. The customer had had credit for four months—the bills taking two months each way—and

9. Cajetan, *In summam theologicam S. Thomae Aquinatis* (Leonine edition), II–II, 78, 1, ad 6.

the bank determined its profit at the end of the *ricorsa* or exchange and re-exchange.[10] This common form of credit had the effect of a short-term loan with an interest rate determined by fluctuations in the exchange market. Its moral lawfulness was in dispute. Clearly condemned by medieval moralists, its admission would remove a large area of commercial banking from the usury doctrine.

Finally, the exchange-banks needed capital for their business, and they were often financed by deposits. These deposits were a *discrezione*, that is, the banker had discretion as to the return paid the depositor, and so, like income bonds, the deposits ran some of the risks of the enterprise.[11] But there was no uncertainty about the banker's obligation to repay the principal. The great moral judge of Florentine banking practice, St. Antoninus, had declared, "Although they call this a deposit, yet it is clearly usury." [12] Yet, clearly, too, the practice of deposit-banking persisted, supported by the sense of the people that profit on a deposit was different from a profit on a loan. At a theological level these contracts received indirect support from the theory of the triple contract and by the argument of Catejan and Navarrus that the triple contract could be found "implicitly" even though the actual spelling out of three separate contracts had not been done.[13]

With the triple contract, annuities, and exchange banking all theologically defended and all presenting ways of avoiding the moral law on usury, Charles Borromeo pressed the Pope to give direction. On November 18, 1567, he wrote Niccolo Ormaneto, the zealous reformer whom he had lent the Pope, as follows:

10. Raymond De Roover, *The Rise and Decline of the Medici Bank* (1963), pp. 110–121.

11. *Ibid.*, pp. 100–102.

12. *Summa sacrae theologiae* (Venice, 1581), 2, 1, 6 and 2.

13. Cajetan, *De societate negotiatoria*, nn. 422–423, in *Opuscula oeconomica-socialia*, ed. cited; Navarrus, *Manuale*, 17, 257; Navarrus, *Commentarius de usuris, Si foeneraveris*, 14, 33.

"Today is the eighth day I have been in Varese, always with constant business. I have found this country full of usury and usurious contracts, made as much by priests as by laymen; and believing that this is caused in good part by the ignorance of many, I would be much satisfied if His Beatitude would put into effect that thought which he has already deigned to communicate to me of wanting to make a general statement on usury; and I recall also that I have named to His Holiness those persons who seem to me good for well chewing over this matter and drawing up the bull. You may now have an hour with a good opportunity to speak a word to His Holiness and to represent to him the need which I see particularly in these parts, which recalls to mind the need which there is everywhere." [14]

Within three weeks Ormaneto could report that there was now a papal commission in existence to study "all the disorders occurring in this matter and above all in annuities, deposits, and exchanges." [15]

Pressure on the Pope to act had come not only from Borromeo, but also from the Jesuits. In 1522 the city of Augsburg had been brought back from Protestant control to a place within the Catholic Empire, and in 1560 the Jesuits, led by the great Dutch reformer Peter Canisius, had come to win back this financial capital, still bitterly divided between Catholics and Protestants.[16] The Jesuits had been pained to discover the general practice prevailed of investing in credit transactions with a 5% return; they were inclined to attribute the custom to pernicious Protestant example. Peter Canisius refused to absolve Catholics taking the 5% "Real usury," he

14. Borromeo to Ormaneto, November 18, 1587, reproduced in Pietro Ballerini, *Vindiciae iuris divini ac naturalis circa usuram* (Bologna, 1747), 4, 2. On Ormaneto's role with Pius V, see Ludwig Von Pastor, *History of the Popes,* trans. F. I. Antrobus, vol. V (St. Louis), pp. 138–139.

15. Ormaneto to Borromeo, December 6, 1587, in *ibid.*

16. James Broderick, *St. Peter Canisius* (1935), pp. 422–435.

told the chapter of Augsburg cathedral, "is here openly committed and the divine commandment 'Lend freely hoping nothing thereby' is violated, whatever is objected by certain men skilled in the law who think according to the prudence of this world that many things of this kind are to be dissimulated, although contrary to the canons and the received opinion of old and new theologians and canonists." [17]

This zeal of the reforming leader of a still new religious order was not shared by all Catholics. The secular clergy of Augsburg continued to object to such rigor, and the Jesuit authorities in Rome counseled Canisius to proceed cautiously. But he would not connive in what he saw as open sin, and a quarrel about the lawfulness of the 5% contract or "the German contract" developed both inside and outside the Jesuit order.[18]

In 1565 Ursula Fugger entered the lists. A member by marriage of the great Fugger banking family, the richest bankers in Europe, she was also a convert of Canisius and a pious benefactress of the Jesuits. It was not easy to be the pious wife of a usurer, for all usury, as ill-gotten gain, was subject to a duty of restitution, and no one could lawfully receive gifts or inheritance made up of usuries. For a decent woman the thought that her husband was daily committing mortal sin in his business was itself anguish. Ursula Fugger wrote directly to the Jesuit General, Francis Borgia, asking his counsel "as to the usurious contracts in which our family is not a little entangled." [19] Borgia replied that these contracts "which

17. Canisius to the Cathedral Chapter of Augsburg, June, 1564, in *Epistolae et acta*, ed. O. Braunsberger (1896–1923), vol. IV, p. 563.

18. Bernhard Duhr, "Die Deutschen Jesuiten im 5%-Streit des 16 Jahrhunderts," in *Zeitschrift für Katholische Theologie*, vol. 241 (1900), pp. 209–248; Ernest Joseph Van Roey, "Le Contractus Germanicus," in *Revue d'histoire ecclésiastique*, vol. III (1902), pp. 901–946 (1903).

19. Ursula of Liechtenstein, wife of George Fugger, to Borgia, April 25, 1565, in Canisius, *Epistolae*, vol. V, pp. 533–534. Ursula Fugger is described by Canisius in *ibid.*, vol. III, pp. 653–654.

are less candid than you wish" would be carefully considered with Canisius and others in Rome.[20] It was plain that the experience of the laity who used these contracts as proper for decent Christians was not to be neglected by the Jesuits at headquarters.

The controversy over the 5% contract continued. In July of 1567 Peter Canisius repeated triumphantly the report that the Pope had decided the question.[21] The rumor was a false one. Only in the winter of 1567 did the combined requests of Charles Borromeo and the Jesuits lead to the constitution of a papal commission. By February 16, 1568, Borgia could assure the Jesuits in Lyons, "Of the deposits and other usurious contracts we expect some speedy resolution, because many theologians are looking at this matter by order of His Holiness, who wants to compose a *motu proprio* or brief." [22] Again on March 15, 1568, Borgia reported the Pope's plan to draft a *motu proprio* on deposits "together with exchanges and annuities." [23]

A commission had, then, come into existence on the main forms of European credit and the common practices of the financial world. The commission's task was to enable the Pope to decide the theological controversies about the moral law which had divided theologians, confused the laity, and threatened to subvert the divine and natural law forbidding men to seek profit on a loan. The commission's head was Cardinal Gugliemo Sirleto, an excellent man whom Borromeo had supported for Pope in the election of 1565.[24] The commission was directed to draw on theologians. It relied on Jesuits, but it also took the counsel of Navarrus, Soto's old foe at Sala-

20. Borgia to Fugger, June 9, 1565, in *ibid.*, vol. V, pp. 535–536.
21. Canisius to Borgia, July 26, 1587, in *ibid.*, vol. V, p. 529.
22. Borgia to the Jesuit House at Lyons, February 16, 1568, in *ibid.*, vol. V, p. 487.
23. Borgia, March 15, 1568, in *ibid.*, vol. V, p. 487.
24. On Sirleto, see Pastor, *op. cit.*, vol. 5, p. 37; on his role in the commission see Ballerini, *op. cit.* The man who was apparently first named as chairman, Cardinal Dolera, died in January, 1588.

manca, now chosen by Borromeo as canonist of the Sacred Penitentiary, a moralist of outstanding acuity.[25] The commission was thus composed of the choices of Borromeo, of Borgia, and of the Pope, and its members were more than routinely distinguished for piety and learning.

The Pope to whom the commission reported, Pius V, had been a Dominican and a high official in the Inquisition. He was not unfamiliar with the main lines of theological thought on usury, but as an especially vigorous administrator he could not have been expected to master the complex distinctions pressed by casuists. Distinctions were the work of theologians; his task was to proclaim the law of God. Pius V was humble, pious, strict, unchangeable in his judgments once they were formed, and with little experience of worldly affairs. Above all, the Pope was marked by his scrupulous care to discharge his office faithfully. He declared once that he would retire into privacy at the Lateran rather than allow anything he considered wrong. As Pastor has remarked, "Pius V was so imbued with the responsibilities of his office that he looked upon it as an obstacle in the way of salvation." [26] To preserve the integral Catholic doctrine on usury Pius V acted upon the report of his commission.

2. A Burden Is Assumed

On January 19, 1569, Pius V issued the bull *Cum Onus*. It began as follows:

Undertaking the burden of apostolic servitude, we have recognized that innumerable contracts of annuity were and are celebrated which are not only not within the limits set by our predecessors

25. On Navarrus, see Mariano Arigita y Lasa, *El Doctor Navarro Don Martin de Azplicueta y sus obras* (1905). On his choice for the Sacred Penitentiary by Borromeo, see *ibid.*, p. 395.

26. *Op. cit.*, vol. 5, pp. 53, 63–66.

for such contracts, but what is worse, by agreements entirely contrary to these limits, due to the burning prick of avarice, show manifest contempt for divine laws. Therefore we—bound as we are to care for the salvation of souls and satisfying the prayer of pious minds—cannot not medicate such a grave disease and deadly poison with a salutary antidote.[27]

The bull closed by saying that for no one was it lawful to infringe what the bull determined or "to contradict it with temerarious audacity." "But if anyone presumes to attempt this he will know that he has incurred the wrath of Almighty God and of His Blessed Apostles, Peter and Paul."

Pius V thus made it evident that he acted in discharge of his apostolic office; that he judged here and now that there were contracts of annuity where certain additional agreements made the contracts offensive to the law of God; that he acted to save souls from mortal sin or "deadly poison"; that he invoked the authority of his office as successor to Peter; and that he called upon all who would dare to go against the teaching not merely ecclesiastical sanction but the wrath of God.

In the body of the bull the Pope decreed that an annuity "can in no way be created except of immovable property or property regarded as immovable, fruitful by nature, and designated for definite ends." He also taught that an agreement binding the seller of the annuity to pay although the property was destroyed was "in no way valid." He also declared that any agreement by the seller to pay interest determined in advance was null. An agreement to permit redemption of an annuity against the seller's will—that is, the forced repayment of the principal—was invalid. Resale of an annuity at a higher or lower figure than the original price, the Pope proclaimed, "can never be done."

Cum Onus was a thorough-going determination that a personal, guaranteed, or redeemable annuity was morally impos-

27. *Bullarium Romanum* (Turin, 1863), vol. VII, p. 737.

52

sible—for by the statement that such could never be done the Pope clearly did not deny that such annuities could be sold, but that such annuities could morally be sold. By this determination Pius V specified the agreements which turned annuities into contracts in contempt of God's law, for it was precisely the agreements which were declared impossible or invalid that turned annuities into the equivalent of loans at a profit. The bull was a rejection of the Tübingen liberals and of the compromisers in the Jesuit order. It was a triumphant vindication of Charles Borromeo and Peter Canisius. It was a definitive theological victory for Navarrus over his old rival Soto at Salamanca. It was established on the basis of divine law that only annuities substantially distinct from loans could be purchased at a profit.

The problems occasioned by exchange-banking were more complex than those of the annuity contracts, and Pius V was unable to fulfill his hope of dealing with all the species of usurious contracts in a single document. Only two years later was he ready to speak specifically on banking. On January 28, 1571, he issued the bull *In Eam*. Like *Cum Onus*, this bull began by setting out that the Pope was discharging an apostolic duty: "We diligently exert ourselves on behalf of our pastoral office so that we do not delay in healthfully applying opportune remedies for the sheep of Our Lord." Like *Cum Onus*, the bull went on to make a judgment that here and now forms of the exchange contract violated divine law: under pretext of exchanges "usurious wickedness is exercised by some." Acting to prevent the practice of mortal sin as he had done in *Cum Onus*, the Pope exercised the office of pastor, striving "in every way to snatch the flock committed to us from the danger of eternal damnation." [28]

As in *Cum Onus*, Pius V was conscious that he was giving moral teaching in his function of Chief Shepherd, that he was judging certain contracts to violate divine law, and that he

28. *Ibid.*, VII, p. 884.

was determining what contracts of credit could avoid the sin of usury. He then taught the moral truth that all "dry exchange" was usurious, defining such exchange to be contracts taking the form of the purchase of exchange in which bills of exchange were not sent to another place or, if they were sent, were not paid there but returned to be paid by the seller of the bill in the same place, as it was agreed or at least certainly intended by the parties. The Pope also taught that the only basis on which foreign exchange prices might vary was distance in space; distance in time of payment could not be made a basis for a change.

In this document, following the example set by Charles Borromeo in the synod of Milan, Pius V made a formal identification of the *ricorsa* with usury, for the expectation of purchaser and seller to pay the bill of exchange after it had not been paid in the foreign city was the essence of the *ricorsa*. The Pope not only taught that this common practice constituted the mortal sin of usury; he also embraced a theory of the true basis for the exchange banker's profit. He adopted the theory that the banker legitimately profited on "virtual transportation" of money, understanding this theory literally —not as a legal fiction, but as an accurate reflection of the way exchange banks worked.[29] He thereby rejected the theory that the banker's profit depended on the supply and demand for money, and he assumed seriously and literally that money distant in space could be the subject of a profit while money distant in time could not. By adopting this assumption and by rejecting the *ricorsa*, the Pope made a sharp distinction between moral profit in exchange banking and sinful usury, and

29. The principal Jesuit adviser of the Pope, Francisco Toledo, in his own later *Summa casuum conscientiae sive Instructio sacerdotum* (Cologne, 1610), stated, "It is not similar as to place and time": there was per se risk and labor in money absent in space, but not absent in time (Book 58, c. 53). The "excess of value ought to be proportionate to the distance" (58.54).

there could be no question of confusing a moral exchange transaction with a loan at a profit.

The triple contract itself was not dealt with. There is some evidence that Pius V personally hesitated more in regard to this practice than in regard to the others.[30] But *In Eam* did speak of deposits, and deposits were a form of commercial contract where the liberals' theory of implicit contract provided the defense of "implicit triple contract." Without adverting to this defense, Pius V simply held "deposits," like dry exchange, to be usurious; and the defense of them fell before this proclamation of their true character.

The triple contract itself was given consideration only fifteen years later in a bull whose history belongs with *Cum Onus* and *In Eam*. In 1586 another friar, this time a Franciscan, another ex-inquisitor, another vigorous reformer was pope—Sixtus V. With his burning zeal to sweep away corruptions of all sorts he issued a bull on usury devoted to the morally impermissible characteristics of contracts of partnership. "Detestable avarice," the bull ominously opened, has inflamed men's hearts, and the devil has led men "to immerse themselves in the whirlpool of usury, odious to God and men, condemned by the sacred canons, and contrary to Christian charity." These avaricious and misled men have used "the decent name of partnership as a pretext for their usurious contracts." In order to stem this "contagious disease" before it spread further, the Pope, "desiring to draw as fully as we can with the favor of God upon the plentitude of apostolic power granted to us," declared that all future agreements "must be condemned," by which "it is guaranteed to persons giving money, animals, or other property in the name of a partnership, that, even if in some fortuitous case some disaster,

30. On April 10, 1568, Borgia wrote Nicholas Lanoius, the Jesuit provincial in Austria, that Pius V, as a "private theologian," not as Pope, approved the triple contract, in Canisius, *Epistolae*, vol. 5, p. 487.

loss, or lack happens to occur, the principal will be always safe and restored entire by the partner receiving it." [31]

The mention of future agreements made the bull appear to be only prospective legislation. But it also dealt with existing agreements of the kind condemned. Any person now enforcing such agreements was to be treated as a manifest usurer and excommunicated and denied Christian burial according to the provisions of the general councils against manifest usurers.

In this bull as in the two documents of Pius V, an apostolic office was discharged—indeed explicitly here the maximum of apostolic power possible was used; certain contracts were here and now judged to be usurious; what these contracts were was determined by the specific provisions declaring the condemned contracts to be invalid; and sanctions were invoked which were founded on the determination made by the Pope that those who used these contracts were in mortal sin, offenders of God and their neighbor. Concretely, by holding usurious any agreement to guarantee the return of partnership principal, *Detestabilis Avaritia* condemned the triple contract.

The three bulls stood together. In a period extending over 17 years these authentic acts of papal teaching authority had repulsed an attempt to subvert the usury prohibition. Faithful to the main lines of theological tradition approved and proclaimed by popes, bishops, and councils for more than a millennium, Pius V and Sixtus V had rejected theories and practices which removed the usury prohibition's rigor from the world of commercial credit. The popes and their advisers had correctly perceived that if the novel theories of the innovating theologians were accepted, the entire moral structure of Catholic thought on economic matter would crumble, that rethinking of the meaning of divine law on lending would be necessary, that the old absolute condemnations of profit on a loan would no longer hold. They saw that to admit a

31. *Bullarium Romanum* VIII, 783–785.

market in money in some forms would be to admit a market in other forms, that it was essential from the viewpoint of existing divine law to maintain a distinction between distance in space and distance in time, that no moral value could be given to the practice of those otherwise decent Christians who invested in credit believing that moderate profit in finance was not a sin, that it was a work of Christian charity to end the confusion and uncertainty caused by rival theological analyses of important issues of conduct.

By means of the bulls' determination of divine law, the ordinary form of commercial credit and government finance in Western Europe were condemned; Christian businessmen, bankers, and investors were told that they were committing sin; their wives and children were informed by the usual rules on unjustly-taken property that they were bound to restitution; their associates, lawyers, notaries, and agents were informed by the usual rules on cooperation that they would have to justify acts of every material cooperation with the condemned practices.[32] While the absolute number of persons affected was not enormous, almost every part of the bourgeois world was affected by the popes' forthright actions.

Challenging established procedures, the popes no doubt anticipated objection and the continuance of sin. But objection could be refuted, sin absolved, and reform effected. With zeal and with serenity the popes assumed that there could be no compromise with evil custom, no abandonment of past theological tradition. The laity must be instructed, the theological innovators repressed.

How did the laity and the theologians respond?

32. On restitution and cooperation, see St. Bernardine of Siena, *De contractibus*, 44, 3, 4, *De evangelio aeterno, Opera omnia*.

3. A Process Is Continued

The first response came from the Jesuits. In April, 1569, three months after the issuance of *Cum Onus*, Peter Canisius treated this declaration of Pius V as ending the 5% controversy. With triumph and compassion, he wrote the General, "I know that for certain ones execution of this recent judgment will be displeasing and harsh . . . but with Christ as our leader we shall overcome these difficulties both on the part of those hearing confessions and on the part of those confessing." [33] But this assurance in the ultimate acceptance of the papal teaching was not shared by all his brethren. From Munich the Jesuit Georg Schorich wrote the secretary general of the Society of Jesus, "These Germans do not desire to understand how lending at 5 florins per hundred is not lawful for them, while in the states of the Church it is 7, 8, 9, and even 10 *scudi* per hundred." [34] At the very moment of Canisius's triumph he was being succeeded by a new provincial, Paul Hoffaeus, who was inclined to take seriously the murmurs of the people that the 5% contract could not always be unjust.[35] To the dismay of Canisius, Hoffaeus began to work for a new decision.

In Rome Pius V himself revealed a strange weakness. Approached again by Francis Borgia, the Pope said orally that "miserable persons" such as wards and widows who invested their funds in the 5% contracts might be "excused." [36] But he vouchsafed no explanation of how intrinsically sinful acts like lending at usury became lawful because the persons engaging in them were poor. The Jesuit theologians must have read this report of papal mildness as a sign that Pius V was himself still unsure of whether lending at 5% could not be

33. Canisius to Borgia, April 2, 1569, Canisius, *Epistolae*, VI, p. 287.
34. Schorich to Polanco, *ibid.*, VI, p. 287.
35. Braunsberger in Canisius, *Epistolae*, VI, p. 287.
36. Borgia to Hoffaeus, June 17, 1510, *ibid.*, VI, p. 410.

analyzed in terms of the other contracts which formally avoided the divine prohibition of profit on a loan.

The Jesuits set up their own commission of theologians to study the problems involved. At its head was one of the brightest of their young theologians, Francisco Toledo, a native of Cordóba, 39 years old in 1571, and Navarrus's counterpart as the theological adviser of the Sacred Penitentiary.[37] To it Hoffaeus forwarded the arguments of the Fuggers' lawyer on behalf of the 5%.[38] The Jesuits also consulted Navarrus as one of the main authors responsible for *Cum Onus* as to whether the bull was "declaratory of natural and divine law, or only constitutive of human law." [39]

In answer to this inquiry Navarrus noted the opening passages of the bull which referred to contracts of annuity made in contempt of divine laws and the conclusion of the bull applying the sanctions against usury to violators of the bull, and judged accordingly that part of the bull must be declaratory of divine and natural law. At the same time he observed that there were a variety of conditions laid down by the bull for a morally lawful annuity, and that as these conditions were to be observed in the future, not all of them were natural and divine law. The necessarily prospective character of some of the requirements showed their merely human character; for what was natural law "began with the beginning of the rational creature." Navarrus's conclusion was that the law set out in *Cum Onus* was partly divine, partly natural, and partly pontifical.[40]

The question this response raised was, What part was only pontifical? Here it was Navarrus's cautious opinion that "it

37. On Toledo, see *Bibliothèque de la Compagnie de Jésus*, ed. C. Sommervogel (1898), vol. 8, p. 64.
38. Hoffaeus to Borgia, June 17, 1571, *ibid.*, VI, p. 416.
39. Navarrus reports only that he was consulted on behalf of the Jesuits by a "friend distinguished for learning and piety." Navarrus, *De usuris*, 22, n. 85, *Opera omnia*, vol. 1, p. 289.
40. *Ibid.*, n. 105, vol. I, p. 295.

seemed to be of natural and divine law" that an annuity b
constituted on fruitful, immobile property. Other require
ments, such that annuities be bought in cash, were purel
pontifical.[41]

The third and key question was, Did the bull then bind i
conscience? Navarrus was clear that to the extent it declare
the divine and natural law, it "bound all, even laymen, i
kingdoms not subject to the temporal domain of the pope.
As to the provisions which were only pontifical law, ther
was an obligation on all Christians to observe them in externa
and internal behavior. Yet since these provisions only pro
vided presumptions as to what was usurious, "no one is to b
judged usurious in the forum of the conscience because o
presumptions induced by this extravagant, if the contrary i
true before God, because no law founded on presumptio
binds someone in the forum of the conscience or of God if th
contrary of what is presumed is, before God, true." [42]

If these answers were taken as a good gloss on the inten
tion of Pius V, a loophole was suggested by Navarrus's lan
guage on the limited force of presumptions created by purely
papal law. Yet respect for the papal intention required finding
some provisions of divine and natural law in the bull. Navarrus
himself thought that his own opinion on the unlawfulness of
personal annuities had been recognized as divine law by the
Pope; he furnished no guidance on how to classify the equally
important prohibitions of guaranteed or redeemable annuities.

The Jesuit theologians acted on the silence of Navarrus,
but not until Pius V was dead. Then on June 22, 1573, there
was a meeting of Toledo's commission—himself, two other
Spaniards, Pedro Paez and Diego Bernal, and one Portuguese,
Leon Enriquez. They were joined by Jesuit provincials from
France and Austria and by Canisius's foe Paul Hoffaeus.
Canisius himself was excluded from the gathering, apparently

41. *Ibid.*, n. 105.
42. *Ibid.*, nn. 106–107, vol. I, p. 296.

design.[43] The group issued a decision written to provide guidance for all Jesuit confessors, preachers, and moralists.

Ex genere, the 1573 Commission declared, a contract for % beyond the principal was morally unlawful. The cases excused by Pius V—wards and widows who could not otherwise support themselves—were specifically condemned. But the triple contract was lawful (this was before *Detestabilis avaritia*), and so was an annuity redeemable by either seller or buyer. In other words, an annuity at 5% where the purchaser could also demand the return of his principal was legitimate. At the same time the theologians added, "Where the Bull of Pius V obliges, the buyer cannot oblige the seller to repurchase." [44]

The decisions of 1573 were a careful step towards undermining the force of *Cum Onus*. The theologians still taught in accordance with the bull and with Navarrus that an annuity was to be founded on "fruitful property"; they did not accept the full-annuity theory of the liberals. But in treating redeemability by the buyer as objectively lawful, they supported the single feature of an annuity contract which made it closest to a loan. Moreover, in the general language "where the bull of Pius V obliges," the Jesuit theologians implied that there were areas where it did not oblige, that it was purely positive law which might not oblige; and they failed to specify what parts of the bull were divine law, what parts purely pontifical law.

This first cautious theological response to the determinations of *Cum Onus* was not decisive enough to end the controversy, but ambiguous enough to sharpen it. In Germany the confusion, uncertainty, and conflict among theologians and laity increased. The rigorist Jesuits, heartened by the bull, con-

43. On the commission and on the exclusion of Canisius, Braunsberger in Canisius, *Epistolae*, VII, pp. 671–672.
44. "Cases Disputed in a Congregation held in the name of the Reverend Father General, June 22, 1573," in *ibid.*, VII, pp. 672–674.

tinued to refuse absolution to persons taking the 5%. They were backed by the bishop of Augsburg who threatened suspension to any priest absolving a man putting out money at 5%.[45] But the bishop died and a new bishop of Augsburg ordered Canisius not to permit teaching against the 5% contract and not to criticize secular priests who did absolve the 5% takers.[46] The papal nuncio, Feliciano Ninguarda, announced that the bull was binding in Germany.[47] A righteous Englishman, a professor at the Jesuit University of Dillingen, Caspar Haywood, became convinced that many of his confrères were unbelievably lax on the subject, that "to save the Company from certain ruin" the 5% contract must be denounced, and that it was his personal mission to war upon the hydra of usury which appeared in these common commercial practices.[48] Pressed to quiet the mounting storm, the new pope, a learned lawyer, Gregory XIII, adopted a *via media*: the Jesuit General was told that the Jesuits should not absolve the takers of the 5%, but the Jesuits should keep from disputing publicly or preaching on the question.[49]

Until 1581 the conservative defenders of medieval theology had won every major controversy taken to the pope. Whatever weakness had been betrayed by Pius V's counsel on the 5% contracts of widows and orphans, whatever prudential circumspection had motivated Gregory XIII's order not to preach, there was an unbroken series of papal decisions rejecting on the merits every contract which substantially approximated a loan for a profit. But one decade after *Cum Onus*, two decades after the controversy had begun in Ger-

45. Broderick, *St. Peter Canisius*, p. 737.
46. Theoderic Canisius, rector of Dillingen, to Edward Mercurian, General of the Society of Jesus, February 17, 1576, in Canisius, *Epistolae VII*, pp. 341–343.
47. Ninguarda to Cardinal Como, December 2, 1580, in Duhr, *op. cit.*, n. 18, p. 282.
48. Duhr, pp. 230, 237.
49. Mercurian to T. Canisius, March 16, 1576, *ibid.*, *VII*, p. 321.

nany, neither the laity nor the theologians were convinced hat the final answer had been given.

In 1581 Gregory XIII acted in response to a plaintive inquiry from Duke William of Bavaria, who was a pious ruler under erious moral pressure from the rigorists Canisius and Heywood.[50] In his perplexity, the Duke first received conflicting advice from the theological faculty of Ingolstadt and then in 1580 received the opinion of a group of Roman theologians which left him still muddled. In desperation he wrote Charles Borromeo describing his plight and how he was working in order that "the Supreme Pastor of the Church with the consent and judgment of his brother cardinals pronounce authentically what must be judged about this kind of usury everywhere and put into practice without discrimination of souls or scruple of conscience." [51]

Again Charles Borromeo took an interest in obtaining a papal judgment. He sent his agent Spetiano at Rome a copy of the Duke's letter, noted that in this business of usury and on the questions raised "by the English Jesuit father," the Duke wanted a decision by the Pope himself, observed that "it would be good that His Beatitude console this Prince in this matter," and instructed Spetiano to speak to the Pope in his name.[52] Again the Pope consulted with Jesuits and other "most learned theologians." [53] Heywood, apparently encouraged by the nuncio Ninguardo and Cardinal Como, intrepidly argued his case in Rome and was benignly heard by the Pope.[54] But the Pope also asked the advice of a select com-

50. Hoffaeus to Oliverio Manareo, Vicar General of the Society of Jesus, October 2, 1580, *ibid.*, *VII*, p. 575.
51. Duke William to Borromeo, February 8, 1581, Appendix to Pietro Ballerini, *De jure divino et naturali circa usuram libri sex* (Bologna, 1747) I, p. 318.
52. Borromeo to Caesare Spetiano, procurator of Borromeo at Rome, February, 1581, in *ibid.*, vol. I, p. 318.
53. Spetiano to Borromeo, March 16, 1581, in *ibid.*, vol. 1, p. 318.
54. Braunsberger in Canisius, *Epistolae*, *VII*, p. 389.

mittee of theologians chosen by the new general of the Jesuit Claudio Aquaviva.[55] This committee had as its most brilliant member Gregorio de Valentia, a 30-year-old Spaniard who had been scandalizing Heywood and others at Ingolstadt by his defense of the German contract.[56] In April, 1581, this committee gave its decision.

The Jesuit Congregation reaffirmed three of the decisions of the Jesuits in 1571: a loan at 5% was "intrinsically evil," the triple contract was permissible, the redeemable annuity was permissible. It went on to teach that an annuity guaranteed to pay a return regardless of what happened to the base was also legitimate. Climatically, it taught that while annuities founded on personal labor were "most dangerous" and "not commonly to be tolerated," they were inherently moral. The cases in which the 5% contract was taken were approved "unless it had the character of a loan"; and the Congregation added that the contract "has not necessarily such a character, unless it is made without respect of persons." The 5% was to be considered usury, if it was sought by force of a loan alone; or if in a loan it was sought without pretext of title, or with false title, or with the deliberate exclusion of all titles, or in a contract not called a loan where no pretext existed. But if the person of the borrower was considered by the parties—that is if the borrower were a merchant, or the owner of fruitful lands, or a working person, and the contract was made with him principally in consideration of his status—the 5% contract could be interpreted as either a triple contract or a real or personal *census*. It would then have "the character of a licit partnership or some tolerable *census*." The Congregation stated specifically that the implicit intention of gaining in a licit way sufficed to justify the contract, and that although they [the parties] do not know of a type [of contract] ex-

55. *Ibid.*, p. 590; see Van Roey, *op. cit.*, n. 18, pp. 939–940.
56. On Gregory de Valentia 1551–1603, Duhr, *op. cit.*, n. 18, p. 233; Sommervogel, vol. 8, cols. 388–349.

pressed in such a way, yet if the circumstances are such on the part of the thing itself, so that they contract with a merchant or person not having fruitful goods, yet having the ability to work, there is no doubt that this 5% is licit."

In other words, wherever the ownership of money was temporarily transferred to a merchant or worker, if the parties intended to act licitly, the contract might be analyzed as a triple contract or *census* and the profit on the contract might be legitimized. The far-reaching implications of this decision are evident, and the influence of the decision was as widespread. In practice, it meant that only loans to aged or infirm persons without property or loans bearing a rate of interest beyond that obtainable in a triple contract or *census* needed to be considered as true loans falling within the usury prohibitions. The old usury prohibition was dead.[57]

How did the Jesuit theologians avoid the teaching of *Cum Onus?* Apparently by assuming that all of the specific provisions of the bull could be treated as purely pontifical law, which had failed to be accepted, the Congregation found no need to mention the bull at all. The more difficult question of reconciling the new Jesuit decision with the earlier teaching of the papal magisterium on the divine law against usury was not faced but left to the ingenuity of theologians.

Gregory XIII had had the advice of the brightest Jesuits. He also knew the mind of Borromeo, for whom he felt "an almost incredible esteem."[58] He knew, too, that the Duke expected support for a strict position. On May 27, 1581, the

57. The decisions are summarized in Franz X. Zech, *Dissertationes tres, in quibus rigor moderatus doctrinae pontificae circa usuras a sanctissimo D. N. Benedicto XIV per epistolam encyclicam episcopis Italiae traditae exhibetur* (Venice, 1762), reprinted in J. P. Migne, *Theologiae cursus completus,* vol. 16 (1841) Dissertation 2, nn. 259–264. See Braunsberger in Canisius, *Epistolae, VI,* p. 590. Evidence of the decisions of 1581 is provided not only by Zech but by a manuscript described by Duhr, p. 240, *Tractatus circa contractum quinque pro centum, ex communi consensu patrum ad id in quarta congregatione generali Societatis Jesu deputatorum, confectus mense Aprili 1581.*

58. Pastor, vol. 19, p. 28.

Pope answered Duke William, congratulated him on his care for the salvation of his people, and gave his judgment. All the Duke had asked for was there in this solemn judgment of the Pope, except that Gregory XIII was cautious enough not to make a bull out of his response. The Pope declared that the contract for 5% could "not be excused by any custom or human law, nor defended by my good intention of the contracting parties, since it is prohibited by divine and natural law." "But if in Germany there is some other contract in which 5% is received, which is celebrated in form and manner different from the aforesaid, we do not by this intend to condemn or approve it, unless it is particularly set out and considered that so what is to be judged in its regard may be decreed, as is decreed in regard to what has been proposed." [59] The response was a classic holding of the line. Gregory XIII had ignored the advice of the Jesuits, invoked divine and natural law, refused to reduce the 5% contract "implicitly" to another licit contract, and not even given approval to other contracts which might be lawful. It is not surprising that the Duke, receiving this severe answer, believed it to be his duty to outlaw the 5% contract of his country and ordered his courts not to enforce existing contracts.[60]

The Duke's sweeping measure hit the commercial life of Bavaria with force. Popular outcry was enormous; the legislature petitioned for the revocation of his measure; and by 1583 in the face of general skepticism as to the soundness of his law following the decision of the Pope, the Duke was compelled to reconsider. Now he knew who to turn to for different theological advice, and he went to Gregorio de Valentia who was still teaching at Ingolstadt. Gregorio gave him the impression that what was decisive was the Jesuit decisions

59. Text of papal brief and accompanying papal judgment in Van Roey, p. 941 and in Ballerini *op. cit.*, n. 50, I, p. 321–322.
60. Zech, Dissertation 2, n. 265–276.

of 1581, not the Pope's judgment.[61] He also provided contract forms which in his opinion met the lenient requirements of the Jesuit theologians. The Duke embraced advice and forms eagerly and told his subjects that while he could never permit usury he would permit the redeemable annuity.[62] The legislature assured him that this was all that it had wanted, and with this wise verbal compromise there was no further confusion among the laity in Germany. The 5% contract or "German contract" was now spoken of as an annuity at 5%; it was everywhere adopted in Catholic Germany; and even the German word for interest, "Zins," was derived from the Latin designation *"census"* for contracts of credit in the form of annuities.[63]

The conservatives among the Jesuits, however, were still uneasy and continued to raise troublesome doubts. But after a majority of the theologians of the German province had agreed with the Roman Jesuits' decisions of 1581, the General Claudio Aquaviva in 1589 ordered the licitness of "the German contract" to be held without dissent by the Jesuits in the province.[64] No papal action was undertaken to challenge this open undermining of Gregory XIII's judgment of 1581—not to mention the complete disregard now manifested of *Cum Onus* or *Detestabilis Avaritia*. A combination of theological and lay opposition had triumphed. Borromeo was not alive to see this end for the program of reform he had begun in 1565.

Later theologians followed the lead of the Jesuit Congregation of 1581 and made explicit the reason it ignored *Cum Onus*. The most acute of Jesuit writers on economic morals, Leonard Lessius, said that the bull had set out positive law

---

61. Valentia to Aquaviva, September 21, 1583, Duhr, p. 242; Van Roey, p. 943.
62. Duhr, p. 244; Zech, Dissertation 2, n. 270.
63. Franz X. Funk, *Zins und Wucher* (Tübingen, 1869), p. 115.
64. Aquaviva to Canisius, March 2, 1589, in Canisius, *Epistolae, VIII*, p. 282.

which had been neither promulgated nor received in Northern Europe; in his country "the contrary practice has always continued." [65] He introduced a defense of the morality of personal annuities by referring to this constant practice in Belgium, Germany, and France and observing that "what so many learned and religious men do in so many provinces is not easily to be condemned." [66]

This approach to *Cum Onus* was not confined to the Jesuits. Martino Bonacina, a Milanese theologian who was a protegé of Cardinal Federico Borromeo and later titular bishop of Utica, taught that personal annuities were formally lawful: "Where the bull of Pius V was received," the contracts were "to be judged usurious." [67] But even in those regions this was a rule only for the external forum; in the internal forum, only a probable opinion held that the bull was binding.[68]

Bonacina adopted an additional technique for reducing the teaching of the bull. The Pope had condemned discounting of annuities. But, Bonacina said, surely this determination could not apply where expense or effort was necessary to collect the return: "this case seems excepted by *epikeia*." [69] By this appeal to exceptions which the legislator equitably must have intended, the way was open for the theologian's judgment as to what cases fell outside the absolute and universal condemnations of the pope.

Bonacina did not identify the countries where *Cum Onus* was even binding as law in the external forum, but by mid-eighteenth century it was apparent that the bull was accepted as law nowhere. Alfonso Ligouri, the most balanced and authoritative of eighteenth-century moralists, reported that the

65. *De justitia et jure ceterisque virtutibus cardinalibus libri quatuor ad 2.2 D. Thomae quaestione 47 ad quaestionem 171* (Lyons, 1630), 2, 22, 12, 98–99.
66. *Ibid.*, 2, 22, 4, 10.
67. *De contractibus* 3, 4, 3, *Opera omnia* (Venice, 1754).
68. *Ibid.*, 3, 4, 46.
69. *Ibid.*, 3, 4, 43.

bull was not binding in Belgium, France, Germany, Spain, southern Italy, and even in Rome itself.[70] Ligouri accepted as probably lawful all of the varieties of annuity which *Cum Onus* had condemned.

Cum Onus was discarded by being reinterpreted as positive pontifical law. *In Eam* was undermined by indirect contradiction and a distinction advanced by the leading Roman canonist, Navarrus. The indirect contradiction occurred in his teaching on the theory justifying exchange banking. The idea that the virtual transportation charge was literally the basis for the banker's profit was not only implied by the bull, but taught expressly by Pius V's Jesuit adviser, Toledo. But Navarrus had taught in 1556 that the price of money on the exchanges depended on the varying supply and demand and added that this was "recognized by the common sense of all good and bad men in Christendom and so, as it were, by the voice of God and nature." [71] When his work was turned into Latin from Spanish following the bull, Navarrus did not change his teaching; the contradiction of Pius V and Toledo was indirect in the sense that Navarrus did not bother to point out that the Pope's notion of a profit founded on distance in space flew in the face of what was determined by God and nature. He tried instead to find a more plausible way of distinguishing between exchange banking and lending at a profit, and later theologians followed his example while ignoring the theory of the Pope. In the words of Lessius, in contradiction to those of Pius V, variation in the price of exchange due to the time of payment "should probably not be disapproved when this variation occurs through the common judgment of merchants for reason which commonly seem just to them." [72]

The distinction which Navarrus advanced was explicitly made to avoid the teaching of the bull. Whatever theory of

70. *Theologia moralis*, ed. Gaudé (Rome 1947), 3, 5, 3, 9, 849.
71. *Commentarium resolutorium de cambiis*, 20, 51 (Venice, 1602), *Opera*, vol. 1. On the dates see Arigita, pp. 276, 520.
72. *De justitia* 2, 23, 91.

exchanges one held, the bull had dealt a mortal blow to banking practice if its condemnation of the *ricorsa* was accepted. Asked about the *ricorsa* some time after the death of Pius V, Navarrus responded that the bull condemned only bills of exchange which were unpaid in another city and returned for payment to the place where the bill was drawn. But suppose, he said, that the bank purchasing the exchange has a branch in the other city which was willing to act as agent for the seller, pay the bill in his name, and draw a new bill for payment by him when the new bill is returned to the home bank; surely in this case there was not a fictitious transaction that deserved the name of dry exchange because the seller actually transferred credit which he possessed in the foreign city in order to make a true payment there of the first bill of exchange. That the branch bank acted as both drawee and drawer was not an objection because one person could act in two different capacities.[73] By this mode of argument, Navarrus justified the usual form in which the *ricorsa* was practiced and at the same time deprived the bull of much practical significance for the bankers.

Bonacina thought such practice "very dangerous" and so advised Federico Borromeo.[74] But he did not dispute Navarrus's basic analysis, and to say "very dangerous" was not to follow Charles Borromeo's synod in declaring the *ricorsa* to be usury. In 1631 Navarrus's approach was formally adopted by a Roman commission of theologians.[75]

Detestabilis Avaritia met an even swifter rejection by the theologians than *Cum Onus In Eam*. By the time it appeared in 1586 the Jesuits had gone on record twice, in the 1573 and 1581 decisions, as approving the triple contract, and both

73. Navarrus, *Consilia*, V, 19, 1, 6–10. This counsel was published posthumously in 1591 and in other later editions of Navarrus's works. Arigita, p. 527.

74. *De contractibus* 3, 5, 1, 10.

75. Juan de Lugo, *Disputationes scholasticae et morales* (Paris, 1893), vol. 8, Disputatio 28, 7, 84.

Toledo and Navarrus were solidly committed to it. The only prominent moralist who had directly challenged it was Soto, and when the bull first appeared it was reported that here Soto's thought had vanquished Navarrus. But Sixtus V was quick to limit the significance of his teaching. He was reported to have said privately that he condemned only what "the classical doctors condemned" [76]—an ambiguous statement because the principles taught by classical doctors like Thomas Aquinas condemned the riskless loan but approved investment in a partnership, and the very question at issue was which principles were to be applied to a relatively new combination of contracts. More strikingly, Navarrus did not revise his teaching, and Toledo, now a cardinal, published an explicit defense of the triple contract in a work for confessors entitled *A Summa of Cases of Conscience, or Instruction for Priests.*[77]

Another technique used by the theologians to correct the teaching of Sixtus V had been used in relation to the other bulls: to describe the document as positive pontifical law. *Detestabilis Avaritia* was found to be accepted nowhere. As lapsed positive law, then, it was found to be not binding.[78]

A second approach was taken by those who thought that the bull insisted too much on its basis in divine law to be merely a pontifical decree. These theologians taught that the bull merely prohibited contracts of partnership which were "naturally usurious"—those contracts where the rate of return did not take into account the guarantee of the return of capital.[79] If the guarantee of capital was properly charged for, as by hypothesis it was charged for in the triple contract, then the bull's condemnation did not apply. This approach was implicit in Toledo's defense of contracts eliminating the risk of capital

76. Ligouri, Book 3, n. 908.
77. *Summa,* 58, 41.
78. Lessius, *De justitia* 25; 33; Book 3, n. 908.
79. Lugo, Disputatio 30, n. 37; Ligouri, Book 3, n. 908.

in partnerships. A footnote referred to the existence of *Detestabilis Avaritia* as though there were no conflict between its denunciation of agreements eliminating the risk of capital and Toledo's defense. By 1602 the Sacred Roman Rota had adopted this approach.[80] In doing so it reduced *Detestabilis Avaritia* as an act of pontifical authority to an aberrant nullity.

4. Conclusion

In the sixteenth century a transition in theological analysis and theological attitude towards lay experience in banking accompanied a change in economic conditions which made the old rule on profit-seeking on a loan obsolete. The theologians were unable to formulate a general theory which could explain how the old rule could change, for they identified this rule as unchanging divine and natural law. Instead of formulating a general theory, they advanced cases where they proposed analyses justifying profit on credit. In these analyses they used principles familiar to their theological predecessors but hitherto restricted to prevent the undermining of the usury prohibition.

When the popes and bishops heard of the theological innovations, they correctly perceived that these devices were inconsistent with the maintenance of what they took to be the divine law on usury. In fulfillment of their duty they acted to repress the innovations. They acted with mature deliberation, after study and report by theologians. Three of the men most responsible for the decisions taken have been subsequently recognized by the Church as saints—Charles Borromeo, Francis Borgia, and Pius V. But neither a sense of duty, nor careful deliberation, nor sanctity, nor fidelity to the theology of the past assured that the papal teaching would

80. "Coram Coccino, June 3, 1602," reported in Zech, *op. cit.*, n. 54, Dissertatio 2, n. 175.

determine in a final way the magisterium of the Church. The papal teaching was an element in a complex process; its effect depended on the response of theologians and laity. Only in action and interaction was the teaching of the Church established.

The theological task was not accomplished at once. It took twenty years of argument before the Jesuit decisions of 1581 were reached. The popes did not formally reconcile themselves to the theologians until the eighteenth century, although in practice by 1589 the theological analysis had replaced the papal one. But no automatic agency or influx of divine grace assumed that all would agree at once or that what the popes had given as authentic teaching would not be repealed.

In five ways—by reducing them to pontifical law (the Jesuit general congregations on annuities), by insisting on distinctions which the bulls had rejected (Navarrus on the *ricorsa*), by appeal to *epikeia* (Bonacina on the discount of annuities), by denying their theoretical assumptions (Navarrus and Lessius on exchange-banking), by restricting them to "naturally usurious" contracts as determined by the theologians' view of nature (Toledo on the triple contract), the theologians successfully resisted the papal attempts to teach what was morally permissible in credit-taking. The theologians' efforts were successful, in part, because they were supported by the highest Jesuit authorities and by bishops like the bishop of Augsburg; they were successful, in part, because Pius V and Sixtus V had short pontificates. But these administrative and personal contingencies should not obscure the fact that the accomplishment of the theologians was basically one of intellectual analysis stimulated by reflection on the common practice of Christians.

The theologians did not form their teaching on a close exegesis of the personal intention of the popes who promulgated the bulls or the personal intention of their advisers; plainly, the popes and the advisers who counseled them

73

conceived of their task as the determination of divine and natural law. But the theologians controlled these personal papal intentions by appeal to a broader context of experience and principle. By this appeal they amended the teaching.

The theologians were weakest in not offering any explanation of the papal language that spoke of divine and natural law. This weakness related to their inability to explain how the whole divine and natural law on usury would not disappear if their approach to annuities, exchange-banking, and commercial credit was adopted. A comprehensive theory of how these laws could be explained in terms of more basic values had to await the work of an eighteenth-century layman, Scipio Maffei, and it was not until the nineteenth century that Maffei's theory became a commonplace of the manuals. But if the question is asked, How and when did the usury prohibition change?, the answer is, It changed in the sixteenth century, and it was changed by the theologians, over stubborn papal resistence, defending forms of behavior where profit was sought in extending credit.

The theologians were strongest in recognizing that the experience and judgments of the laity had a value for moral teaching, in not abandoning principles or insights of their theological predecessors even when these principles led to results clearly undermining the usury rule, and in rejecting a facile but untrue explanation of the nature of banking. Thus, appealing to the experience of the faithful, Navarrus argued that an "infinite number of decent Christians" engaged in exchange-banking, and he objected to any analysis which would "damn the whole world." Thus the principles permitting partnerships, insurance, the sale of rights, and the sale of exchange were not abandoned by any major theologian, although the implications of these principles undercut the usury rule. Thus, the Pope's attempt to rest the distinction between exchange-banking and lending upon an alleged distinction between distance in space and distance in time was ignored.

In this development of moral doctrine the three authentic acts of papal teaching, *Cum Onus*, *In Eam*, and *Detestabilis Avaritia* served the purpose of engaging theological attention in a close study of the conditions in which credit was extended. The weak, scrupulous, or badly informed were probably led by these bulls to abstain from contracts which those with access to more expert theological advice felt free to enter. In a short space of time—thirty years at the most—the bulls were deprived of force to influence anyone's behavior. Acts of papal authority, isolated from theological support and contrary to the conviction of Christians familiar with the practices condemned, could not prevail, however accurately they reflected the assumptions and traditions of an earlier age. The theologians were to have the last word, because acts of papal authority are inert unless taught by theologians, because those who cared consulted them, because they taught the next generation, and because the very categories in which the papal teaching was put were shaped by Christian experience and theological analysis.

The Case of Robert Grosseteste [1]

"Because of the obedience by which I am bound to the Apostolic See . . . filially and obediently, I do not obey, I oppose, I rebel." [2] When, in 1253, Robert Grosseteste wrote these words of defiance in reply to a command of Pope Innocent IV, he stood at the height of his fame as one of the most distinguished scholars and bishops of Christendom. Nowadays, perhaps, Grosseteste is remembered most of all as one of the first great pioneers of modern scientific methodology. In his own day he was renowned throughout Europe as a philosopher and biblical scholar. Moreover, in his capacity as bishop of Lincoln, he was one of the most eminent prelates of England and he played a major role in English affairs of state. He was also an exemplary diocesan administrator and a vigorous reformer. In the years immediately after his death there were

1. This paper is based on an article originally published in *The Journal of Ecclesiastical History*.
2. *Roberti Grosseteste Episcopi Quondam Lincolniensis Epistolae*, ed. H. R. Luard (Rolls Series, 1861), Ep. 128, 436. The passage continued, "You cannot take any action against me for my every word and act is not rebellion but the filial honour due by God's command to father and mother. As I have said, the Apostolic See in its holiness cannot destroy, it can only build. This is what the plenitude of power means; it can do all things to edification. But these so-called provisions do not build up, they destroy. They cannot be the work of the blessed Apostolic See, for 'flesh and blood', which do not possess the Kingdom of God 'hath revealed them', not 'our Father which is in heaven'." Trans. in F. M. Powicke, *King Henry III and the Lord Edward* (Oxford, 1947), I, p. 286.

many reports of miracles at his tomb in Lincoln and Grosseteste's friends urged that he be canonized. The Roman authorities received this suggestion with a notable lack of
enthusiasm and no steps were taken in the matter.[3]

The command of Innocent IV which evoked Grosseteste's
protest required the bishop to appoint the Pope's nephew,
Frederick of Lavagna, to a vacant canonry in the cathedral
church of Lincoln. (Of course, Frederick of Lavagna had no
intention of moving to England and taking up residence in
Lincoln. He would live as an absentee and enjoy his benefice
as a sinecure.) Grosseteste was not stirred to resistance, however, merely by this one papal command. For years he had
been growing increasingly opposed to a policy, deliberately
conceived and executed by Innocent IV, of using the Pope's
supreme power in the Church to appoint absentee clerics to
benefices all over Christendom. Such "papal provisions" were
extremely useful to the Pope. They helped Innocent IV to
maintain his curia and to bribe allies to fight in the Pope's
endless wars against the emperor Frederick II. But Grosseteste
thought—quite rightly as it turned out—that a continuance of
the papal policy would weaken the whole pastoral mission of
the Church. That was the basis of his protest.

Grosseteste's letter has attracted the attention of a long line
of distinguished scholars. But it has never been adequately
analyzed from one important point of view, as an extreme
example of the exercise of a right that was deeply engrained
in the theory and practice of the medieval Church—the right
to resist unjust commands of a divinely ordained power. The
case can be called extreme both because of the status of the
parties involved and because of the nature of the correspon-

3. On the various facets of Grosseteste's career, see the essays collected
in *Robert Grosseteste: Scholar and Bishop*, ed. D. A. Callus (Oxford,
1955). The outstanding work on Grosseteste as scientist is A. C. Crombie,
Robert Grosseteste and the Origins of Experimental Science (Oxford,
1953). This book contains an excellent bibliography of modern work on
Grosseteste.

dence that passed between them. Grosseteste was an eminent bishop and he acknowledged the pope to be vicar of Christ and head of the Church on earth. There did exist, already by this time, trends of thought that sought to limit the pope's power by associating the cardinals with him in the exercise of *plenitudo potestatis* or by alleging the superior authority of a general council. But Grosseteste's writings display little sympathy with such ideas. On the contrary, he accepted wholeheartedly, and expressed in language that reflects his own metaphysical preoccupations, the high doctrine of papal sovereignty in the ecclesiastical sphere propounded by Pope Innocent III at the beginning of the thirteenth century.[4]

Moreover, the Pope's command in the matter of Frederick of Lavagna was exceptionally clear and unambiguous. In Grosseteste's day there already existed an elaborate jurisprudence concerning the validity of papal rescripts. Not every papal command imposed an immediate obligation of obedience on the recipient; the principle laid down in the Decretals was, "Papal commands are to be obeyed or letters sent ex-

4. For Innocent III's doctrine see, for example, Migne, P.L., ccxv, col. 279 (Ep. 1), "Petrum caput ecclesiae . . . qui . . . in membra diffunderet ut nihil sibi penitus deperiret, quoniam in capite viget sensuum plenitudo, ad membra vero pars eorum aliqua derivatur." See J. Rivière, "In partem sollicitudinis . . . évolution d'une formule pontificale," *Revue des Sciences Religieuses*, V (1925), 210–231. Grosseteste's very high conception of the papal authority is in evidence all through his letters. See especially Ep. 127, 364, ". . . sicut autem dominus Papa se habet ad universalem ecclesiam in potestatis plenitudine, sic se habet episcopus in potestate accepta a potestate apostolica ad suam diocesim . . ." 389–390, "Quemadmodum igitur sol, quia non potest ubique super terram simul et semel praesentialiter lucere . . . de plenitudine luminis sui, nullo per hoc sibi diminuto, lunam et stellas illuminat . . . Ita dominus Papa, respectu cujus omnes alii praelati sunt sicut luna et stellae, suscipientes ab ipso quicquid habent potestatis ad illuminationem et vegetationem ecclesiae, suam exhibit praesentiam . . ." The image of the Holy See as a sun radiating light and life throughout the Church also occurs in the exhortation read at the papal curia in 1250, see Edward Brown, *Fasciculus Rerum Expetendarum et Fugiendarum* (London, 1690), II, 254. W. A. Pantin's translation of the relevant passage is quoted by Sir Maurice Powicke, "Robert Grosseteste, Bishop of Lincoln," *Bulletin of the John Rylands Library*, xxxv (1953), 482–507 at 505.

plaining why they cannot be obeyed." [5] Canon law provided numerous grounds for contesting the validity of a papal instruction.[6] The pope's letter might conflict with another papal command, it might have been obtained by misrepresentation, it might conflict with the common law of the Church concerning the qualifications of clerks for benefices, and so forth. Only when all previous privileges and all canonical impediments were explicitly abrogated by a *nonobstante* clause, and when the pope affirmed that he was acting *ex certa scientia*, was his mandate to be regarded as an incontestable expression of the *plenitudo potestatis*. But that was precisely the sort of letter Grossesteste had to deal with; it was indeed the use of the non *obstante clause* in such a fashion as to bar any appeal to the common law of the Church that drove him to the point of rebellion. From every point of view the issue stands out simply and starkly. The pope was the supreme embodiment of God's authority on earth; his command was explicit, its rejection uncompromising.[7]

In explaining this paradox modern historians have usually adopted one of three positions. Grosseteste was not a faithful Catholic; or he did not write the letter attributed to him: or —if he was a Catholic and did write the letter—he fell into flagrant self-contradiction. The modern controversy began about a hundred years ago. At that time, while archdeacon Perry was devoting himself to the then fashionable sport of discovering premature Protestants among the leaders of medieval Catholicism, Charles Jourdain was arguing that a bishop of Grosseteste's Catholic convictions could never have written

5. I, iii, 5, "Qualitatem negotii pro quo tibi scribitur, diligenter considerans, aut mandatum nostrum reverenter adimpleas aut per litteras tuas, quare adimplere non possis rationabilem causam praetendas."

6. Such points were discussed at length in the Gregorian Decretals, especially in the title, *De Rescriptis,* and in the glosses and *summae* on this title.

7. The fact that Grosseteste's letter was addressed to the Pope's notary. Master Innocent, not to the Pope himself, does not materially affect the issue. The Pope sent his command through this agent; Grosseteste replied through the same man.

such a letter to a reigning pope.[8] Given the whole background of Grosseteste's life and work, the first position need not be taken seriously and the arguments advanced by Jourdain based on the manuscript tradition of Grosseteste's letter have proved untenable in the light of subsequent research.[9] If the authenticity of the letter is to be called into question it must be on the basis of the inherent improbability of its contents.[10] A. L. Smith, for instance, wrote, "It is unlike Grosseteste to lay down, with no philosophical and scriptural arguments to back it up, so new a proposition . . ." [11] More recent scholars have come to accept the crucial letter as undoubtedly genuine; but it is so different in tone from other writings of Grosseteste that they have been compelled either to postulate a radical change in Grosseteste's attitude to the papacy in the last years of his life[12] or, granted that he retained to the end his

8. G. G. Perry, *The Life and Times of Robert Grosseteste* (London, 1871). Jourdain's criticisms were originally published in 1868 in the *Bulletin de l'Académie des Inscriptions et Belles-Lettres* and were reprinted in his *Excursions Historiques à travers le Moyen Âge* (Paris, 1888), pp. 147–171.

9. S. Harrison Thomson, *The Writings of Robert Grosseteste* (Cambridge, 1940), pp. 171, 193, 212–213. Jourdain's arguments were criticised by J. Fehlten, *Robert Grosseteste, Bischof von Lincoln* (Freiburg, 1887), pp. 109–112. See also F. S. Stevenson, *Robert Grosseteste, Bishop of Lincoln* (London, 1899), pp. 315, 316, 319ff.; F. M. Powicke, *King Henry III and the Lord Edward* (Oxford, 1947), I, 285, n. 3.

10. This was, indeed, Jourdain's principal argument in *Excursions Historiques*, 170–171, "Un point demeure constant, c'est que les écrits contre la cour de Rome, attribués à Robert Grosse-Tête aussi bien que les faits correspondants, racontés dans l'*Historia major* et dans l'*Historia minor* sont en contradiction manifeste avec les opinions qui se font jour à chaque page de la correspondance authentique de l'évêque de Lincoln. La critique est donc en droit de rejeter ces écrits commes apocryphes. . . ."

11. *Church and State in the Middle Ages*, Ford Lectures delivered in 1905 (Oxford, 1913), pp. 104–105.

12. L. Dehio, *Innocenz IV. und England* (Berlin-Leipzig, 1914), pp. 75–81. See W. Stubbs, *Constitutional History of England*, 3rd ed. (Oxford, 1887), ii. 314, "Certainly as he grew older his attitude to the pope became more hostile." Mandell Creighton, *Historical Lectures* (London, 1903), p. 148, "Grosseteste, devoted to the existing ecclesiastical system as he was, an absolutely devout son of the pope," yet was driven in spite of himself into antagonism to that system. . . ."

high conception of papal *plenitudo potestatis*, to charge him with a logical inconsistency in committing an act of disobedience. This latter view was forcefully expressed long ago by Maitland. "The more we make of Grosseteste's heroism in withstanding Innocent IV the worse we think of his logical position. And bad enough it was. He had conceded to the apostolic see a power of freely dealing out ecclesiastical benefices all the world over and then had to contend that this power should be used, but not abused. Instead of the simple statement that the pope cannot lawfully provide clerks with English benefices . . . we find this indefensible distinction between use and abuse. . . . The bishop who makes a stand against the pope at the line between use and abuse is indeed heroic; but his is the heroism of despair." [13]

The most recent writer on the problem, Professor Powicke, if we have understood him rightly, takes up a position that does not differ essentially from that of Maitland, though it is expressed in language more sympathetic to Grosseteste. With his gift for writing thirteenth-century history "from the inside," Professor Powicke enables us to see how Grosseteste's protest was in accordance with all his moral convictions on the episcopal duty of pastoral care, and how his very exaltation of the papal dignity led him to react with unusual vehemence when confronted with abuses of papal power. But Powicke seems concerned to show that Grosseteste's attitude was psychologically comprehensible rather than that it was logically consistent. He points out that, in the thirteenth century, "Orthodox minds were more outspoken than they were in post-Tridentian times in their criticism of papal behaviour." [14]

---

13. F. W. Maitland, *Roman Canon Law in the Church of England* (London, 1898), pp. 66–67. See Stevenson, *Robert Grosseteste*, p. 312, "Although the language of the letter is full of vigour, the sequence of the thoughts is less logical than when Grosseteste's faculties were in their prime."

14. F. M. Powicke, "Robert Grosseteste, Bishop of Lincoln," *Bulletin of the John Rylands Library*, XXXV (1953), pp. 482–507.

This is very true and very relevant. It explains Grosseteste's "sermon" to the papal curia; it would explain a vigorous protest against any specific papal action of which he disapproved; but it does not seem adequately to explain an act of direct disobedience to an authority whose divinely conferred power to command Grosseteste had acknowledged over and over again. And, in the matter of Frederick de Lavagna, he did not merely protest; he flatly refused to obey. One is still left with the problem that Mandell Creighton formulated in discussing Grosseteste's position. "If we grant spiritual supremacy and unlimited power, is it possible to define either the contents or the limits and restrictions of that power?" [15]

One might observe at this point that, if the question at issue were one of disobedience to the unjust command of a temporal ruler, it would present no great problem or paradox, at least to the historian of political theory. We have been told often and emphatically—perhaps too emphatically—that the Middle Ages had no true conception of secular sovereignty, that the authority of a king was limited by custom and natural law, that the ruler who governed unjustly became a tyrant whose commands carried no obligation of obedience. Such limitations on kingship are familiar enough; but there has been no comparable enquiry into the influence of these medieval preconceptions on the theory of papal authority that was built up by Grosseteste's contemporaries in the first half of the thirteenth century. It has usually been vaguely assumed that the powers attributed to the pope as vicar of God were such as to exclude any possibility of legitimate disobedience to a papal command. As Fritz Kern put it, ". . . on the whole, the contrast between the ecclesiastical and the secular authorities was considered to lie in the fact that the former, being in the last resort infallible, was worthy of unconditional obedience, whilst the latter, being fallible, was not to be ac-

15. M. Creighton, *Historical Lectures*, 148.

cepted without conditions." [16] It is this underlying assumption
—that all papal commands were issued by divine authority—
that has made Grosseteste's letter seem illogical to some critics
and unauthentic to others; some further enquiry into its validity may help to explain both the position that Grosseteste
adopted and the arguments by which he defended it.

It is to the canon lawyers that we must turn for the most
penetrating discussions on problems of papal authority in the
age of Innocent III and Innocent IV. Grosseteste himself was
no professional lawyer indeed (and he had hard things to say
about the canonists on occasion) but we may be sure that, as
an active administrator, frequently immersed in legal business,
he was familiar with the basic principles of ecclesiastical law. [17]

16. F. Kern, *Gottesgnadentum und Widerstandsrecht im früheren
Mittelalter* (Leipzig, 1914), p. 183. The translation is that of S. B. Chrimes,
Kingship and Law (Oxford, 1939), p. 89. See also Chrimes, 112: "In the
Church papal infallibility and exemption from every jurisdiction were
claimed and unconditional obedience was demanded from the laity." In
a note to the first quotation (*Gottesgnadentum*, 183, n. 337) Kern pointed
out that the infallibility (*Unfehlbarkeit*) of the Church was not held
necessarily to reside in the person of the pope. Perhaps the use of the
word infallibility at all, with its overtones of modern controversies is
unfortunate; the doctrine concerning the indefectibility of the whole
Church, which was commonly held in the early Middle Ages, had little
to do with the question at issue. See A. Van Leeuwen, "L'Église, règle
de foi chez Occam," *Ephemerides Theologiae Lovanienses*, XI (1934),
pp. 249–288, A. M. Landgraf, "Scattered remarks on the development of
dogma and on papal infallibility," *Theological Studies*, VII (1946), pp.
577ff. The question of the right to resist a tyrannical pope was also raised
briefly by Gierke, but he referred only to the doctrines of fourteenth-
and fifteenth-century conciliarists on this point, see Gierke-Maitland,
Political Theories of the Middle Ages (Cambridge, 1900), p. 36: "Gradually also the doctrines of Conditional Obedience, of a right of resistance
against Tyranny, of a right of revolution conferred by necessity were
imported into the domain of ecclesiastical polity" (referring to the works
of Ockham, Gerson, Dietrich of Niem, Andreas Randulf, Antonius de
Rosellis, Nicholas of Cues).

17. The letter of Giraldus Cambrensis to the bishop of Hereford on
behalf of the young Grosseteste referred not only to his skill in the
liberal arts but also to his usefulness "in the decision of cases," *Giraldi
Cambrensis Opera*, ed. J. S. Brewer (Rolls Series 1861), I, 249. Grosseteste's familiarity with *Decretum* and Decretals is especially in evidence
in Ep. 72 (Luard, 205–234).

Nor need we doubt that, in his younger days, as a brilliant scholar and teacher with an exceptionally enquiring mind, he would have been familiar with at least the major controversies concerning the right government of the Church that were being vigorously pursued in the law schools of Paris and Oxford as well as at Bologna around the turn of the twelfth and thirteenth centuries. The canonists of that period were putting forward ever more extreme claims for the papacy, especially in the realm of temporal affairs, but they never altogether lost sight of the possible dangers to the Church that could arise from abuse of the great powers they conceded to the pope. They did, in fact, think it possible to develop a most exalted doctrine of papal *plenitudo protestatis*, but still to "define the contents" and even the "limits and restrictions" of that power.[18]

Although the precise issue of resistance to papal commands has attracted little attention, it has sometimes been pointed out in standard histories of political theory that the authority attributed to medieval popes, even by their most enthusiastic supporters, was never wholly irresponsible nor wholly arbitrary.[19] A pope could be deposed, at least in the one case of heresy,[20] and he was bound by the ancient law of the Church,

18. On their views see my *Foundations of the Conciliar Theory* (Cambridge, 1955), and "Pope and Council: Some New Decretist Texts," *Mediaeval Studies,* XIX (1957), pp. 197–218.

19. A. J. Carlyle, *A History of Mediaeval Political Theory in the West* (London, 1928), II, pp. 164–178, provides a discerning analysis of Gratian's views on the pope's authority in relation to existing canon law. Carlyle's discussion of the Decretists' treatment of the question (178–194) is interesting but based on a very narrow selection of texts. C. H. McIlwain also discussed the theoretical limits to the pope's competence in *The Growth of Political Thought in the West* (New York, 1932), pp. 279, 283–284. His illustrations were taken from the works of fourteenth-century papal publicists but their arguments in turn were usually borrowed from thirteenth-century canonistic sources. See also Maitland, *Canon Law in England,* pp. 11–12; A. L. Smith, *Church and State,* pp. 85–91; F. Gillmann, "Romanus pontifex iura omnia in scrinio pectoris sui censetur habere," in *Archiv für katholisches Kirchenrecht,* XCII (1912).

20. This was universally acknowledged in the Middle Ages. A selec-

at least in two defined spheres of activity. Gratian wrote at one point of the *Decretum* that only those papal decretals were binding "*in quibus nec praecedentium patrium decretis nec Evangelicis praeceptis aliquid contrarium invenitur*,"[21] and went on to cite the case of a pope who was punished by God and repudiated by the Church because he acted "against the decrees of God and of his predecessors and successors." But, in a later, more detailed discussion, Gratian maintained that the Roman church was not bound by the earlier canons since it was the source of their authority: "*Sacrosancta Romana ecclesia ius et auctoritatem sacris canonibus impertitur, sed non eis alligatur.*"[22] The commentators on the *Decretum*, faced with these apparently contradictory opinions, evolved a doctrine that became generally accepted in the early thirteenth century. They held that, although the pope was not bound by every detail of the early canons and could normally grant special dispensations contrary to their general provisions, nevertheless he was bound by them in matters touching the Christian faith and also in matters touching the "general state of the Church." "*Nec a papa quidem canones possunt abrogari, puta de articulis fidei vel de generali statu ecclesiae.*"[23] There was also much elaborate discussion concerning possible limi-

---

tion of canonistic texts illustrating the point was printed by J. F. v. Schulte, *Die Stellung der Concilien, Päpste und Bischöfe* (Prague, 1871), pp. 253–269. For further references see Gierke-Maitland, *Political Theories*, p. 154, n. 176.

21. *Dist.* 19 *dictum Gratiani post* c. 8.

22. 25 q. 1 *dictum Gratiani post* c. 16.

23. Huguccio, *Summa ad Dist.* 4 *post* c. 3, MS. 72 of Pembroke College, Cambridge, fol. 119ra, and again *ad Dist.* 15 c. 2, fol. 125vb, *ad Dist.* 16 c. 9, fol. 126rb, *Dist.* 40 c. 6, fol. 147vb. These limitations on the pope's authority were commonly recognized, e.g. by Rufinus, *Summa*, ed. Singer (Paderborn, 1902), *ad Dist.* 4; *Glossa Palatina ad* 25 q. 1 c. 3 and 25 q. 2 c. 17, MS. 0.10.2 of Trinity College, Cambridge, fol. 35vb and fol. 37va; Joannes Teutonicus, *Glossa Ordinaria ad* 25 q. 1 c. 3, 25 q. 2 c. 17; Tancred, Gloss *ad Comp. III*, II. VI. 3, MS. 17 of Gonville and Caius College, Cambridge, fol. 197vb; Bernardus Parmensis, *Glossa Ordinaria ad Decretales*, II. XIII. 13, III. VIII. 4; Hostiensis, *Summa Aurea*, Venetiis 1570, *De Constitutionibus*, fol. 7vb.

tations on papal authority by the precepts of Scripture and by natural law (especially in the matter of oaths and vows). The tendency was to concede to the pope the maximum freedom of action in such matters, but some limits were always recognised, at least in theory. It was usually held, for instance, that a pope could not dissolve a consummated marriage nor dispense from a vow of chastity, and that the pope's powers did not license him to sin or to lead others into sin.[24] Such specific limitations were recognised even by a canonist like Tancred who, when indulging in rhetorical generalities, carried the exaltation of papal *plenitudo potestatis* to the utmost peak in phrases that passed into the *Glossa Ordinaria* on the Gregorian Decretals, and subsequently became a part of the standard equipment of the fourteenth-century papal publicists: "*In is gerit vicem dei quia sedet in loco Jesu Christi qui est verus deus et verus homo . . . item de nichilo facit aliquid. . . . Item in is gerit vicem dei quia plenitudinem potestatis habet in rebus ecclesiasticis. . . . Item quia dispensare potest supra ius et contra ius. . . . Nec est qui dicat ei, cur ita facis.*" [25] In spite of such sentiments Tancred thought that the pope could not dispense *contra articulos fidei vel generale statutum ecclesiae*, nor in questions of monastic poverty and chastity.[26]

24. For typical discussions of such questions see Bernardus Parmensis, *Glossa Ordinaria ad* I. VII. 2, I. IX. 11, II. XIII. 13, II. XXIV. 18, III. VIII. 4, III. XXXV. 6. It was often held that the pope could not annul natural law or divine law but that he could interpret them: for example, Raymundus de Pennaforte, *Summa Iuris,* ed. J. R. Serra (Barcelona, 1945), p. 38, "Licet autem dixerim nullam dispensationem admittendam contra ius naturale tamen papa potest ipsum interpretari. . . ." The power to "interpret" might in practice prove very elastic, as was emphasized by W. Ullmann, *Medieval Papalism* (London, 1949), pp. 50–75, but it was never altogether limitless. On the bounds of the pope's dispensatory authority see J. Brys, *De dispensatione in iure canonico praesertim apud Decretistas et Decretalistas usque ad medium saeculum decimum quartum* (Bruges, 1925).

25. Gloss *ad Comp. III,* I. v.3, Caius MS. 17, fol. 147va. Repeated by Bernardus Parmensis, *Glossa Ordinaria ad* I. VII. 3.

26. Gloss *ad Comp. III,* II. VI. 3, Caius MS. 17, fol. 197vb, "Dominus papa potest dispensare in omnibus quae non sunt contra articulos fidei vel generale statutum ecclesiae . . . nec in his quae sunt contra substantiam

All this is relatively straightforward. Maitland observed that, 'As a matter of fact, popes do not attempt to repeal the ten commandments"; and we need not be surprised to find even the medieval canonists pointing out that it was improper for them to do so. Of course, a pope was not expected to teach heresy or to issue unjust commands or to bring ruin on the Church. But what if he did? There is the crux of our problem —and Grosseteste's; and it was a problem quite familiar to the medieval canonists as well. The whole question of unjust decisions by ecclesiastical superiors was raised by Gratian in the third *Quaestio* of *Causa* II of the *Decretum*. He first cited some forty texts tending to prove that even unjust sentences were to be respected and unjust commands obeyed; but then, following his normal dialectical technique, he went on to argue the other and stronger side of the case. "*Quod autem iniustae sententiae parendum non sit, multis auctoritatibus probatur*"; [27] and there were even more texts cited in support of this point of view. Perhaps the one that expresses the essence of the argument most succinctly is c. 92: "*Non semper malum est non obedire praecepto, cum enim Dominus iubet ea quae sunt contraria Deo, tunc ei obediendum non est.*" However, all this argumentation dealt with obedience in general, not with the specific issue of disobedience to papal commands. If the question had been simply whether one should obey God or man, no medieval lawyer or theologian would have hesitated; the problem of disobedience to a pope was so difficult precisely because the pope was said to "stand in place of Jesus Christ who is true God and true man," because, as the canonists were fond of pointing out, his edicts were promulgated not by human but by divine authority. If that dictum had been applied to every papal command, there could evidently have been no basis for licit disobedience in any circumstances,

---

monachatus ut monachus haberet uxorem vel proprium . . . nec in his quae in sui natura sunt mala ut quis sine peccato posset adulterari."

27. 11 q. 3 *dictum Gratiani post* c. 43.

but the canonists did not in practice press it so rigorously. The *Glossa Ordinaria* to the Decretals, for instance, declared that, "*quod fit auctoritate Papae dicitur fieri auctoritate Dei,*" but added at once, "*et est verum,* si iusta causa hoc faciat." [28]

Grosseteste based his whole case on the assertion that not every command emanating from the pope was supported by the divine authority of the Apostolic See: ". . . *contra Ipsum autem nec est nec esse potest Apostolicae sedis sanctitas divinissima. Non est igitur praedictae literae, tenor Apostolicae sanctitati consonus. . . .*" [29] And this led him to his concluding declaration that, precisely in order to remain loyal and obedient to the apostolic see, it was necessary for him to disobey that particular command of the pope. One might have expected that this sharp distinction between the person of a ruler and the institution that he represented would have attracted the attention of constitutional historians, coming as it does from a most influential bishop about half a century before the English barons declared that their allegiance was owed to the crown, not to the person of the king, and that, in defense of the crown, they might lawfully take up arms against the king. But Grosseteste's argument has usually been passed over as a piece of "epigrammatic and paradoxical language," "a strange form of words," "a curious formula." The distinction between the pope and the apostolic see upon which he relied was in fact no invention of Grosseteste but was well established in the glosses of the preceding half century. Huguccio, commenting on an assertion that all the decrees of the Apostolic See were to be obeyed, put the point quite explicitly. "*Hoc non fit ratione papae sed propter auctoritatem sedis, unde caute dixit apostolicae sedis et non dixit apostolici.*" [30] Laurentius, approaching the question from a different angle, explained that it was possible to distinguish between

28. Bernardus Parmensis, *Glossa Ordinaria ad* I. VII. 2.
29. Luard, Ep. 128, 434.
30. *Summa ad Dist.* 19 c. 2, Pembroke MS. 72, fol. 128rb.

the source of authority of an office and that of the individual who occupied the office.[31] There is, moreover, an interesting English gloss written in the last years of the twelfth century which seems precisely to anticipate Grosseteste's argument that one could resist the pope while remaining in communion with the see of Peter. The author was considering the case of the Roman clergy who deserted the erring Pope Anastasius, and suggested that they sinned in doing so since all Catholics were required to remain in communion with the apostle Peter or with *"eo qui sedet pro Petro."* His reply was that, in this case, *"Anastasius non fuit de societate Petri, sed cardinales. errant . . ."* [32] Finally, Joannes Teutonicus, in his *Glossa Ordinaria* to the *Decretum,* maintained that, in promulgating a law that endangered the Church, a pope stripped himself of the authority pertaining to the head of the Church, so that the law was of no effect.[33] A good deal of the "illogicality" of Grosseteste's attitude disappears when one realises that, according to the prevailing opinion of the time, there was no certain presumption that every papal command was consistent with the divine will nor supported by divine authority. After all, the

31. His view was cited by S. Mochi Onory, *Fonti canonistiche dell' idea moderna dello stato* (Milan, 1951), p. 196, ". . . set dic quod aliud est ipsa iurisdictio per se inspecta, que a Deo processit, et aliud, quod ipsius iurisdictionis executonem consequatur aliquis per populum . . . Nam populus per electionem facit imperatorem, set non imperium, sicut cardinales per electionem preferunt aliquem sibi ad iurisdictionem, que a Deo data est, exercendam."

32. The gloss was commenting on 24 q. 1 c. 27, "Quicunque ab unitate fidei vel societatis Petri Apostoli quolibet modo semetipsos segregant, tales nec vinculi peccati absolvi. . . ." It runs, *"societatis,* i.e. ab eo qui sedet pro Petro sed tunc 19 *dist. Anastasius* contra. Solutio, Anastasius non fuit de societate Petri sed cardinales erant." Caius MS. 676, fol. 166ra. On the date and provenance of this work see S. Kuttner and E. Rathbone, "Anglo-Norman Canonists of the Twelfth Century," *Traditio,* VII (1949–1951), pp. 279–358 at 317.

33. *Glossa Ordinaria ad Dist.* 40 c. 6. After setting out the usual doctrine that a pope could be deposed for heresy Joannes Teutonicus went on, "Item nonquid papa posset statuere quod non posset accusari de haeresi. Respondeo quod non, quia ex hoc periclitaretur tota ecclesia quod non licet . . . quia hoc fit in eo casu quo desinit esse caput ecclesiae et ita non tenet constitutio."

crimes and errors of several popes had been described in *Decretum;* there were elaborate discussions concerning the steps to be taken against a pope who fell into heresy; and, though one text of the *Decretum* declared that the pope was to be presumed holy, the *Glossa Ordinaria* rather drily commented, "It does not say that he is holy but only that he is to be presumed holy until the contrary is established." [34]

One is left with the problem of whether, and in what circumstances, a subject could take it upon himself to assume that the pope was so grievously at fault that there was a duty to disobey his command. Once again, if one looks only at the canonistic generalities—"*Nemo iudicabit primam sedem,*" "*Papa a nemine potest iudicari*"—it would seem that there could be no such right or duty; but, again, one finds that the generalities were considerably modified in discussions on particular cases. The issue was posed for the Decretists by two consecutive chapters which Gratian cited in support of the proposition, "*Quod absque discretione iustitiae nulli agere licet.*" The first declared,

Quidquid ergo sine discretione iustitiae contra huius (Romanae ecclesiae) disciplinam actum fuerit, ratum habere ratio nulla permittit.[35]

The second, in the same strain, laid down that,

Praeceptis Apostolicis non dura superbia resistatur sed . . . quae . . . Apostolica auctoritate iussa sunt salutifere impleantur.

Having regard to the context it would seem that Gratian meant to suggest that *cum discretione* or *sine dura superbia* it might be permissible to resist, and this was assumed without question by earlier commentators like Rufinus and Stephanus

34. *Glossa Ordinaria ad Dist.* 40 c. 1, "Sed non dicitur hic quod sancti sunt sed quod sancti praesumuntur donec contrarium constet."
35. *Dist.* 12 c. 1.

Tornacensis.[36] Huguccio, however, would have none of this. No one could judge the act of the pope, he argued, and so it was impossible to act *cum discretione* against the discipline of the Roman church, and Gratian was wrong to envisage such a situation.[37] The suggestion that one might resist the pope, not with pride but with humility, evoked the same comment from Huguccio.

. . . *non esset humilitas sed superbia, non esset discretio sed indiscretio si ei resistatur, et sic non facit ad propositionum Gratiani.*[38]

Yet, when he came to consider the words *iussa sunt salutifere,* Huguccio did acknowledge the possibility of licit resistance in some circumstances.

SALUTIFERE. *Si contra salutem aliquid praecipitur non est parendum, et est argumentum quod non omnia statuta a praelatis sunt observanda sed tantum illa quae statuenda sunt salutifere.*[39]

Commenting on these passages a century later, Guido de Baysio observed that Huguccio first contradicted Gratian and then contradicted himself.[40] It would seem more correct to

36. Rufinus, *ed. cit., ad Dist.* 12, "Dictum erat quod nulli preter consuetudinem romane ecclesie faciendum est; sed ne hoc omnino absolute intelligeretur, determinat quod cum discretione iustitie aliquando secus licet." Stephanus Tornacensis, *Summa,* ed. Schulte (Giessen 1891), *ad Dist.* 12 c. 1, "*Sine discretione.* Alterum cum discretione fieri. . . ."

37. *Summa ad Dist.* 12 c. 1, Pembroke MS. 72, fol. 124ra. Huguccio drew a distinction between following a local practice different from that of the Roman church, but not forbidden by it, and acting against the discipline of Rome. "Sed nunquid cum discretione licet agere contra disciplinam romanae ecclesiae, nunquid licet alicui judicare de facto papae? . . . Dico ergo vacat argumentum a sensu contrario nec facit ad propositum magistri . . . licet ergo cum discretione aliter agere quam romana ecclesia teneat, sed nec cum discretione nec sine discretione licet agere contra disciplinam eius."

38. *Summa ad Dist.* 12 c. 2, Pembroke MS. 72, fol. 124ra.

39. *Ibid.* The argument recurred in very similar form in Ockham's *Breviloquium,* ed. L. Baudry (Paris, 1937), II. XXI, 61. See "Ockham, the conciliar theory, and the canonists," 45–46.

40. *Rosarium seu in Decretorum Volumen Commentaria* (Venetiis, 1577), *Dist.* 12 cc. 1, 2, fol. 15ra–15rb.

suggest that he was shifting the emphasis from the subjective disposition of the recipient of a command to the objective nature of the command itself. In all these discussions one is aware of the intense medieval conviction of an objective moral law whose tenets were accessible to a man of good will and good sense, and whose precepts were to be obeyed in preference to those of any human superior, whether prince or pope.

In the next generation the *Glossa Ordinaria* sharply denied any right to disobey.

Nunquid ergo cum discretione iustum est contra illam agere? Certe non . . . unde vacet hic argumentum a contrario sensu.[41]

This view was also held by Joannes Faventinus,[42] but it does not reflect a general consensus of opinion. The *Glossa Palatina* repeated Huguccio's argument that a command *contra salutem* was not to be obeyed, and added the suggestion that a papal command *contra ius* should not be obeyed at once, but a second message awaited;[43] Goffredus Tranensis returned to the old point of view that *cum discretione* resistance was permissible. The discussion was continued in glosses on the Gregorian Decretals with special emphasis on the proper attitude to a papal rescript *contra ius*. Raymundus de Pennaforte the compiler of the Decretals and, incidentally, a correspondent of Grosseteste,[44] wrote in his early *Summa Iuris* that such a rescript should be rejected,[45] and Goffredus Tranensis

41. *Glossa Ordinaria ad Dist.* 12 c. 1.
42. For his view and that of Goffredus Tranensis, see *Rosarium ad Dist.* 12, fol. 15ra.
43. Vatican MS. Pal. Lat. 658, fol. 3rb, Gloss *ad Dist.* 12 c. 1; "Quid ergo quod romana ecclesia aliquid praecipit contra ius. Dico quod non statim est faciendum sed secunda responsio est expectanda." Gloss *ad Dist.* 12 c. 2; "*Salutifere impleantur* . . . et est argumentum quod non quaecumque a praelatis statuuntur observare tenemur, nisi salutifere sint statuta."
44. Luard, Ep. 37, 128.
45. *Summa Iuris, ed. cit.,* 28; "Si dubitatur utrum rescriptum habeat vim constitutionis, videas utrum sit secundum ius, aut preter ius, aut

expressed the same opinion, taking up a similar position in his *Summa* on the Decretals to that expressed in his gloss on *Dist.* 12 of the *Decretum*.[46] Hostiensis held that a rescript destructive of divine law should be utterly rejected. "*Si sit destructivum iuris Evangelici vel Apostolici omnino respuitur.*"[47] (One is reminded of Grosseteste's ". . . *his quoque quae mandatis Apostolicis adversantur, parentalem zelans honorem, adversor et obsto.*"). Hostiensis also, in his discussion on the title, *De Maioritate et Obedientia*, provided a brief treatise on the whole principle of canonical obedience which included a discussion on the proper limits of that obedience. An evil command was not to be obeyed, he wrote, provided that there was no doubt whatsoever as to its injustice; if there was any doubt it was better for the subject to obey.[48] The same reservation was put forward by Bernardus Parmensis in his *Glossa Ordinaria* on the Decretals. He was discussing the text, "Qui non obedierit principi morte moriatur," and, after explaining that *princeps* in this context could be taken to mean the pope, he went on,

Vel dic qui non obedierit iusto praecepto, 11 q. 3 si dominus. Si est iniustum et hoc manifestum, non obediat ut ibi et c. Iulianus.

---

contra ius. In primo et secundo casu est epistola decretalis, et habet auctoritatem canonis in causis definiendis. . . . In tertio casu, scilicet cum est contra ius, reiciendum est."

46. *Summa super titulos Decretalium* (Venetiis, 1601), fol. 4, n. 6.

47. *Summa Aurea* (Venetiis, 1570), *De Rescriptis*, fol. 11va.

48. *Summa Aurea, De Maioritate et Obedientia*, fol. 90vb–fol. 93ra, ". . . secularis vero et regularis consequenter obedire debet preceptis maioris in his quae pertinent ad divinum cultum, vel respiciunt utilitatem communem . . . ideo si quid precipiat maior quod canonicis obviet institutis servandum non est . . . hoc si certum est quod iniustum sive iniquum sit . . . nonquam enim propter obedientiam malum committendum, licet bonum aliquando debeat intermitti . . . alias in dubio obediendum est . . ." (fol. 92rb). Hostiensis, one of the most eminent jurists of the thirteenth century, lived for several years in England in the service of Henry III. The most recent survy of his life and thought is that of C. Lefebvre, *Dictionnaire de Droit Canonique* (1953), s.v. "Hostiensis." On his stay in England see F. M. Powicke, *King Henry III and the Lord Edward*, I, 272–273; N. Didier, "Henri de Suse en Angleterre," *Studi in Onore di Vincenzo Arangio-Ruiz* (Napoli, 1953), pp. 333–351.

Si dubium esset praeceptum principis, propter bonum obedientiae quod sibi praecipit, faciat . . .[49]

These texts suggest that, according to canonistic doctrine the obedience due to the pope was subject to qualifications and limitations. However, we have not so far mentioned the canonist whose views on the whole question must seem most interesting and relevant in the present context—that is, of course, Grosseteste's adversary, Pope Innocent IV himself Matthew Paris has left us a vivid if not wholly reliable account of the great pontiff's angry reaction when he learned of Grosseteste's defiance; there is a certain piquancy in investigating his treatment of the question at issue when, as one of the greatest lawyers of his age, he reviewed it dispassionately in the calm of the study. Needless to say, Innocent was, in theory as well as in practice, an extreme exponent of the theory of papal *plenitudo potestatis*. Even if one sets aside the difficult question of his conception of the temporal power of the papacy, it is still clear that he pressed the papal claims beyond all previous bonds. In his *Commentaria* the limits of the pope's dispensatory authority were stretched further than ever before; [50] the pope's immunity from all human judgment was vigorously reemphasised; and, characteristically, Innocent showed himself less willing than his predecessors to condone resistance to papal commands even when there was just cause for disobedience. Even then, he held, it was sinful for the subject to disobey unless he was permitted to do so by the

49. *Glossa Ordinaria ad* I. XXXIII. 2. Bernardus expressed himself more ambiguously in his gloss *ad* I. XIV. 4: "Si enim ex certa scientia scriberet papa pro minori eius mandato esset obediendum quia sacrilegii instar obtinet, dubitare an is sit dignus quem Princeps eligit. . . . Praeterea contra ius et contra publicam utilitatem est tale rescriptum et ideo non valet. . . . Item est hic argumentum quod non est obediendum semper mandato Papae . . . sed non dicitur mandatum, quando ignoranter mandat."

50. For example, in the matter of monastic poverty and celibacy. *In Quinque Libros Decretalium Commentaria* (Venetiis, 1570), p. 517, ad III. XXXV. 6.

uthor of the command,[51] and, apparently, papal rescripts *ontra ius vel publicam utilitatem* were to be held valid pro-ided only that they were issued *ex certa scientia.*[52]

But even Innocent IV found it necessary to admit certain xceptions to this general rule. For instance, he acknowledged hat monks who were commanded to act in violation of their nonastic vows ought not to obey even if the command came rom the pope: "*Quia etiam si papa mandaret eis aliquid, quod esset contra substantiam ordinis, vel peccatum, non de-erent obedire.*"[53] There was an interesting discussion too :oncerning the pope's authority in relation to episcopal ights. Innocent raised the question whether a pope could ake away a bishop's power to administer the sacrament of :onfirmation, and argued that, while the pope could not abolish he sacrament itself, he could make such regulations concern-ng its administration as to exclude any particular bishop from :onferring it. But he went on,

Tamen si papa talia faceret sine causa magna et aliis nota non debet ustineri tanquam faciens contra generalem statum ecclesiae.[54]

The words "*non debet sustineri*" seem to imply a right of esistance, but Innocent did not pursue the question further t this point. His most detailed treatment of the whole prob-

51. *Commentaria ad* I. IV, *Rubrica,* 40: "Vel dicas et melius quod :ontra iura et contra praecepta venire licet his, quibus licitum est novam egem et specialem introducere contra illud ius vel praeceptum similiter, t novam consuetudinem. Sed si tale esset, quod contra illud ius vel praeceptum non licet sine peccato legem specialem statuere; et ad hoc, t non peccet ille qui contra ius vel praeceptum domini papae facit, opportet quod ex aliqua iusta causa faciat, et volens consuetudinem intro-ducere, et superiore consentiente, scilicet eo qui legem fecit, vel qui ootestatem habet condendi legem contra illud ius, vel mandatum."
52. *Commentaria ad* I. XIV. 4, 125: "Non enim semper literis papae obediendum est, quia decipi potest papa . . . sunt enim literae aliquando :ontra ius vel publicam utilitatem, unde non valent, nisi ex certa scientia facta inde mentione quod pro minus literato vel minore scriberet."
53. *Commentaria ad* V. III. 34, 601.
54. *Commentaria ad* I. IV. 4, 41.

lem was reserved for the last pages of his treatise. C. 44 of th
title, *De Sententia Excommunicationis* in the Decretals deal
with the case of a man who, after his marriage, discovered
the existence of an impediment which rendered the marriage
invalid. The decretal laid down that it was then his duty
under pain of mortal sin, to abstain from conjugal relation
with his wife, and—provided he was acting with certain
knowledge—he was required to do so in the face of any
ecclesiastical sentence to the contrary, even to the point o
undergoing excommunication if necessary.[55] As the *Glossa Ordinaria* commented, "*potius debet omnia mala pati quam contr
conscientiam peccatum operari mortale.*"[56] Innocent took
this case, which so clearly raised the issue of the subject'
conscience, as the basis for further enquiries into the limits o
the obedience due to an ecclesiastical superior. What if a

[55]. V. XXXIX. 44: "In primo casu debet potius excommunicationi
sententiam humiliter sustinere, quam per carnale commercium peccatum
operari mortale." It is interesting to note that this authoritative decretal
of Innocent III directly contradicts a twelfth-century opinion quoted by
A. L. Smith, *Church and State,* pp. 54–55: "A *Summa Quaestionum,* a
book of problems more than thirty years before the Lateran Council,
had put the case of a man bound to adhere to a wife whom he knows
to be not really his wife. 'Yet he sins not if he is obeying a command of
the Church. . . . If the objection be raised that he is acting against his
conscience and therefore sins, we answer he must let conscience go'."

[56]. *Glossa Ordinaria ad* V. XXXIX. 44. Grosseteste, indeed, did not
profess himself willing to undergo punishment for his disobedience, but
rather declared in advance that no action could be taken against him for
his conduct. Luard, Ep. 128, 437: "Nec ob hoc potest inde vestra discretio quicquam durum contra me statuere, quia omnis mea in hac parte
et dictio et actio, nec contradictio est nec rebellio, sed filialis divino
mandato debita patri et matri honoratio." But the whole issue of "passive
resistance" as against "active resistance" assumed a different form when
the penalty involved was a spiritual one whose main sanction was its
effect on the soul of the excommunicated party; for the question naturally arose whether an unjust sentence of excommunication could be
binding in the eyes of God even though promulgated by the pope. The
point was often discussed by the canonists in connection with the words,
"Quodcumque ligaveris super terram erit ligatum et in caelis." The more
common opinion held that an unjust papal excommunication might bind
as regards the Church Militant, but not as regards the Church Triumphant. This was the view, for example, of Joannes Teutonicus, *Glossa
Ordinaria ad* 11 q. 3 c. 48, 24 q. 1 c. 5, c. 6.

bishop issued, under pain of excommunication, an unjust command whose fulfilment did not actually involve the subject in mortal sin? He need not obey, wrote Innocent, but should appeal to a superior for absolution from the sentence. That led inevitably to the next question. What if the command came from the pope who had no superior?

Sed quid si papa iniustum praecipiat qui superiorem non habet cum quo agi possit. Potest dici quod si de spiritualibus vel ecclesiasticis personis aliquid praecipit, etiam iniustum, illud servandum est quia nemini licet de eius factis iudicare 40 dist. si papa, 9 q. 3 c. cuncta et multis aliis cc . . .

So far it was merely a reassertion of the claim that even unjust commands of the pope were to be obeyed; but the conclusion of the passage introduced very significant reservations.

. . . nemini licet de eius factis iudicare . . . nisi mandatum haeresim contineret, quia tunc esset peccatum, vel nisi ex praecepto iniusto vehementer praesumeretur statum ecclesiae turbari, vel etiam forte alia mala ventura esse, quia tunc peccant obediendo . . .[57]

Nisi . . . vehementer praesumeretur statum ecclesiae turbari. That is exactly what Grosseteste did presume! *Quia tunc peccant obediendo.* That was the whole substance of Grosseteste's protest. One is faced with the irony that his conduct can be justified out of the writings of Innocent IV himself, for Grosseteste defended his "rebellion" on precisely the ground that Innocent conceded as justifying disobedience to a papal command. He was vehemently convinced that the Pope's policy was disrupting the peace and order of the Church.

57. *Commentaria ad* V. XXXIX. 44, 661. The edition cited has "nisi ex praecepto *iusto* vehementer praesumeretur." *Iniusto* is given in the edition of Frankfurt 1570 and seems obviously preferable in this context. There is no critical edition of Innocent's work.

. . . primo, quia de illius literae et aliarum ei consimilium longe lateque dispersarum superaccumulato Non obstante *. . . scatet cataclysmus inconstantiae, audaciae, et procacitatis etiam inverecundae mentiendi et fallendi, diffidentiae cuiquam credendi vel fidem adhibendi, et ex his consequentium vitiorum, quorum non est numerus, Christianae religionis puritatem et socialis conversationis hominum tranquillitatem commovens et perturbans.*[58]

And, accordingly, he argued that obedience to the pope's command would involve mortal sin, and, moreover, a sin more damnable and detestable than any since Lucifer's.

Praeterea, post peccatum Luciferi . . . non est nec esse potest alterum genus peccati tam adversum et contrarium Apostolorum doctrinae et Evangelicae . . . quam animas curae pastoralis officio et ministerio vivificandas et salvandas, pastoralis officii et ministerii defraudatione mortificare et perdere.[59]

Even a brief survey of contemporary opinions on the limits of the obedience due to the pope makes it possible to reconsider some of the arguments that have been advanced against the authenticity of Grosseteste's letter. Some critics have emphasised the "general" language in which it was written, and have suggested that, if Grosseteste wrote it at all, it was intended as a protest against the papal policy as a whole, not as a direct refusal to a specific command.[60] It seems more probable that Grosseteste, taking the extreme step of resisting the Pope, was couching his letter in the language best calculated to justify such resistance. Like most of his contemporaries, he had conceded that the pope normally possessed

58. Luard, Ep. 128, 434.
59. *Ibid.*
60. This argument was advanced by H. K. Mann, *Lives of the Popes* XIV, 263: "This language, which under the circumstances must be set down as too general, has led some authors to regard the letter as a forgery, or at least as a mere literary exercise. It may perhaps with more justice be said to be a letter in which Grosseteste was dealing, not with the particular case of Frederick, but with the whole method of procedure of the papal commissioners."

he right of distributing ecclesiastical benefices; but he also followed the common opinion of the time in holding that no exercise of papal power should be endured which threatened the well-being of the Church, which was, as the canonists put it, "*contra generalem statum ecclesiae,*" or, in Grosseteste's words (borrowed from St. Paul), "*non in aedificationem sed in destructionem.*" The specific act of disobedience could be most effectively defended by an emphasis on the injury to the Church as a whole arising from the papal policy.

The comment that "It is unlike Grosseteste to lay down, with no philosophical and scriptural arguments to back it up, so new a proposition . . ."[61] is evidently wide of the mark. There was no new proposition in Grosseteste's letter. But A. L. Smith's further argument that Grosseteste's defiance of the Pope reflects an attitude of mind radically different from that implied by his other, more deferential, letters of protest concerning papal appointments does present a serious difficulty. Once again, however, the problem can be resolved by reference to the contemporary doctrine on canonical obedience. The prevailing opinion held that resistance to an ecclesiastical superior could be justified only by certain knowledge that he had commanded something evil or injurious to the "state of the Church"; there was a strong presumption in favor of the superior, and if there was any trace of doubt in the mind of the subject it was his duty to obey. Grosseteste, one may suppose, was driven only very slowly and reluctantly to the conclusion that God's own vicar was using his plenitude of power for the "destruction" of the Church. It is not quite accurate to say that he based his disobedience on an "indefensible distinction between use and abuse." The line at which disobedience became a duty was drawn by the law and doctrine of the Church; the burden that lay on Grosseteste's conscience was to determine whether the Pope had crossed

61. See above, note 11.

that line. As long as the Pope's demands seemed merely inconvenient and inconsiderate Grosseteste felt bound to obey. It was only when submissively worded letters of protest had been brushed aside, when even personal exhortation at the papal curia had proved ineffective, that he was forced to the certain conviction that further compliance would actually endanger the Church. But once Grosseteste was so convinced his proper course of action was clear; according to the common doctrine of the time—according to the teaching of Innocent IV himself—it was his duty to disobey the Pope. We need not wonder that the letter recording his outraged decision was filled with a grief and bitterness that set it apart from the rest of his correspondence.

Our investigation of Church law in the thirteenth century shows that it is not necessary to accept any of the three modern interpretations of Grosseteste's conduct outlined above—that is, that he did not write the letter attributed to him or that he was not a faithful Catholic or that he contradicted his own beliefs. On the contrary, Grosseteste did write the letter; he was a profoundly Catholic pastor of souls; and he was never more Catholic than when he refused to injure the Church at the behest of the Pope. In disobeying Innocent IV, Grosseteste was neither rejecting his own inner convictions in a moment of anger nor formulating a novel principle of resistance to papal authority. He was acting in accordance with a widely accepted and well-developed doctrine of the Church which could find support even in the writings of Innocent himself. It is rare indeed to find the doctrine so uncompromisingly acted upon by a medieval bishop—but then Grosseteste was a man of rare courage. Perhaps one day he will be canonized after all.

ORDINARY PAPAL
MAGISTERIUM AND RELIGIOUS ASSENT

Humanae Vitae is a document about marriage, love, and procreation, but the controversy that has followed its publication
has not centered around those matters, but around authority in
the Church and, specifically, around the authority to teach.
The questions now under discussion are not new, but the
encyclical has forced them to be asked with a concern and
an urgency that have been lacking in the recent past. This
article speaks of some of those problems.

1. Lumen Gentium, 25

In paragraph 28 of *Humanae Vitae*, Pope Paul VI urges
priests to "loyal internal and external obedience to the teaching authority of the Church." "That obedience, as you well
know," the Pope continues, "obliges not only because of the
reasons adduced, but rather because of the light of the Holy
Spirit, which is given in a particular way to the pastors of the
Church in order that they may illustrate the truth." A footnote
at this point refers to paragraph 25 of *Lumen Gentium*, where
the Second Vatican Council teaches:

Religious allegiance of the will and intellect should be given in an
entirely special way to the authentic teaching authority of the
Roman pontiff, even when he is not speaking *ex cathedra;* this
should be done in such a way that his supreme teaching authority

is respectfully acknowledged, while the judgments given by him are sincerely adhered to according to his manifest intention and desire, as this is made known by the nature of his documents, or by his frequent repetition of the same judgment, or by his way of speaking.

That it is to this statement about *religiosum voluntatis et intellectus obsequium* that the Pope is referring, and not to other statements in paragraph 25, is clear from the Pope's own manner of speaking in the encyclical and from the remarks of Monsignor Lambruschini in presenting the encyclical to the press. In order to understand what response the Pope himself is seeking, then, it will be of aid to examine the background and import of paragraph 25.

A section dealing with the ordinary teaching authority of the pope was included in the original *schema, De Ecclesia et de B. Maria Virgine,* presented to the council at the first session in 1962:

To the authentic teaching authority of the Roman pontiff, even when he is not speaking *ex cathedra,* religious allegiance of will and intellect should be given; this should be done in such a way that his supreme teaching authority is respectfully acknowledged, while the judgment given by him is sincerely adhered to according to his manifest intention and desire, as that is made known by the nature of the documents, by his frequent repetition of the same judgment, or by his way of speaking. The intention and desire of the Roman pontiffs is made manifest especially through those doctrinal acts that concern the whole Church, such as certain apostolic constitutions or encyclical letters or their more solemn addresses; for these are the principal documents of the ordinary teaching authority of the Church, they are the principal ways in which it is declared and formed, and what is taught and inculcated in them often already belongs, for other reasons, to Catholic doctrine. And when the Roman pontiffs go out of their way to pronounce on some subject which has hitherto been controverted, it must be clear to everyone that, in the mind and intention of those pontiffs, this subject can no longer be regarded as a matter for free debate among theologians.[1]

In support of the general obligation of assent, the text refers to the First Vatican Council, the Code of Canon Law, Leo XIII's *Sapientiae Christianae*, and Pius XI's *Casti Connubii*.[2] A second footnote identifies the last lines of the passage as a direct citation from Pius XII's *Humani Generis*.[3]

The first *schema* on the Church was rejected by the council at the first session. Between the first and second sessions a new *schema* was elaborated, which was presented to the second session and accepted as a basis for discussion. In the new *schema*, the paragraph on the teaching office of the Church (no. 19) was entitled, "*De Episcoporum munere docendi*," and formed part of the new chapter III, "*De Constitutione Hierarchica Ecclesiae et in specie de Episcopatu*." The section on the ordinary magisterium of the pope is the last part of paragraph 19 and is, except for very minor differences, the same text cited above from *Lumen Gentium*.[4] But it should be noted that in the new *schema* the explanation of the concrete mode of exercise of the magisterium and the warning against continued public theological discussion are both omitted. Apparently the warning was not dropped without opposition, for among the suggested *emendationes* distributed along with the second schema was that of five bishops who ask that the statement from *Humani Generis* be replaced in the text.[5] This suggestion was not accepted, nor was that of

1. *Schemata Constitutionum et Decretorum de quibus disceptabitur in Concilii sessionibus: Series Secunda, De Ecclesia et de B. Maria Virgine* (Vatican Press, 1962), pp. 48–49.
2. *Ibid.*, p. 57.
3. *Ibid.*
4. *Schema Constitutionis Dogmaticae De Ecclesia*, Pars I (Vatican Press, 1963), p. 30.
5. *Emendationes a Concilii Patribus scripto exhibitae super schema Constitutionis Dogmaticae De Ecclesia*, Pars I (Vatican Press, 1963), pp. 43–44.

Bishop Cleary who proposed that the text include a statement about freedom of investigation.[6] No explanation for either refusal is given.

The last stage in the history of *Lumen Gentium* was the presentation and acceptance of the revised second *schema* at the third session. Very slight changes were made in the text of the section on the ordinary magisterium of the Pope (now no. 25); but its position in the paragraph was changed, so that, as it was explained, "it might be clearer that the discussion of the teaching office of the Roman Pontiff was being carried on *in the context of the teaching office of the entire college of bishops*, which is the subject of this paragraph." [7]

Three *modi* were presented to the doctrinal commission for paragraph 25. The *modi* and the answers they received are important for our purpose:

Modus 159 is the suggestion of three bishops who "invoke the particular case, at least theoretically possible, in which an educated person [*eruditus quidam*], confronted with a teaching proposed non-infallibly, cannot, for solid reasons, give his *internal* assent." The response of the commission is, "For this case approved theological explanations should be consulted." [8]

Modus 160 is the proposal of three bishops that the text read: "and that the judgments given by him are sincerely adhered to, *although not with an absolute and irreformable* assent." The reason for the addition is to make clear the

6. *Ibid.*, p. 43. Bishop Cleary's proposed text reads: "Romani Pontificis authentico magisterio, etiam cum non ex cathedra loquitur, religiosum obsequium iuxta regulas prudentiae praestandum est; sed nihil impedit quominus periti omni qua par est moderatione et temperentia, argumentis hinc inde accurate perpensis, rem plenius investigent, dummodo profiteantur se paratos esse stare iudicio Ecclesiae."

7. *Schema Constitutionis De Ecclesia* (Vatican Press, 1964), p. 96; italics in the original text here and elsewhere unless otherwise indicated.

8. *Schema Constitutionis Dogmaticae De Ecclesia: Modi a Patribus conciliaribus propositi a commissione doctrinali examinati, III: Caput III: De constitutione hierarchica Ecclesiae et in specie de Episcopatu* (Vatican Press, 1964), p. 42.

distinction between the response owed to the infallible magisterium and that owed to the authoritative but non-infallible magisterium.[9] The reply is, "The ordinary teaching office often proposes doctrines which already belong to the Catholic faith itself; so that the proposed addition would itself have to be completed. Therefore, it is better to refer to the approved authors." [10]

Finally, *modus* 161 is the proposal of one bishop that an addition be made indicating the freedom to be permitted for further investigation and for doctrinal progress. The reply is, "The observation is true, but does not need to be brought in at this point." [11]

This review of the *modi* and the replies they received indicates that paragraph 25 of *Lumen Gentium* is to be read in the light of the presentation of the ordinary magisterium given by the *auctores probati*. The problems that arise when an educated person cannot assent to a non-infallible declaration and the differences between the various kinds of responses expected from a Catholic to the magisterium are all to be studied from the manuals. It is not, then, an idle exercise in historical theology to examine the manuals' presentation, but a work that is necessary in order correctly to understand the teaching of Vatican II on the subject.

2. The "Auctores Probati"

For the sake of clarity, "manuals" here will be understood as textbook-presentations of theology, usually intended for use in seminary theology courses. They are a distinct *genus litterarium*, whose historical origin, methodological presupposi-

9. *Ibid.*, p. 42.
10. *Ibid.*
11. *Ibid.*

tions, and theological *Denkformen* deserve study.[12] The manuals used for the following study date from 1891 to 1963, and do not represent any particular "tendency," whether theological or regional.[13]

In the first place, the manuals describe the "ordinary" teaching office of the Church as the day-to-day proposal of the faith that the pope carries out in his sermons, addresses, and encyclicals, "that exercise of his teaching office by which the pope intends to teach, but does not make clear his intention of imposing his judgment as absolutely definitive and irreformable." [14]

The ordinary teaching office of the pope is commonly regarded by theologians as being non-infallible.[15] But, the manualists say, even when it is non-infallible, the pope's ordinary teaching office is "authoritative," that is, unlike the teacher whose teaching stands or falls by the merit and strength of the arguments he presents, the pope has been given an authority to teach which can require assent even when his reasons are not in themselves convincing.[16] His is a *magisterium au-*

12. See Y. Congar, "Théologie," in *Dictionnaire de Théologie Catholique*, XV, cols. 431–44 (ET: *A History of Theology* [New York, 1968], pp. 177–95). Karl Rahner's strictures against *Schultheologie* are well known.

13. D. Palmieri, *De Romano Pontifice cum prolegomeno De Ecclesia* (2nd ed.; Prato, 1891); C. Pesch, *Praelectiones Dogmaticae*, I: *Institutiones Propaedeuticae ad Sacram Theologiam* (Freiburg, 1915); H. Dieckmann, *De Ecclesia*, II (Freiburg, 1925); J. M. Hervé, *Manuale Theologiae Dogmaticae*, I (Paris, 1934); L. Lercher, *Institutiones Theologiae Dogmaticae* (5th ed. by F. Schlagenhaufen), I (Barcelona, 1951); J. Salaverri, "De Ecclesia Christi," in *Sacrae Theologiae Summa*, I (Madrid, 1955); F. A. Sullivan, *De Ecclesia*, I: *Quaestiones Theologiae Fundamentalis* (Rome, 1963).

14. Sullivan, p. 349; see Lercher, p. 296, and Dieckmann, p. 91. Congar remarks that the distinction between ordinary and extraordinary magisterium, always implicit *via facti*, was not made in those explicit terms until Pius IX's *Tuas libenter* in 1863. See *La Foi et la Théologie* (Tournai, 1962), p. 158.

15. For the discussion, see Sullivan, pp. 348–352; Salaverri, pp. 709–710; J. Hamer, *The Church is a Communion* (New York, 1962), pp. 29–34.

16. Palmieri, p. 719; Pesch, p. 370; Dieckmann, p. 116; Lercher, pp. 297–298; Salaverri, pp. 716, 718; Sullivan, pp. 345, 348.

thenticum, where *authenticum* means not "authentic," but "authoritative" or "official." [17]

To every authority there corresponds an obligation on the part of its subjects. In the case of the ordinary magisterium, the obligation is to "internal, religious assent." Assent is required, that is, an act "by which what is contained in the decree is affirmed to be true." [18] The assent must be internal and sincere; external conformity or respectful silence are not sufficient.[19] Finally, the assent is termed "religious," because its motive lies in the fact that the pope has been given authority to teach by Christ.[20]

But this "internal religious assent" must be distinguished from the assent of divine faith.[21] The motive for an act of divine faith is the unfailing authority of God; the motive for "internal religious assent" is the authority of the teaching office in question.[22] Divine faith is absolutely certain and *super omnia firma*; internal religious assent is not absolutely or metaphysically certain.[23] Most of the authors speak of it as

17. The manuals distinguish between a *magisterium mere docens seu scientificum*, to which assent is given because of the reasons the teacher offers, and a *magisterium auctoritativum*, to which assent is given because of the authority of the teacher. See Sullivan, pp. 258–259; Salaverri, pp. 662–663; Lercher, pp. 158, 275; Palmieri, p. 167.

18. Lercher, p. 297; see Dieckmann, p. 116; Salaverri, p. 716; Sullivan, p. 347.

19. Palmieri, p. 719; Pesch, p. 370; Dieckmann, p. 116; Lercher, p. 297; Salaverri, p. 716; Sullivan, p. 347.

20. Pesch, p. 370; Dieckmann, p. 116; Lercher, p. 297; Salaverri, p. 716; Sullivan, p. 347, and see 345, 259. Palmieri (p. 719) calls the assent "religious" both because of its object and because of its motive, Christ's establishing of teachers in the Church and God's special providence over them.

21. There has long been a dispute whether between divine faith and "religious assent" there is not a third category of assent, called "ecclesiastical faith," which regards those infallible statements of the Church that do not concern matters formally revealed. See Congar, "Faits dogmatiques et 'foi ecclésiastique'," in *Catholicisme*, IV, cols. 1059–1067, reprinted in *Sainte Eglise* (Paris, 1963), pp. 357–373. This discussion is not of importance for this study.

22. Palmieri, p. 719; Pesch, p. 393.

23. Palmieri, p. 719; Pesch, p. 370; Dieckmann, p. 116; Salaverri, p. 716

"morally certain," [24] that is, not excluding the possibility of error but only its present likelihood. Finally, divine faith is given without qualification or condition; but this is not true of internal religious assent. Most of the authors say explicitly that it is conditional; [25] Palmieri and Pesch do not use that word but imply it by the mere fact that they acknowledge the possibility of dissent.[26]

While the manualists agree that internal religious assent has its conditions, they are rather general in describing them. Salaverri expresses the condition as "unless by an equal or superior authority the Church should decree otherwise." [27] For Sullivan, it is "unless the Church should at some time decide otherwise or unless the contrary should become evident." [28] For Lercher, it is "unless a grave suspicion should arise that the presumption is not verified." [29] Pesch speaks of the binding force of pronouncements "so long as it does not become positively clear that they are wrong," and adds that "assent is prudently suspended when there first appear sufficient motives for doubting." [30] Straub is quoted by Salaverri as holding that it is licit to dissent, to doubt, or to continue to regard the opposite opinion as probable, "if the decree should appear to someone to be certainly false or to be opposed to so solid a reason that the force of this reason cannot be shat-

24. Palmieri, pp. 719, 720: "maxime probabile causas erroris deesse"; Pesch, p. 370: "certitudine morali quadam latiore"; Dieckmann, p. 116; Sullivan, p. 348; Salaverri's "certitudo relativa" is identical with what the others mean by "certitudo moralis." Lercher speaks of religious assent as "non objective certus" because resting "upon a motive that does not exclude the possibility of error and is known to be such." The presumption, however, is that in any concrete case the magisterium is not in error (p. 297; see p. 275).
25. Dieckmann (quoting Maroto), p. 116; Lercher, p. 297; Sullivan, pp. 348, 354; Salaverri, pp. 716, 719, where he cites other authors.
26. Palmieri, p. 719; Pesch, p. 370.
27. Salaverri, pp. 716, 720.
28. Sullivan, pp. 348, 354.
29. Lercher, p. 297.
30. Pesch, p. 370.

tered even by the weight of the sacred authority." [31] And Palmieri says that "religious assent is owed when there is nothing which could prudently persuade one to suspend his assent. . . . The assent is morally certain; therefore, should motives appear, whether they be true or false (but from inculpable error), motives which persuade one to a different view, then in those circumstances the will would not act imprudently in suspending assent." [32]

Apart from Salaverri, then, the manualists admit the possibility of a Catholic's having reasons which could justify his withholding his assent to a teaching of the ordinary magisterium of the Pope. Dieckmann and Salaverri suggest that only a theologian could find himself in such a position; [33] the others are quite general in their statements. Nor do these authors suggest that the reasons for dissent must be new ones, not previously considered by the magisterium. [34]

On the other hand, the authors insist that the presumption in the beginning is always with the teaching of the ordinary magisterium, and that assent may not be suspended rashly, casually, out of pride, "excessive love of one's own opinions," or "over-confidence in one's own genius." [35] Generally, they think it extremely unlikely that error would ever be taught officially by the ordinary magisterium. [36] Palmieri, however, at least suggests that certain historical cases, such as Celestine III's permission of divorce and remarriage in the case of the heresy of a spouse, or the Galileo case, may prove "both the

31. See Salaverri, p. 719; Straub's manual, De Ecclesia Christi, published in 1912, was not available for my use.

32. Palmieri, p. 719.

33. Dieckmann (again quoting Maroto), p. 116; Salaverri, p. 720; see Hervé, p. 523.

34. Diekamp, who can be cited in favor of restricting the possibility of dissent to the scholar, does not require new reasons to justify such dissent but only "a new, scrupulous examination of all the elements." See F. Diekamp, Katholische Dogmatik, I (11th ed.; Münster, 1949), p. 64.

35. Lercher, pp. 298, 307; Salaverri, p. 720.

36. See Lercher: "periculum erroris fere nullum," p. 298.

exception that we have allowed for and that metaphysically certain assent is not required." [37] And Sullivan implies error in the ordinary magisterium on the part of Liberius, Vigilius, and Honorius.[38]

The manuals are generally rather negative on the possibility of public dissent or disagreement. The only one that can be regarded as leaving any door open for public dissent is Hervé, who speaks of "external reverence" [39] where the others require *"obsequium silentii"*; but his mention of the possibility of one's presenting one's reasons to the proper authorities leaves reason to doubt that he is any more liberal on the point than the others. Palmieri would permit public discussion if the pope should allow it, and he suggests two reasons among others why the pope might allow it: "either so that the truth might shine out more clearly or in order to complete the stage of investigation before a solemn definition." [40]

Three of the manuals explore more fully than the others the possibility of error and of its correction. Sullivan admits the possibility of a pope's making a mistake on one or another occasion, but not that it would ever become the "constant and traditional teaching of the Holy See." [41] Against the claim of infallibility for the ordinary magisterium of the pope, he argues:

It seems to be possible that a pope, teaching *modo ordinario*, might propose a judgment that would have to be corrected afterwards, without the whole Church being drawn into error thereby. In such a case, the divine assistance would be enough to assure that the error would be corrected before it was generally accepted by the Church and to prevent the erroneous teaching from becoming the traditional teaching of the Holy See.[42]

37. Palmieri, p. 721; see pp. 731–737.
38. Sullivan, pp. 349–350; see pp. 331–340.
39. Hervé, p. 523.
40. Palmieri, p. 719.
41. Sullivan, p. 345.
42. *Ibid.*, p. 350.

On the following page, he acknowledges again that "an error in the ordinary magisterium could be corrected before the whole Church were led into error." [43] But at no point does he indicate how that might be accomplished in fact.

Dieckmann makes a rather important statement in a discussion of the assistance of the Holy Spirit that accompanies the daily exercise of the ordinary magisterium:

It must be conceded that the influence of this assistance cannot be determined accurately, so that each doctrinal act could be said to have been made under this special assistance which preserves one from error. If that were true, all the acts would be infallible. The assertion is rather a universal one: generally the Holy Spirit will preserve the organs of the authoritative magisterium from error, especially in those decisions which are prepared and issued with the necessary diligence, caution and scholarship.[44]

The remark is chiefly of value against the assumption that to acknowledge the possibility or fact of error is to deny the assistance of the Holy Spirit.

In Pesch the problem is also approached obliquely, in a discussion of inquiry into the reasons for a pronouncement:

Since the pope's congregations [45] do not *per se* supply an absolutely certain argument for their teaching, one can and, it may be, one must inquire into the reasons for the teaching. In this way it may come about either that the teaching in question will slowly be received by the whole Church and thus be raised to the level of infallibility, or that the error will be detected.[46]

When error is present, it can be detected by inquiry into the reasons for some pronouncement.

43. *Ibid.*, p. 351.
44. Dieckmann, pp. 117–118.
45. Pesch's exposition of "internal religious assent" is made in terms of the respect due to the papal doctrinal congregations, but he adds that his remarks "nullo negotio applicantur ad decreta summi pontificis, quae non pro suprema sua auctoritate emittit" (p. 370).
46. Pesch, p. 370.

111

What the other three authors are perhaps only hinting at is stated more explicitly by Lercher:

If the supreme pontiff, exercising his authority, but not at its highest level, obliges all to assent to a thing as true (because revealed or coherent with revelation), he does not seem to be infallible *de jure;* nor is it necessary to say that the Holy Spirit would never permit such a decree to be issued, if it should be erroneous.

It is true that the Holy Spirit will never allow the Church to be led into error by such a decree. The way in which error would be excluded would more probably consist in the assistance of the Holy Spirit given to the head of the Church, by which such an erroneous decree would be prevented. But it is not entirely out of the question that the error might be excluded by the Holy Spirit in this way, namely, by the subjects of the decree detecting its error and ceasing to give it their internal assent.[47]

A few lines earlier, Lercher had made a similiar comment about the decrees of the papal congregations made *in forma communi:* "If by such a decree the affirmation of the truth of some matter should be prescribed for the whole Church and the thing should be objectively false, the Holy Spirit would not permit error: probably by his assistance he would not move the bishops and faithful to give a firm internal assent." [48] A few pages later he repeats the notion: "It is not out of the question that the Holy Spirit might assist individual bishops or even individual members of the faithful, so that they would not err, when the magisterium teaches authoritatively but not infallibly." [49]

The cogency of these statements is not affected by the fact that Lercher is extremely skeptical that such a situation will ever arise. He is the only manualist who explicitates how concretely the Church might correct an error taught by the ordinary magisterium. That correction would be the work of

47. Lercher, p. 297.
48. *Ibid.,* p. 297.
49. *Ibid.,* p. 307.

the Holy Spirit and it would take the concrete form of refraining from internal dissent. It should also be noted that Lercher does not exclude the faithful from the possibility of such dissent for the sake of preserving the Church from error.

Lercher's position, acknowledging at least the possibility of the Church's correcting the pope, fits in well with such views as Newman's "on consulting the faithful in matters of doctrine," or even with the insistence of Bishop Gasser, the official *relator* at Vatican I, that the pope has a moral obligation to consult the Church before approaching an infallible declaration.[50] But it calls to mind even more a set of traditional discussions which recent scholarship has recalled to our attention. I am referring to the discussions, which can be fully documented from the eleventh century on, of the possibility of a pope becoming a heretic or a schismatic.[51] Popes, canonists, and theologians can be cited who acknowledged the possibility of heresy or schismatic action in a pope; and some nine centuries of theological and canonical discussion have included consideration of what the Church at large could do in such a case.[52] The whole discussion demonstrates at least this

50. See *Collectio Lacensis,* vol. VII (Freiburg, 1892), p. 401.

51. See B. Tierney, *Foundations of the Conciliar Theory* (Cambridge, 1955); H. Küng, *Structures of the Church* (New York, 1964), pp. 249–319. See also the controversy about the force and significance of the *"Sacrosancta"* decree of the Council of Constance, for example in P. de Vooght, *Les pouvoirs du Concile et l'autorité du Pape au Concile de Constance* (Paris, 1965), or the reviews of this book in *The Downside Review* 84 (1966), pp. 432–435, and in the *Revue des Sciences Religieuses* 40 (1966), pp. 195–196. Nor was this discussion only within the context of conciliarism; see the references to Adrian II, Gratian, and Innocent III below.

52. The problem did not concern the pope only as *persona privata;* see A. Duval, *De Suprema R. Pontificis in Ecclesiam Potestate* (1614), 19th ed. (Paris, 1877), pp. 255–257. And the remarks of Adrian II about Honorius cannot be restricted to his "private" opinions: "Siquidem Romanorum Pontificum de omnium Ecclesiarum praesulibus judicasse legimus, de eo vero quemquam judicasse non legimus. Licet enim Honorio ab Orientalibus post mortem anathema sit dictum, sciendum tamen est quia fuerat super haeresi accusatus, propter quam solam licitum est minoribus majorum suorum motibus resistendi vel pravos sensus libere respuendi." *PL* 129, 110.

much: that there do remain within the Church at large norms of doctrine and practise which are not dependent on the pope; that there are circumstances (however unlikely one may judge them to be) in which it could be necessary for the Church to judge and correct the pope;[53] and that the Church is not unreservedly committed into the hands of any pope.[54] By no means is this digression meant to suggest that the present circumstances constitute a case of heresy or schism; it is merely intended to recall that quite traditional positions in canon law and in theology acknowledge that there could be circumstances in which the Spirit might not be speaking or acting through the pope but through the bishops and/or faithful in opposition to the pope.

So far as I know, the history of the theology of the teaching

53. See Gratian, "Cunctos ipse Papa judicaturus a nemine est judicandus, nisi deprehendatur a fide devius." *Decretum*, dist. 40, c. 6; or Innocent III, "In tantum fides mihi necessaria est, ut cum de ceteris peccatis solum Deum iudicem habeam, propter solum peccatum quod in fide committerem, possum ab Ecclesia iudicari." *PL* 217, 656.

54. See the interesting reply of the doctrinal commission at Vatican II to Pope Paul VI's suggested formula on the pope: "ipse uno Domino devinctus." After observing that the intention of the proposed formula, namely, to exclude any higher human authority, is sufficiently expressed in earlier statements, the commission replies: "Formula est *nimis simplificata:* Romanus Pontifex enim etiam observare tenetur ipsam Revelationem, structuram fundamentalem Ecclesiae, sacramenta, definitiones priorum Conciliorum, etc. Quae omnia enumerari nequeunt." *Schema Constitutionis De Ecclesia* (Vatican Press, 1964), p. 93. See also Karl Rahner's comment on the relationship between the pope and the college of bishops: "There are no juridical norms for the behaviour of the Pope with regard to the college of bishops whose breach could invalidate his actual decision about the amount of cooperation allowed them. There is no process of law through which the Pope in such a case could be made answerable to an earthly authority distinct from himself. But the Pope is obviously bound by the ethical norms of the gospel, justice, fairness and the objective relationships which result from the fact that an entity founded by Christ with a constitution . . . may not be condemned to atrophy by being disregarded and left out of account, or allowed to exist only in name. . . . And though there is no legal authority to see that these ethical norms are observed, and to question the validity of the Pope's decisions if they are not, the charismatic and prophetic quality of the Church still makes 'open opposition' (Gal 2, 11) possible." *Commentary on the Documents of Vatican II*, ed. H. Vorgrimler, vol. I (New York, 1967), p. 202.

114

office in the Church still remains to be written. The manuals offer no help in tracing the tradition they endorse back beyond 1863, and the single encyclopedia article I have discovered to treat the matter at all is too sketchy to be of much use.[55] Congar observes that the explicit distinction between an "extraordinary" and an "ordinary" papal magisterium dates only from the mid-nineteenth century.[56] If that is so, it is understandable that there is so little evidence for our subject in such post-Tridentine writers as Bellarmine, Duval, Billuart, and P. Ballerini. These authors normally distinguish only between the pope as a *doctor privatus*, capable of error, and the pope as *caput Ecclesiae*, acting and speaking infallibly.[57] The center of controversy for these men was the *locus* within the Church of a *judex controversiarum infallibilis*, and this context did not suggest such distinctions as we make today.

Whatever the earlier history may reveal, it was not until the middle of the nineteenth century that the duty of internal religious assent to non-infallible teaching is stated explicitly in Church documents. The earliest references anyone gives are to Pius IX's "Munich Brief" and its restatement in the Syllabus of Errors.[58] After those references, the manuals also

55. See E. Dublanchy in *Dictionnaire de Théologie Catholique*, VII, cols. 1710–1711.

56. See above, note 14. It is surely not accidental that the distinction was explicitated at the same time that the most frequently used means of ordinary teaching by the popes, encyclical letters, was coming into its own under Gregory XVI and Pius IX. See Congar, *La Foi et la Théologie*, p. 159.

57. For example, Billuart, *Cursus Theologiae iuxta mentem Divi Thomae*, vol. V (Paris, 1839), p. 174; P. Ballerini, *De vi ac ratione Primatus Romanorum Pontificum* (1766), in Migne, *Theologiae Cursus Completus*, III (Paris, 1842), cols. 1217–1218. A study of the ecclesiology of this period is much needed, for it is the immediate background of the nineteenth century and of Vatican I.

58. DS 2879–2880, 2895, 2922. A study of the reaction to the "Munich Brief" and to the *Syllabus of Errors* provides an excellent background for the contemporary discussion. For the reaction in England, see J. Altholz, *The Liberal Catholic Movement in England* (London, 1962); H. A. MacDougall, *The Acton-Newman Relations* (New York, 1962); D. McElrath, *The Syllabus of Pius IX: Some Reactions in England* (Louvain, 1964).

refer to a *monitum* at Vatican I,[59] and to documents of Leo XIII, Pius X, Pius XI, and Pius XII.[60] To these can now be added the *Constitution on the Church*, paragraph 25, the doctrinal statement of the Synod of Bishops,[61] and *Humanae Vitae*. The theological note attached to their thesis by the manuals varies from Lercher's *doctrina communis et satis certa* to Sullivan's and Salaverri's *doctrina catholica*.[62] It might then, be remarked that the obligation of "internal religious assent" to the ordinary magisterium has never been taught by the extraordinary magisterium (with the consequence that internal, religious assent and not divine faith is due to the proposition that "internal religious assent" is due to the ordinary magisterium).

The tradition reflected by the manuals, then, teaches at once the duty of internal religious assent to ordinary teaching and the possible legitimacy of dissent. Any author who discussed the authority of such teaching also considered (at least *in abstracto*) the circumstances under which it would no longer require assent.[63] It was to this tradition that the 650 theologians who have signed the American theologians' statement were appealing when they said, "It is common teaching in the Church that Catholics may dissent from authoritative, noninfallible teachings of the magisterium when sufficient reasons for so doing exist." The same tradition underlies the

59. DS 3045; see *Collectio Lacensis*, vol. VII, pp. 83–84, 209–212.

60. Leo XIII, *Immortale Dei*, DB 1880; *Sapientiae Christianae*, *ASS* 22 (1889–1890), p. 395; Pius X, *Lamentabili*, DS 3409–3410; *Praestantia Scripturae*, DS 3505; Pius XI, *Casti Connubii*, AAS 22 (1930), p. 580; Pius XII, *Humani Generis*, DS 3885.

61. "Omnes autem christifideles clare edocendi sunt, modis mentalitati hodiernae adaptatis, de filiali obedientia et sincera adhaesione quae declarationibus magisterii Ecclesiae praestanda est, ratione utique diversa pro diversis earum indole." II, 2.

62. Lercher, p. 298; Sullivan, p. 354; Salaverri, p. 717.

63. See also the following encyclopedia articles: O. Karrer, "Papst," in H. Fries (ed.), *Handbuch Theologischer Grundbegriffe*, vol. II (Munich, 1963), p. 274; J. R. Lerch, "Teaching Authority of the Church," in *New Catholic Encyclopedia*, vol. XIII (New York, 1967), pp. 364–365; S. E. Donlon, "Freedom of Speech," in *ibid.*, vol. VI, pp. 122–123.

1967 statement of the German bishops [64] and the statement of the Belgian hierarchy on *Humanae Vitae*.[65] This tradition did not find its way into the 1967 pastoral of the American bishops.[66]

After this review of the manuals, something should be said of the perspective in which they discuss the matter. That perspective suffers from some serious philosophical and theological limitations. For one thing, the manuals' analysis of the nature of assent is quite inadequate and quite unaware of the kind of questions raised by Newman in *A Grammar of Assent*.[67] They tend to pass rather quickly over the problems

64. See *Documentation Catholique* 65 (1968), pp. 321–324.

65. "If we do not find ourselves considering a statement which is infallible and therefore unchangeable . . . we are not bound to an unconditional and absolute adherence such as is demanded for a dogmatic definition. Even in the case, however, where the pope . . . does not use the fullness of his teaching power, the doctrines which he teaches, in virtue of the power entrusted to him, demand in principle on the part of the faithful, strengthened by a spirit of faith, a religious submission of will and mind. . . . This adherence does not depend so much on the arguments proposed in the statement as on the religious motivation to which the teaching authority, sacramentally instituted in the Church, appeals. Someone, however, who is competent in the matter under consideration and capable of forming a personal and well-founded judgment —which necessarily presupposes sufficient information—may, after a serious examination before God, come to other conclusions on certain points. In such a case he has the right to follow his conviction, provided that he remains sincerely disposed to continue his inquiry. Even in this case, he must maintain sincerely his adherence to Christ and to his Church and respectfully acknowledge the importance of the supreme teaching authority of the Church. . . . He must also beware of compromising the common good and the salvation of his brothers by creating an unhealthy unrest or, *a fortiori*, by questioning the very principle of authority." (As quoted in the *National Catholic Reporter*, September 11, 1968, p. 7)

66. *The Church in our Day* breaks with the usual theological vocabulary to speak of "religious assent" as a generic term including at once the faith that responds to an infallible dogmatic definition (such as the real presence), the response due to the ordinary magisterium, and obedience to disciplinary decisions (such as clerical celibacy). This new use could easily confuse what must be kept distinct. Despite a long treatment of conscience, supposedly under the guidance of Newman, the document does not mention the possibility of dissent.

67. What, for example, would the manualists have made of Newman's view that assent is by nature unconditional? "No one can hold conditionally what by the same act he holds to be true." *A Grammar of Assent*

117

created by using such words as "authority" and "obedience" when speaking of "teaching." [68] Not much effort is expended in distinguishing the part of the mind and the part of the will in assent, with the result that the movement from "assent" to "obedience" and vice versa is often made too easily. Perhaps these difficulties derive from a too close association (not to say identification) of the magisterial and juridical functions of authority.[69] Such an association would cause misgivings even if the notion of law involved were properly intellectualist, but when it is voluntaristic itself the danger is greatly increased of a voluntaristic notion of truth as whatever authority happens to be teaching.[70] All these questions are much too large for extensive discussion here. For our purposes, it is enough to have shown that even within the perspective of the manuals, dissent from authoritative teaching is not regarded as entirely out of the question.

(London, Longmans, Green & Co., 1906), p. 172. The discussion of what Newman terms "opinion" is also of interest to the discussion of "assent" that is the "presumption" of truth. *Ibid.*, pp. 58–60.

68. The association of the words "teaching" and "authority" is not without its ambiguity. Surely the use of the word "authority" with regard to teaching is at best only analogous to its use with regard to law. Does "authority" to teach derive from another source than from the possession of truth? The manuals seem to think so; Palmieri (pp. 240–241) and Pesch (pp. 193–194) add to the obligation to assent to a word from God that derives from natural law (not to mention common sense) another obligation that derives from the "authority" of the Church. The manuals can argue from the fact that the magisterium possesses a *vis coactiva* to its infallibility, for otherwise the whole Church would be required to assent to error. Is not the sole ground on which a person (whether God, the pope, or a private individual) can claim assent his assurance of possessing the truth?

69. For the discussion of the relationship between these two functions, see Salaverri, pp. 964–987 and Hamer, pp. 118–124. Hamer's discussion of the Thomist virtue of "*docilitas*" (pp. 25–26) is illuminating.

70. On the dangers of "juridicism" in the interpretation of Church documents, see Congar, *The Meaning of Tradition* (New York, 1964), pp. 120–124; W. Kaspar, *Dogme et évangile* (Tournai, 1967); and the remark of a prominent contemporary theologian, "Rome seems to regard truth as a law to be imposed." The shift in theological ideal from the medieval quest for understanding to the post-Tridentine passion for certainty is also not without its importance for the development of the kind of perspective present in the manuals.

118

3. Some Perspectives from Vatican II

The possibility of dissent is, if anything, strengthened by more recent theological developments in ecclesiology and especially by several positions adopted by the Second Vatican Council. The following paragraphs briefly indicate a few of those positions.

There is, first of all, the very experience of the Council. The conciliar documents did not descend full-grown from above, but were arrived at only after long and sometimes bitter debate. If we believe the Spirit to have presided over Vatican II, it remains true that the Spirit guided its course precisely through the human dialectic of disagreement, discussion, and compromise. Nor was this dialectic a closed debate among members of "the teaching Church"; it involved consultation with theologians, with the non-Catholic observers present, and even, through the press, with the non-Christian world. Whatever progress was made at the Council was in varying measures due to all these factors, and it would be difficult to restrict the working of the Spirit to any single one of them.

Secondly, there is the perspective in which Vatican II discussed the infallibility of the Church. *Lumen Gentium* deliberately refrained from speaking of the infallibility of the Church *in credendo* as a "passive" thing, deriving from the "active" infallibility of the magisterium as an effect from a cause.[71] The council fathers do indeed speak of the Church's "faithful obedience" to "the guidance of the sacred teaching authority" (*Lumen Gentium* 12), but they do so in a context in which it has also been explained to them that respected post-Tridentine theologians saw no danger to the hierarchy in arguing "from the faithful to the hierarchy" or from infallibility *in credendo* to infallibility *in docendo*.[72]

71. See *Schema Constitutionis De Ecclesia* (Vatican Press, 1964), p. 46.
72. *Ibid.*, p. 46.

119

Along the same lines is the council's insistence on the freedom and responsibility of the laity to make known to Church authorities their needs, desires and opinions. (*L. G.* 37) In *Gaudium et Spes* (62), the council refers to that paragraph in *Lumen Gentium* to indicate that "all the faithful, clerical and lay, possess a lawful freedom of inquiry and of thought, and the freedom to express their minds humbly and courageously about those matters in which they enjoy competence." [73] Such comments are, perhaps, not without connection with conciliar statements on charisms in the Church (*L.G.* 12).

In such statements the council may be considered to be thematizing its own experience. Another indication of the same thing can be found in the council's acknowledgement that it is not only from within the Roman Catholic Church that proceed the forces leading towards the growth of the Church's understanding of itself and of its mission and message. God's grace and truth also exist outside the Roman Catholic community: in non-Catholic Christians and their communities (*Unitatis Redintegratio* 3, 20, 21; *L.G.* 8, 15–16; *G.S.* 40), in non-Christian religions (*Nostra Aetate* 1–2), and in the world (*G.S.* 22, 26, 34, 36, 38). From dialogue with non-Catholics, the Church grows in its self-knowledge and self-criticism (*U.R.* 4, 9). With the world and aided by it, the Church, which does not have solutions to all men's problems, commits itself to search for them (*G.S.* 10, 11, 33). From the world which she helps, the Church has, in her turn, derived abundant and various helps in preparing the way for the

---

73. See the use of this text in the first draft of the doctrinal report of the Synod of Bishops: "As far as doctrine is concerned, we must distinguish between truths infallibly defined by the magisterium of the Church and those which are authentically proposed but without the intention of defining. While preserving that (*sic*) obedience to the magisterium, 'the just freedom of research is recognized for faithful and clerics, as also freedom of thought and of expressing their opinion with courage and humility in those matters in which they are competent.'" See P. Hebblethwaite, *Inside the Synod: Rome, 1967* (New York, 1968), pp. 132–133.

Gospel (*G.S.* 40, 44, 57) and even in her presentation of the knowledge of God (*G.S.* 62).

The chief point of this brief summary is to recall that the Second Vatican Council, while restating the place and role of the teaching office in the Church, at the same time recognizes and emphasizes, as the manuals did not, the activity of the Spirit in many and differing ways in the Church and in the world. It is from all these workings of the Spirit that the Church grows in its understanding and accomplishment of its mission, and it may be suggested that by all these workings the Spirit might operate for the correction of mistaken teachings.

4. Some Objections

Arguments can be brought against the position maintained in the previous pages, and in considering them, it might be well to make the discussion concrete by particular reference to *Humanae Vitae*.

An important objection asks: If *Humanae Vitae* does not require assent, is there any teaching of the ordinary magisterium of the pope which must be considered to require assent? It can be replied that *Humanae Vitae* does require assent, in the sense outlined above; that is, the fact that the encyclical comes from the supreme teacher in the Church, whose office was instituted by Christ and is guided by the Holy Spirit, establishes a presumption in favor of its truth. Therefore, assent to it can be suspended only because serious, personally convincing arguments lead a person to believe that the general presumption is not verified in this instance. Further, depending on the weight of the authority in question in each case, any other authoritative teaching also requires assent and can be dissented from only for reasons that are similarly sound and convincing. Nor does this reply

121

say anything that is not already implied in the recognition that such teaching is not infallible. If it is fallible, it may be mistaken. If it may be mistaken, no unqualified assent may be given to it. If it is mistaken, it has no claim on assent.[74] If a person is convinced that it is mistaken, then he may, indeed he must, suspend assent to it. This is the teaching of the manuals, the teaching presupposed by *Lumen Gentium* 25; and it is hard to see how *Humanae Vitae* can be exempted from it. It does not undermine papal teaching authority to maintain that in one or another, even in a very serious case, it has been wrong. The authors of the manuals could consider the possibility without suspecting that they were thereby undermining the papal teaching office.

Secondly, it may be objected that if the papal position on artificial birth control is wrong, we are faced with an extremely serious doctrinal error. For many centuries the Church would have been giving incorrect moral guidance; and there are theologians who believe it impossible for the Spirit ever to permit the Church to fall that seriously into error. In reply, it can be pointed out that it is a very risky business to try to predict how much of evil (whether the evil of sin or the evil of error) God might permit to creep into the Church.[75] There are enough cases in which the Church has been wrong in the past, and there are no *a priori* grounds on which it can be demonstrated that it could not be wrong again.

74. See St. Thomas: "Notandum autem quod cum multi scriberent de catholica veritate, haec est differentia, quia illi qui scripserunt canonicam Scripturam, sicut Evangelistae et Apostoli, et alii hujusmodi, ita constanter eam asserunt quod nihil dubitandum relinquunt. Et ideo dicit, 'Et scimus quia verum est testimonium ejus' (Gal 1:9). 'Si quis vobis evangelizaverit praeter id quod accepistis, anathema sit.' Cujus ratio est quia sola canonica scriptura est regula fidei. Alii autem sic edisserunt de veritate, quod *nolunt sibi credi nisi in his quae vera dicunt.*" *Super Ioannem XXI*, lectio VI, 2; no. 2656 in the Marietti edition; my emphasis.

75. Compare J. M. Cameron's criticism of Charles Davis for failing to place ecclesiastical failure and sin against the larger background of the enormous evils that exist in the world but do not shake our belief in God's existence or providence. *New Blackfriars* 49 (1968), p. 333.

Others object, however, that even if the teaching of *Humanae Vitae* is reformable, even if objectively it is wrong, still this encyclical represents what the Spirit, speaking through the Pope, wants us, historically conditioned creatures that we are, to do here and now. We must live by our present lights, and this is all the light the Spirit is now giving. In reply, it can be noted that, first of all, the teaching of *Humanae Vitae*, as any other teaching, requires assent only to the extent that it is objectively true; that, while one may be required to obey a *law* that one may believe to be incorrect, no one can be required to assent to a *teaching* he believes to be incorrect. Secondly, it cannot be excluded *a priori* that the Spirit may make his will known independently of the Pope; it cannot be demonstrated *a priori* that it is not the Spirit who is leading individuals to dissent in this case; and therefore it cannot be excluded *a priori* that the Spirit may be using such dissent to correct more quickly than would otherwise be possible a teaching that is, as all agree, at least reformable and possibly incorrect.

5. The Question of Public Dissent

We have already seen that the authors of the manuals generally do not allow public disagreement to authoritative teaching. With regard to the manuals, however, it should be recalled that Palmieri had offered two reasons why the pope might feel it helpful to permit public discussion, to confirm the truth of the teaching or to prepare the way for an infallible statement.[76] Pesch, similarly, saw as one of the possible results of inquiry into the reasons for a teaching its acceptance by the whole Church, but saw another one in the possible detection of its error.[77] Further discussion and inquiry, then, could either confirm the truth or discover a mistake, but in either

76. Palmieri, p. 719.
77. Pesch, p. 370.

case the Church would only be served. Both possibilities ought to be kept in mind in the debate about the legitimacy of making the inquiry and discussion public.

To advance a first, less important argument in support of public dissent, the fact that the discussion of *Humanae Vitae* concerns a matter that is not speculative and practically in-different (such as, for example, subsistent relations in the Trinity, or the quality of Adam's original justice), but rather a matter of immediate and urgent practical consequence for millions of persons, both Catholic and not, has already moved the matter from the remote and private rooms of the theologians out into the forum of public concern.

Secondly, for what it is worth, it should be recalled that a prohibition of further public discussion after a papal pro-nouncement, included in the first draft of the Constitution *De Ecclesia* at Vatican II, was dropped in the second *schema*.

More importantly, arguments in favor of public discussion and dissent can be drawn from points already touched upon: the necessity of dialogue between teaching and believing Church and the possibility, acknowledged by all,[78] that the teaching of *Humanae Vitae* may be incorrect. Dialogue has always played a major role in the development of Church teaching in the past, as the most casual reading of the history of the councils makes abundantly clear. Defined Catholic teaching generally represents a consensus arrived at by an all too human dialectic of disagreement and debate, of compro-

78. There is the possibility that some would maintain that the practical conclusions of *Humanae Vitae* are infallible not because of the encyclical but because of a constant tradition in the Church. Obviously, I have assumed throughout that the practical conclusions are not infallible. In 1964 Pope Paul VI, by speaking of a possible duty to reform the tradi-tion, implied that the tradition to that point was not irreformable. Noth-ing in the subsequent discussion can be said to have strengthened the force of the tradition. And in *Humanae Vitae* itself, Paul's quest for assent is built not upon the infallibility of the tradition or of his restate-ment of it, but upon the authority of the ordinary magisterium. This is also the assumption of the great majority of those bishops who have commented on the encyclical and its authoritative force.

mise and conciliation, of honesty and humility. An end to such a process was considered to have come only with a definitive pronouncement of pope and/or council. There is no reason why such a dialogue should be stopped before such a pronouncement in the present case.

Now it must be granted that such a dialogue could continue without having to be public and that the dialogue would eventually make the truth or error of the teaching clear. But it may be suggested that if the dialogue is conducted in private, the process of confirmation or of correction would take a much longer time. While the Church might not suffer if the process of confirmation were to be prolonged, it would be hard to establish that whatever value there may be in private discussion outweighs the harm that could be done to the Church if the process of correction were prolonged. The general good of the Church can be invoked on both sides.

Again, given the real possibility of error, is there not a responsibility imposed upon each qualified member of the Church, who believes he has detected an error, to seek to correct it? Does he not have this responsibility to truth itself? *Magis amica veritas.* By the same token, does he not have a responsibility to the Church, "light of the world," "pillar and ground of truth"? Does not the qualified person who believes dissent to be necessary have a responsibility towards the members of the Church who regard a particular teaching as unacceptable and, because of it, are tempted to leave the Church? Finally, does not the more qualified person have the obligation to speak publicly to avoid misunderstandings and oversimplifications which can so readily occur in the mass media? In the light of an affirmative answer to these questions, what I have called the possibility of public dissent can well be described as the right, or indeed the obligation to dissent publicly.

Further, if there is a real possibility of error, may it not be argued that the Church has nothing to fear from public discussion? If the teaching is correct, the Spirit will show (as has not yet been shown) why it is correct. If the teaching is incorrect, it can only be correted if there is given to bishop and to theologian the freedom to explore the matter. Since collaboration is a necessary part of the theological endeavor, it is difficult to see how such exploration can remain private. No theological journal is so abstruse and no language so arcane that its publications cannot overnight become known to the world. It is not certain that one can even speak of private discussion or dissent any longer.

Finally, much of the fear expressed about the laity's losing respect for the teaching authority of the Church when debate is public, arises at least in part from the fact that the faithful have not generally been taught what are the respective and mutual roles of teacher and believer in the Church. Commonly they are unaware that all pronouncements on religious matters are not of equal authoritative weight and that the response they owe differs accordingly. If they were to possess a more adequate notion of the teaching office, then perhaps the danger of scandal and disrespect might be considerably less than many feel it to be today. It was also the strong recommendation of the Synod of Bishops in 1967 that "clearly and in ways adapted to the contemporary mentality" the faithful be taught their responsibilities before the magisterium.[79] Even if, therefore, someone may still be convinced that public dissent in the Church may do more harm than good, only good can come from a clear and intelligent explanation of the various responses a Catholic owes to the various exercises of the Church's teaching office, an explanation that would have to include as well a discussion of the circumstances under which it is quite legitimate and even necessary for a Catholic to suspend his assent.

79. See Hebblethwaite, p. 155.

DANIEL C. MAGUIRE MORAL INQUIRY AND RELIGIOUS ASSENT

The tragedy of the encyclical *Humanae Vitae* and the debate it has engendered "before angels and men" is that the insights that make both the encyclical and the debate unnecessary have long enjoyed a prominent existence in the human community. A debate is a happy event when it is sparked by discovery and points to enriching expansion of communal consciousness. But this debate is sad, precipitated as it is by the appearance under high auspices of old problems that linger with us, scandalously unresolved.

The well-known conclusions of the encyclical concerning artificial birth control are based on particular natural-law traditions. The arguments employed have won scant applause even from those who support the Pope's specific conclusions. Instead, the issue has become one of authority, and paragraph 25 of the *Constitution on the Church* has quickly become the most quoted passage in the Second Vatican Council. This passage speaks of the "religious assent" that is due non-infallible pronouncements of the hierarchical magisterium. Such a defense is in accord with the encyclical itself. The Pope says that "internal and external obedience" is due "not only because of the reasons adduced, but rather because of the light of the Holy Spirit, which is given in a particular way to the pastors of the Church in order that they may illustrate the truth" (28). Also, the encyclical dismisses the majority position of the special commission "above all" because it "departed from the moral teaching on marriage proposed with constant firmness by the teaching authority of the

Church" (6). However ambiguous the notion of natural law is, the Pope claims to be teaching it here "by virtue of the mandate entrusted to us by Christ" (*ibid.*).

On the issuance of the encyclical, Monsignor Lambruschini granted that the document was not an infallible definition. In spite of its admitted fallibility, however, "This decision binds the consciences of all without any ambiguity." Lambruschini continued:

In particular, it can and must be said that the authentic pronouncement contained in the encyclical *Humanae Vitae* excludes the possibility of a probable opinion, valid on the moral plane, opposed to this teaching—and that notwithstanding the number and the authority (hierarchical, scientific, and theological) of those who have in recent years maintained that it is possible to have such a probable opinion.

Those who have been convinced and have taught that artificial conception could at times be a moral option for spouses "must now change their attitude." This involves no "servility" but is rather a case "of essential loyalty and consistency in the profession of Catholic doctrine." [1]

A pertinent background to the matter of religious assent is offered in the American bishops' pastoral letter, *The Church in Our Day*. There it is said that religious assent is due to decisions touching on dogma such as the eucharistic presence and also for decisions affecting, disciplines such as priestly celibacy in the Western Church. This latter decision should be seen "as God's will for our time." The authority enforcing this discipline should be acknowledged "as the instrument of God." [2]

The defense of *Humanae Vitae* has become a defense of a

1. *L'Osservatore Romano*, Weekly Edition in English, August 7, 1968, p. 7.
2. *The Church in Our Day*, United States Catholic Conference (Washington, 1968), pp. 71–73.

theology of the magisterium that is heavy with problems. Three critical problem areas seem to call for special attention: (1) the concept of handing down a deposit of wisdom in which "the natural law" is somehow contained; (2) the notion of "assistance of the Holy Spirit" which somehow guarantees even the fallible utterances of Church officers; (3) the juridical paradigm by which official teaching is conceived and explained. My remarks are primarily directed to the problem of religious assent to moral teaching but are not without relevance to other doctrinal matters.

1. The Deposit Handed Down

As the early Church became aware of the possibility of doctrinal decay, the notion developed of an apostolic *paradosis* which was to be preserved against the "fierce wolves" (Acts 20, 29).[3] This was the beginning of the notion of a deposit that was given, in Jude's words, "once for all" (v. 3). The expression *"quasi per manus traditae"* became classical to describe the handing on of the truth of the deposit. The expression "faith and morals," which was already common in the twelfth and thirteenth centuries, came to describe the nature of the truths preserved in the Church. The meaning of this expression, however, was not precise and varies considerably in history. At the time of the Council of Trent, for example, "morals" in this expression signified not "the natural law" but the practices and customs of the early Church, including points of liturgy, doctrine, and discipline.[4]

In Vatican I, the object of infallibility was declared to be *"doctrinam de fide vel moribus"* (DS 1839). No effort was

3. See Jude 17; 1 Tim. 1, 3–4; 2 Tim. 2, 1; 4, 1–8; Titus 3, 9–11; 1 John 2, 18–19; 4, 1–6; 2 John 7.
4. See J. L. Murphy, *The Notion of Tradition in John Driedo* (Milwaukee, 1959), pp. 292–300.

made to clarify the meaning of "*moribus*." [5] It was said, however, that the teaching role of the pope was to guard and explain the deposit of faith handed down by the apostles (D 1836). This idea of guarding the deposit is found again in Vatican II's treatment of infallibility.[6] Theologians who say that the Church can speak infallibly in specific issues of morality are constrained to say that the natural moral law is "virtually" or "implicitly" contained in this deposit.[7]

The notion of "the natural law" being somehow contained in the deposit of revelation is more than a little baffling. First of all, the natural law cannot be spoken of as though it were a univocal and neatly determined reality. Even Thomas Aquinas has several working definitions of what natural law is.[8] It is not a code of specific principles admitting of universal application. Traditional natural law ethicists have managed to agree that changeable circumstances are essential to "the moral object." This is to say that empirical data have ethical import and meaning, that ethical inquiry is inductive as well as deductive. Whether a moralist plies natural law or situation ethics (another ambiguous and polyvalent term), he must allow that his ethical conclusions are organically dependent on the existential context as well as on the insights contained in traditional moral principles. These morally significant circumstances cannot be anticipated or pre-contained in a deposit.

This is one of the reasons why no Church (much less a

5. See Mansi 52, 1235. Cardinal Berardi calls attention to the ambiguity of this part of the definition. No account was taken of his remarks by the *Deputatio de fide*.

6. See the *Dogmatic Constitution on the Church*, paragraph 25.

7. See my essay, "Moral Absolutes and the Magisterium," in *Absolutes in Moral Theology*, ed. Charles E. Curran (Washington, 1968), pp. 78–80; 85–87.

8. See Charles E. Curran, "Absolute Norms and Medical Ethics," in *Absolutes in Moral Theology* (see above, note 7), pp. 114–120; Jean Marie Aubert, "Le Droit Naturel; ses avatars historiques et son avenir," in *Supplement de la Vie Spirituelle*, 81 (1967), pp. 298ff.; Odon Lottin, *Le Droit Naturel chez Saint Thomas d'Aquin et ses prédecesseurs* (2nd ed.; Bruges, 1931), p. 62.

Church officer) can claim to be able to teach infallibly the natural law and its application to specific cases. To do so would require an omniscient grasp of the ethical import of all the morally relevant circumstances of all possible cases. I have argued this point at length elsewhere.[9]

A second difficulty in handing down moral wisdom arises from the role of affectivity in the perception of moral truth. The New Testament does not offer precise distinctions of intellect and will such as developed in later scholasticism. It does, however, link the knowledge of the Good News to the affections of the heart. It is when you are "planted in love and built on love" that you will know what is "beyond all knowledge" (Eph. 3, 18). It is the morally right and pure of heart who will see. St. Thomas, writing of wisdom, says that rightness of judgment can come about in two ways: through study or through a certain connaturality to the subject matter, as when a truly chaste man judges rightly of things pertaining to chastity, by being connaturally attuned to these matters (II II, q. 45, a. 2). This connatural rapport achieved through moral experience yields another way of achieving moral truth aside from ethical inquiry. It is knowledge achieved through connatural affinity (see *In III Sent.*, dist. 35, q. 2, a. 1, 1).

Prudence, for Thomas is directive of practical morality and has both affective and intellectual elements (I, q. 22, a. 1, ad 3; I II, q. 56, a. 2, ad 3; q. 57). Its tie to the affections is such that it cannot achieve its intellectual role without love (II II, q. 47, a. 1, ad 1) and cannot exist apart from the moral virtues (I II, q. 57, a. 4).

John of St. Thomas, the most thorough of Thomas's commentators on knowledge by way of connaturality, says that there is a formal distinction between knowledge attained through a right functioning of the intellect and knowledge that is attained affectively. The influence of the will in intellection is such as to formally distinguish the knowledge that

9. See my essay referred to in note 7 above.

arises "*ex affectu*" and "*in affectu*" from knowledge that is not "*affective attacta.*" [10] For John of St. Thomas, knowledge can be increased and formally distinguished by the affections so that affective knowledge is a normal possibility and not a contradiction in terms.

Henri Bergson says that there is "a genius of the will as there is a genius of the mind." [11] John Macquarrie puts it this way: "We are disclosed to ourselves, and being is disclosed, in affection and volition as well as in cognition, or perhaps better expressed, all affective and conative experience has its own understanding." [12]

Moral wisdom involves an affective experience of value and because of this fact it is impossible to commune perfectly with any past appreciation or to compare our contact with it to the handing down of a material heirloom. The radically personal aspect of moral perception is such as to render it only partially communicable. When the two Vatican councils speak of the Church's authority to teach doctrine "*de moribus,*" there is every indication that morality is being thought of as a given body of truth which the Church can guard and apply. The subtle and personal affective component of moral insight is not considered.

This is not to suggest that past wisdom is all lost but that it is ever losable. To recapture it in some way requires openness of heart as well as of mind. It demands receptivity to the Spirit of truth and love whose grace is the primary Christian moral law. However helpful the hierarchical magisterium may be, it cannot guarantee that the Master's moral

10. ". . . voluntas formaliter non illuminat intellectum, sed tamen potest causaliter majus lumen praebere seu perficere, quatenus reddit objectum magis unitum sibi per amorem et immediatius in se attactum et gustatur . . . et hoc modo ex affectu sic uniente diversitas formalis objecti, scilicet ut uniti et experti . . ." *In I II*, disp. XVIII, a. 4, n. 15. See *ibid.*, a. 2, nn. 29, 30; a. 4, nn. 6, 11, 42.

11. *The Two Sources of Morality and Religion* (New York, 1956), p. 58.

12. *Principles of Christian Theology* (New York, 1966), p. 88.

vision has not been blurred in the consciousness of an imperfectly loving Church. It cannot claim to have "handed it down" with unflagging fidelity. If a sinful Church required proof of this fact, its history supplies such in abundance.

For similar reasons, none of the magisterial offices in the Church could assume for itself the task of applying moral insights from the past to all individual cases. Perceptivity sharpened by love, feeling, intuition, and personal experience and reasoning all have their irreplaceable function in assessing the somewhat unique circumstances of each individual case. But since neither man nor his decisions can exist outside of a community context, a magisterium can valuably assist man's moral decision-making by giving voice to the moral experience of the community. The role of a Christian magisterium, therefore, would be to struggle to recreate as far as possible the genetic Christian moral experience, to allow this experience to shape the liturgical and social life of the community so as to make the Church a truly Christianizing context for decision making.

A third source of ambiguity in the "handed down" approach to cognitive contact with the past is in the conception of language and thought. Knowledge and its expression are essentially conditioned by the flowing context. The meaning-giving context of each historical moment involves the crisis-crossing patterns of reaction and counter-reaction that make every time somewhat unique and unrepeatable. Each age has its dominant images and cognitive archetypes. So too it has dominant emotional fields which affect reality perception in ways we can only partially recreate in another situation. Significant relationships change and in this flux, insights can wane or deepen as points of reference and analogy fade or grow clear.

Meaning can slowly detach itself from the formulations that once bodied it forth. Persons who operate from a static world view would never suspect that cherished formulations now house a different meaning from that intended by the original formulators. These formulations might be dogmatic formulations or traditional moral principles. In either case continuity with the original knowing experience is a problem. Men with little feel for the processual quality of the real long for "definitive," "irreformable" expressions of the truth. Naïvely, they employed a literary genre which showed undue confidence in the perfection of language. Thus anyone who "says" anything different is a candidate for anathema. "*Si quis aliter* dixerit . . . *anathema sit.*"

Formulations of religious or moral truth are verbal symbolizations of realities that are not entirely "effable." No such verbalization is irreformable or definitive. This is not to say that they are to be discarded; they may be our principal contact points with the past experience. But they are to be recognized as inevitably imperfect expressions. Traditional formulations of morality, then, call for distrust as well as trust. Even if we are rather successful in discovering their original import they may be seen to have the deficiencies of an old photograph. The "real" that they partially portrayed has changed.

2. *The Assistance of the Holy Spirit*

The *Humanae Vitae* debate has not been centered on natural law but on ecclesiology. The defense of the encyclical rests on the notion of "assistance"; because of this assistance, the Pope's conclusions are said to merit "religious assent." The term "assistance" is of rather recent coinage in theology, as is our very technical use of the term "magisterium." The early Church was convinced that the Holy Spirit was active in the Church. The inspirations and revelations of the Spirit were not limited to the pages of Scripture. Neither was the work of the Spirit necessarily tied to the appointed officeholders of the Church. The gift of the Spirit was abundant. Quickly, of course, it became difficult to determine who was speaking in the Spirit and who was not. Criteriologies for the discernment of the Spirit developed and the ordering influence of special ministries was soon in evidence.[13] Indeed, up until the Council of Trent, the terms "inspiration" and "revelation" were used rather freely to describe the utterances of Fathers, councils, and outstanding churchmen.[14] The Nicene Creed is, for St. Athanasius, "the word of the Lord." The early councils were commonly called "inspired." The Spirit was seen as "instructing," "dictating," and "preaching" in the workings of these councils. The work of Church fathers and, at times, of outstanding theologians is sometimes listed as pertaining to the *divine pagina*.[15] There is talk in medieval times of the "many things" revealed to Sts. Gregory and Augustine. Even disciplinary decrees were credited to the Holy Spirit.

This faith in the active presence of God took a new form in the heavily juridical ecclesiology that grew out of the eleventh and twelfth century reforms. After studying this period closely, Yves Congar finds in it "the transition from an appreciation of the ever active presence of God to that of juridical powers put at the free disposal of, and perhaps even handed over as its property to 'the Church,' i.e., the hierarchy. For the Fathers and the early Middle Ages, the sacred actions

13. For an extensive study of the development of ministries in the early Church, see Hans Küng, *The Church* (New York, 1967).

14. See Y. Congar, *Tradition and Traditions* (New York, 1967), pp. 119–137. In this excursus Congar documents the permanence of *revelatio* and *inspiratio* in the Church and gives a bibliography for further documentation.

This essay can touch only lightly on the complex history of ministries and the historical theology of the discernment of the assistance of the Spirit. Aside from Congar's monumental *Tradition and Traditions*, see his *Lay People in the Church* (Westminster, 1957). Useful essays and bibliographies can be found in *Concilium* (Glen Rock), vol. 7, *Historical Problems of Church Renewal* (1965), and vol. 34, *Apostolic Succession* (1968).

15. *Ibid.*, p. 92.

are performed in the Church . . . But their subject is God, in an actual and direct way. Ecclesiastical structures are much more the manifestation and form of God's action than a subject whose internal quality or power could constitute an adequate basis for the certain production of the expected effect." [16]

After this transition there is a tendency to see the teaching acts of popes and bishops as divinely guaranteed. The teaching of Church officers seems to enjoy an inalienable presumption in its favor, a certain authenticity that other Christian teaching does not have. The magisterial role of the Church at large is neglected in the stress on the prerogatives of officers. This hierarchical emphasis was intensified in the panicked reaction to the Reformation.

Gradually, the terms "inspiration" and "revelation" were replaced by "assistance" in explaining the teaching powers of the hierarchy. The term "assistance," however, failed to be precisely explained and there were such as Suarez who said that it was "equivalent to revelation." [17] In the eighteenth century Billuart stressed that traditions do not constitute a rule of faith unless they have been proposed by a magisterium.[18] The official proclamation constitutes the truth proposed as normative. In the nineteenth century the influential Franzelin distinguished between the preservation of truth in the whole Church and the binding promulgation of the truth by the hierarchy.[19] Billot, reacting to the Modernist threat, gave a powerful role to the assisted hierarchical magisterium.[20] In the early Church, "the rule of faith" referred to the content of the faith itself; by the time of Billot it was the assisted

16. *Ibid.*, p. 135.
17. ". . . aequivalet revelationi vel consummat illam, ut ita dicam." *De Fide*, disp. III, sect. 2, n. 11 (Opera, ed. Vives, vol. XII, p. 100).
18. *Cursus theologiae*, Tract. De Regulis Fidei, Diss. II, a. 1.
19. *De Divina Traditione et Scriptura*, thesis XI, p. 96 (2nd. ed., 1875).
20. *De Sacra Traditione contra novam haeresim Evolutionismi* (Rome, 1904); in the second edition of this work, 1907, the title was changed to *De immutabilitate Traditionis contra modernam haeresim Evolutionismi*

magisterium. In the writing of Irenaeus the "charism of truth" referred to the power of the truth given in Christ; in modern times it refers to the teaching power of the hierarchy.

The definition of infallibility of Vatican I was based on the theology of "assistance." Through the assistance of the Spirit the pope can faithfully guard and expose the sacred deposit of doctrine concerning faith and morals (DS 1836, 1839). The *acta* reveal much of the theological state of this unique council. Two trends which are not easy to reconcile appear. On the one hand, the limits of the teaching office are expressed. D'Avanzo, speaking for the Deputation of the Faith, admits that assistance is not a new revelation but a manifestation of the truth which is already contained in the deposit of revelation. For this reason, the Pope may not omit the necessary diligence and care to discover the truth. He must take suitable means to see what is the genuine mind of the Church (Mansi 52, 764). Gasser makes the same point. The pope has neither inspiration nor revelation to support his utterances. Hence he is bound to use apt means to discover the truth. Consultation with bishops, cardinals, and theologians are among the "apt means" suggested (1213). Gasser also says that the definition does not separate the pope from the consent of the Church: "We are not able to separate the pope from the consent of the Church because this consent can never be lacking to him" (1214). When the pope defines, he does so "in relation to the universal Church" (1213) and "representing the universal Church" (*ibid.*).

On the other hand, whatever limits these spokesmen concede, their notion of assistance carries with it extraordinary guarantees. D'Avanzo tells the bishops that they are infallible too if confirmed by the pope. The pope, however, needs only the assistance of the Holy Spirit. "He teaches and is not taught; he confirms and is not confirmed" (764). Gasser, after mentioning the "apt means" the pope must use to find truth, says that we must piously believe that the promise of assistance includes a promise that suitable means will always undergird the papal pronouncements.[21] We need not worry about whether the pope has fulfilled his obligation to use the proper means. The nature of the assistance is such that a negligent pope would be impeded from making a pronouncement that would be wrong or destructive. If, whatever the preparation, the pope manages to make a definition, it would be infallible.[22]

In Vatican II's *Constitution on the Church*, paragraph 25 says that religious assent must be given to "authentic" teaching of the pope even when he is not speaking *ex cathedra*. This assent must be in accordance with "his manifest mind and will. His mind and will in the matter may be known chiefly either from the character of the documents, from his frequent repetition of the same doctrine, or from his manner of speaking."

It is to be noted that Vatican I and II speak of "assistance" with an air of peaceful possession, as though the theology thereof were developed and problem-free. In point of fact, the development is slight and the problems are many. Faith in the active presence of the Spirit in the Church is not at issue. What is at issue is a particular theology of spiritual discernment that has not achieved a balance between the magisterial role of the hierarchy and the witness of the magisterial Church at large.

First of all, the notion of assistance operative in the recent past is tendentially quietistic in its attitude towards human cooperation with divine activity. The defense of *Humanae*

21. ". . . pie debemus credere quod in divina assistentia Petro et successoribus eius a Christo Domino facta, simul etiam contineatur promissio mediorum, quae necessaria aptaque sunt ad affirmandum infallibile pontificis judicium." Mansi 52, 1213.

22. "Sed idea nil timendum, ac si per malam fidem et negligentiam pontificis universalis ecclesia in errorem circa fidem induci posset. Nam tutela Christi et assistentia divina Petri successoribus promissa est causa ita efficax, ut iudicium summi pontificis, si esset erroneum ea ecclesiae destructivum, impediretur; aut, si reapse pontifex ad definitionem deveniat, illa infallibiliter vera exista." Mansi 52, 1214.

Vitae often seems to suggest that the encyclical has an authority that is independent of its arguments, of the history of natural law, of the historical fact that the position on contraception was borrowed from philosophies long since discredited. Also deemed irrelevant is the ecclesiology that controlled the production of this document, that lifted this topic from open conciliar treatment, that had the encyclical written in nervous secrecy, that dismissed the witness of good theologians, spouses, Protestant Christians, and non-Christians. This says, in effect, that the assistance promised to the pope is such that his teaching is effective regardless of the means used to arrive at it. The assistance of the Spirit frees the hierarchical magisterium from the pitfalls of research and from the vagaries and uncertainties of theology and philosophy.

Pope Paul on October 1, 1966, gave his views on the subject of the magisterium. Speaking to theologians gathered in Rome, the Pope spoke of the magisterium and of theology as adequately distinct realities. He allowed that the work of theology is convenient and useful for the magisterium.[23] The magisterium, however, could do without theology! It could, unaided by this science, protect and teach the faith. This it could achieve by the charism of assistance of the Spirit.[24] The magisterium is, in fact, the representative of Jesus and his instrument.[25]

Aside from the failure to realize that any explanation of

23. "Quapropter Ecclesiae Magisterium magnum commodum utilitatemque capit ex fervidis et operosis theologorum studiis, atque et eorum socia libentique opera." *AAS*, 58 (1966), p. 892.

24. "Magisterium enim absque sacrae Theologiae auxilio poterit quidem fidem tueri atque docere, sed magna cum difficultate illam altam plenamque cognitionem pertingere, qua indiget, ut muneri suo cumulate satisfaciat, cum non charismate Revelationis vel inspirationis ditatum se reputet, sed tantum charismate adsistentiae Spiritus Sancti." *Ibid.*, p. 893.

25. ". . . Magisterium dicimus, quo in Ecclesia ipsius Christi Magistri persona geritur." *Ibid.*, p. 894. ". . . fidem dicimus, Magisterio Ecclesiae tribuendam, quod illam cum auctoritate explanat et interpretatur, cum Christum Iesum Magistrum repraesentet eiusque sit quasi instrumentum." *Ibid.*, p. 896.

belief is theological and that even Scripture contains various theologies, this position claims for the hierarchical magisterium a power to attain truth outside the human processes if not in contradiction to these processes. God's assistance is not seen here as given "according to the disposition and cooperation of each" (Trent) but as supplying for the defects of disposition and cooperation. In a manner that is richly redolent of magic (which seeks to achieve ends without proportionate means), the preter-theological magisterium is seen as immune to the hazards of thought and sin. It enjoys a kind of disincarnate power to judge scientific theology (*ibid.*, p. 892) without using or essentially depending on scientific theology. Instead, it uses the "charism of assistance."

This does not mean that the bishops must be scientific theologians in order to teach. Theirs is a legitimate pastoral teaching office. The Christian proclamation of faith does not require scientific expertise. The magisterial role of the hierarchy is distinct from the magisterial role of the theologians. The teaching roles of hierarchy, laity, theologians in the Church are distinct. They can be said to constitute distinct but complementary magisteria of a Church that is by vocation magisterial. Difficulties arise when one magisterium exceeds the limits of its own competence.

Underlying this claim is the confidence expressed by Gasser in Vatican I that a papal pronouncement would be impeded if it would be destructive or wrong, even if the normal means available were not employed. The fact that a doctrine has been officially taught (and thus has not been "impeded") introduces presumptions of divine approbation. It does not seem too much to say that there are hints of presumption here as well as what the old manuals called "*tentatio Dei*." It would be far truer to the Christian vision to see God working "with us" and in us and not *substituting for* work that we leave undone.

Equally unhelpful are the criteria offered in Vatican II for

140

determining when the "charism of assistance" has been activated with binding force. The clear implication of paragraph 25 cited above is that the charism is activated if the pope wills it to be; hence the necessity of analyzing the mode and language of his statement. There is also care taken to see if some phrase indicates that the pope activated his charism to the point of infallibility, thus lifting the contended issue forever beyond the disputations of men. In such a theory the role of the theologian devolves into a studious determination of the "manifest mind and will" of the pope to see how much charismatic authority might accrue to his statement. If the pope gives evidence of having seen contrary arguments and dismissed them, these arguments may no longer be offered to counter the papal position. It is as though his rejection strips them of their probative force. Those who continue to press those arguments are accused of a lack of faith in the papal authority. In a confusion of the juridical and epistemological orders (which we will discuss in a moment) the pope's teaching is said to command obedient acceptance.

Again, there appear in all of this strains of a quietism which abandons normal human effort, confident that God will act in the void. Such thinking furthermore seems affected by a deviant supernaturalism which is pessimistic about nature and reason and sees God's intervention in grace as a substitute for nature. The magisteriology in question would seem comfortably germane to those species of Augustinianism which were so impressed with grace as to deny even the possibility of pure nature and which saw much of man's native potential as forfeited by the fall. Man in such straits would require a divine refuge from the deceits of "that harlot, reason" (Luther's phrase). The philosophies of this fallen world's order would matter little in comparison to the words of the divinely guarded magisterium. It would not be surprising if the words of the magisterium were found to be in frontal conflict with the "natural" wisdom of men.

The ability to admit in practice a kind of radical discontinuity between the wisdom of faith and natural knowledge is basically opposed to the traditional Catholic teaching about the unity of truth, as expressed, for example, by St. Thomas: "*Ea quae ex revelatione divina per fidem tenentur non possunt naturali cognitioni esse contraria*" (*Contra Gentiles, I, 7*).

The second major weakness in the common notion of assistance by the Spirit is its innocence of history. Statements about the assisted magisterium imply that the Holy Spirit has a very low tolerance of error in hierarchical teachers. A chastening trip through history serves theory well in this regard. Pope St. Gregory the Great in his influential *Pastoral Rule* warned couples that if any pleasure were mixed with their marital intercourse, they "transgressed the law of marriage." They have "befouled" their intercourse. Consistently, this same Pope taught that couples could not receive communion after marital copulation. Blessed Urban II, with the hearty endorsement of the Council of Clermont, sought to establish Jerusalem as the center of Christian holiness by means of the crusading sword. Indulgenced warriors were assured that killing infidels merited heaven. Boniface VIII in his *Unam Sanctam* taught that temporal authority should be subjected to the spiritual authority of the Church. He said: "We further declare, state, define, and pronounce as entirely necessary for salvation that every human creature be subjected to the Roman Pontiff." (DS 469).[26]

Innocent III and the Fourth Lateran Council taught that it was absurd for a Jew to have authority over Christians and banned Jews from public office. Jews were also required

---

26. It would be unhistorical to suggest that Boniface here was merely asserting the ecclesial dimension of grace or some such palatable modern conception. The *Unam Sanctam* was based on the writings of Aegidius Romanus who said: "Totum posse quod est in Ecclesia reservatur in summo pontifice." See *De ecclesiae potestate*, III, 9, ed. R. Scholz (Weimar, 1929).

by this council to wear distinctive dress, a prescription that was later extended to heretics, prostitutes, and lepers. A series of popes banned the taking of even a little interest on a loan as mortally sinful. Until this century all official Church teaching denied accused persons the right to silence. Pope Innocent IV, in fact, said that torture could be used to extract confessions. Gregory XVI and Pius IX both condemned notions of religious liberty and freedom of conscience later to be blessed in Vatican II.

It is, I trust, generally accepted that assent is no longer due to these teachings, even when the word "define" was used by the teaching pope. All of these teachings affected critical areas of human conduct. Often they touched on matters clearly contained in Scripture, such as love of neighbor and the freedom of man. In these instances the popes were applying the message of the gospel to their day in a way that we now acknowledge as erroneous. If we use Vatican II's criteria to see how binding their teaching was, we find no problem in discerning the "manifest mind and will" of these teachers. What, then, of those who at that time, through the grace of God, were able to anticipate the present day attitudes of Christians towards ecumenism, liberty, and the rights of conscience? Should they have repressed their insights in favor of the authority of the Roman See? It would seem rather that the Church would have been well served if, in those sad moments of our sinful past, an intelligent dissent had been effectively and prophetically voiced.

Dissent to these old official teachings is a fact in the Church. Dissent to *Humanae Vitae* has shocked many. Is the passage of time necessary to make dissent respectable? No. Time is not an essential factor in judging dissent. Those old moral teachings were abandoned when new data showed them wrong. When we learned more about Scripture, ecclesiology, anthropology, relevant scientific and sociological data, we were

143

led to new conclusions. With *Humanae Vitae* the grounds for dissent were seen by many as having developed in the human community long before the encyclical.

History embarrasses those in whose ecclesiology eschatological straining has been dissipated in triumphalism. When the Church ceases to realize that it is most truly that which it is called to be; when it ceases to look longingly to the coming of the Lord, it is tempted to glorify its current forms. It takes a healthy eschatological spirit to keep ecclesiology honest. Error and sin are hidden and denied when the Church, tired of awaiting the divine visitation, divinizes itself. Gregory XVI in his *Mirari Vos* illustrates this attitude when he says of the Church:

. . . it is obviously absurd and most injurious to her to demand some kind of "restoration and regeneration" as necessary for her existence and growth—as if it were possible for her to be subject to defect, to decay, or other such deficiencies. By these attacks the innovators would lay the foundations of a new human institution, and what Cyprian detested would come about, namely, that from being something divine "the Church would become human" (Letter LII).[27]

A realistic loyalty to the Church does not permit us to pretend that the Church is or has ever been without spot or wrinkle. It should be possible to share the wholesome realism of an anonymous twelfth-century writer who, upon discovering egregious errors in the fathers of the Church, could say without loss of faith: "The Holy Spirit does not always succeed in touching the hearts of his saints."

3. Teaching and the Juridical Paradigm

A practical mind is comfortable with juridical categories. It was during the times of practical reform (for example, in

27. *Readings in Church History*, vol. III, ed. Colman J. Barry (Westminster, 1965), p. 40.

the twelfth century and after Trent) that the Church most readily expressed its self-understanding in juridical terms. Juridicism so flourished and dominated ecclesiology that even the teaching offices came to be seen in a way that confused juridical notions with cognitive and epistemological considerations. A modern dictionary can even describe the magisterium as a teaching competence "juridically embodied." [28]

It is characteristic of a juridical magisteriology to see official teaching in terms that are more proper to a legislative act. So in discussions of ecumenical councils it is the authoritative approbation by a pope that is seen as making the council genuinely and authentically ecumenical. No one could object if this approbation were seen as manifesting the approbation of the universal Church. The difficulty is that the approbation tends to be viewed as a juridical act with the mind and will of the pontiff being the point at issue. This procedure effectively bypasses the root ecclesiological question of the relationship of papal teaching to the faith of the universal Church.

At Trent, this canon was proposed: "If anyone says that a legitimately convened Council does not represent the universal Church, let him be anathema." [29] Bellarmine said that a council is void if not approved by a pope.[30] Some ecclesiologists have felt the need to stretch the data of history to show that all the "ecumenical" councils had papal approbation. It is as though a council could not bear witness to the Christian experience of the Church at a particular time without a kind of juridical validation.

This type of thinking is less than realistic. The proposed

---

28. Karl Rahner, Herbert Vorgrimler, *Theological Dictionary* (New York, 1965), p. 268.
29. Hubert Jedin, *A History of the Council of Trent*, vol. II (St. Louis, 1957), p. 347.
30. R. Bellarmine, *De conciliis* (Paris, 1870), lib. I, cap. 12, p. 211. See Hans Küng, *Structures of the Church* (New York, 1964), pp. 319–341, for other examples of this kind of thinking.

canon from Trent which said that a legitimately convened council represents the Church was a strange inversion of the truth. It would seem, rather, that a council can be legitimately convened if it is representative of the Church to a reasonable degree. The approbation does not make it representative, nor does it make all councils equally representative and equally valuable. Approbation by pope and bishops does not, by a sort of transsubstantiation, supply for the deficiencies of the council. For example, an assessment of the significance of Vatican I must take realistic account of the problems of that council, viz., simplistic approach and fundamentalism in the use of Scripture and the fathers; the role of Pius IX and the limited freedom of the council; the consideration of the papacy outside of a treatment of the whole Church; the influence of the critical deputation of the faith which was staffed with guaranteed "infallibilists"; the prevailing philosophical presuppositions; and others. These serious defects gravely limited the council. The final vote did not eliminate their pejorative influence. At most, papal approbation could proclaim the presence of "ecumenicity." The doctrinal value of Constance does not depend on whether Martin V or subsequent popes "validated" it. It was as valuable as it was representative of truly Christian viewpoints. The moderate conciliarism that was expressed there has a value deriving from its own logic and its long and honorable development in medieval Church thought. It is valuable for the insights it contains. It is valuable as a safeguard against absolutist papal pretensions. This value abides with or without a particular act of approbation. The canons of the councils of Carthage and Orange are generally thought of as having a dogmatic and genuine value. Yet clear evidence of formal papal approbation is lacking. More relevant to a dogmatic evaluation in these instances is the general acceptance of these councils by the Church.[31]

31. Peter Fransen, "The Authority of the Councils," in *Problems of Authority,* ed. John M. Todd (Baltimore, 1962), pp. 63–64.

Lambruschini's statement that *Humanae Vitae* "excluded the possibility of a probable opinion, valid on the moral plane, opposed to this teaching" is unintelligible. The juridical and the epistemological are here confounded. Opinions are not probable or non-probable by way of permission. The system of probabilism is concerned with the gradual emergence of truth in areas of moral complexity. The system realistically allows for the appearance of new insights amid the "infinite diversities" (St. Thomas) that characterize moral questions. Lambruschini's comment might imply a variety of things; it might be a prediction that no contradictory insights will appear, or that if they do, they can have no relevance. Only those insights count that are willed into legitimacy by the proper Church officers. Consistently, then, those who have seen the matter differently must now "change their attitude." They are, in effect, ordered not to see. In all of this, the roles of intellect and will are confused and the science of moral inquiry is submerged in a kind of juridical positivism and crass voluntarism.[32]

It is small wonder that the average person, untrained in theology or ethics, sees the *Humanae Vitae* controversy in terms of positive law and obedience. The calls for obedience and submission that have come out in support of the encyclical support this confusion. It is not usually acknowledged, of course, that such an interpretation of the matter opens the way to *epikeia* and the traditional notion of the excusing cause.

A further difficulty of the juridical notion of teacher is its abstractionism and Platonic separateness. A juridically explained magisterium functions outside of community relationships and history. The juridicist abstracts from the processuality of human existence and basks in a static view of life. His vision is like that attributed by Bergson to his "first

---

32. Note the stress on the will of the teacher in paragraph 25. Note the same in John C. Ford and Gerald Kelly, *Contemporary Moral Theology*, vol. 1 (Westminster, 1964), pp. 3–41.

morality." This morality "is supposed to be immutable. If it changes, it immediately forgets that it has changed, or it acknowledges no change. The shape it assumes at any given time claims to be the final shape." [33]

The juridical mentality, in its evasion of the real order of things, is equipped with a protective poor memory. It is shy of speculation and threatened by creative thought. It can give only lip service to freedom of inquiry.

It is to be understood that the weaknesses of juridicism to which we allude are not to be seen as an indictment of law. Law is essential to love, to morality, and to society. Law must be revised but not abandoned in the evolving societies of man. However, there is always the danger that the juridical estimates that make law operable will come to dominate rather than serve the good of man. And when the office of teacher is juridically described, the teacher whose task is to serve men by opening them to the truth can come to be seen as a rather independent, "official" source of truth.

In conclusion, there is need for teaching officers in the Church to give voice to the truest insights of the community by stimulating the magisterial potential of the whole Church. There is no room for teaching officers whose claim to an *ex officio* grasp of truth prescinds from the nature of language, the limitations of thought, the blinding presence of sin, or the authentic breathings of the Spirit in the universal Church and in the universal society of man. Christian hope points us to the day when the Spirit of truth will reign among men. Christian realism reminds us, however, that the Holy Spirit is remarkably tolerant of both sin and error in the meantime. Until the victory of the Spirit is complete, then, reverence for a teaching Church will not always exclude dissent.

33. *Op. cit.,* p. 58.

PART TWO

The Encyclical "Humanae Vitae"

CHARLES E. CURRAN NATURAL LAW
AND CONTEMPORARY MORAL THEOLOGY

Pope Paul's encyclical *Humanae Vitae* explicitly employs a
natural law methodology to arrive at its particular moral conclusions on the licit means of regulating births. The encyclical
admits that the teaching on marriage is a "teaching founded
on natural law, illuminated and enriched by divine revelation"
(*H.V.* 4). The papal letter then reaffirms that "the teaching
authority of the Church is competent to interpret even the
natural moral law" (*H.V.* 4). Recently, Catholic moral theologians have been reappraising the notion of natural law.[1] The
sharp response to the papal letter indicates there is a great
divergence between the natural law methodology employed
in the encyclical and the methodology suggested by recent
studies in moral theology. The natural law approach employed in the encyclical raises two important questions for
moral theology: (1) the place of natural law in the total
understanding of Christian ethics, (2) the concept of natural
law itself.

1. Natural Law in the Total Christian Perspective

The recent papal pronouncement realizes that natural law
forms only a part of the total horizon of moral theology. The

1. For example, *Light on the Natural Law*, ed. Illtud Evans (Baltimore,
1965); *Das Naturrecht im Disput*, ed. Franz Böckle (Düsseldorf, 1966);
"La Nature fondement de la morale?", *Supplément de la Vie Spirituelle*,
81 (May 1967), pp. 187–324; *Absolutes in Moral Theology*, ed. Charles
E. Curran (Washington, 1968).

apostles and their successors have been constituted "as guardians and authentic interpreters of all the moral law, not only, that is, of the law of the Gospel, but also of the natural law, which is also an expression of the will of God" (*H.V.* 4). Although the terminology (moral law) seems to imply a deontological approach to the moral life, the encyclical admits there is a source of ethical wisdom and knowledge for the Christian apart from the explicit revelation of the Scriptures.

There have been some theologians especially in the more strict Protestant tradition who would tend to deny any source of ethical wisdom and knowledge which Christians share with all mankind.[2] Such theologians based their position on the uniqueness and self-sufficiency of the scriptural revelation, the doctrine of justification, and an emphasis on sin as corrupting whatever exists outside the unique revelation of Jesus Christ.[3] However, Protestant theologians today generally maintain the existence of some ethical wisdom apart from the explicit revelation of God in the Scriptures and in Christ Jesus, even though they may avoid the term "natural law."[4] Protestant theologians have employed such concepts as the orders of creation (Brunner), the divine mandates (Bonhoeffer), love and justice (Reinhold Niebuhr), love transforming justice (Ramsey), common ground morality (Bennett), and other similar approaches.

The natural law theory as implied in the encyclical has the theological merit of recognizing a source of ethical wisdom for the Christian apart from the explicit revelation of

2. Edward LeRoy Long Jr., *A Survey of Christian Ethics* (New York, 1967); Thomas G. Sanders, *Protestant Concepts of Church and State* (Garden City, 1965).

3. Such emphases can still be found, although not in an absolute sense, in the writings of Niels H. Söe. See Söe, "Natural Law and Social Ethics," in *Christian Social Ethics in a Changing World*, ed. John C. Bennett (New York, 1966), pp. 289–309. The same article with a response by Paul Ramsey appeared in *Zeitschrift für Evangelische Ethik*, 12 (März 1968), 65–98.

4. John C. Bennett, "Issues for the Ecumenical Dialogue," in *Christian Social Ethics in a Changing World*, pp. 377, 378.

God in Christ Jesus. The difficult question for Christian theology centers on the relationship between the natural law and the distinctively Christian element in the understanding of the moral life of the Christian. The same basic question has been proposed in other terms. H. Richard Niebuhr describes five different models of the relationship between Christ and culture.[5] An older Catholic theology spoke about the relationship between nature and grace, between the natural and the supernatural. Niebuhr has described the typical Catholic solution to the question of Christ and culture in terms of "both-and"—both culture and Christ.[6] Such an approach corresponds with an unnuanced understanding of the relationship between nature and grace. The two are neither opposed nor identical; but they exist side by side. Grace adds something to nature without in any way destroying it. A simplistic view of the supernatural sees it as something added to the natural. But the natural retains its own finality and integrity as the substratum to which the supernatural is added.[7]

In such a perspective the natural tends to be seen as something absolute and sufficient in itself to which the supernatural is added. The natural law thus exists as a self-contained entity to which the law of the gospel or relevation is then added. *Humanae Vitae* seems to accept such a "both-and"

5. H. Richard Niebuhr, *Christ and Culture* (New York, 1956).

6. Niebuhr actually describes the Thomistic approach as "Christ above culture." He goes on to explain that "Thomas also answers the question about Christ and culture with a 'both-and'; yet his Christ is far above culture, and he does not try to disguise the gulf that lies between them" (p. 129).

7. One cannot simplistically condemn the nature-grace and natural-supernatural distinctions. In their original historical contexts such distinctions tried with considerable success to describe and synthesize this complex reality. Although such distinctions do have some meaning today, many Catholic theologians realize the need to reinterpret such distinctions in the light of different metaphysical approaches. See the three articles by Bernard Lonergan, which appeared in *Theological Studies*, 2 (1941), pp. 307–324; 3 (1942), pp. 69–88, 375–402. For an exposition of the thought of Karl Rahner on this subject, see Carl J. Peter, "The Position of Karl Rahner Regarding the Supernatural," *Proceedings of the Catholic Theological Society of America*, 20 (1965), pp. 81–94.

153

understanding of the relationship between natural law and the gospel or revelation. "All the moral law" is explained as "not only, that is, of the law of the Gospel, but also of the natural law, which is also an expression of the will of God . . ." (H.V. 4). The papal letter calls for an anthropology based on "an integral vision of man and his vocation, not only his natural and earthly, but also his supernatural and eternal vocation" (H.V. 7). The "both-and" relationship appears again in paragraph 8 which refers to "the entire moral law, both natural and evangelical."

Not only the wording of the encyclical but the methodology presupposed in the argumentation employs a "both-and" understanding of the relationship of natural law and evangelical law. Monsignor Lambruschini, who explained the encyclical at a press conference, said that purposely no mention was made of scriptural arguments, but the entire reasoning was based on natural law.[8] Bernard Häring [9] has criticized the encyclical because it does not even mention the admonition of St. Paul that husband and wife should "not refuse each other except by mutual consent, and then only for an agreed time, to leave yourselves free for prayer; then come together again in case Satan should take advantage of your weakness to tempt you" (1 Cor. 7, 5). The *Pastoral Constitution on the Church in the Modern World* did take heed of Paul's admonition. "But where the intimacy of married life is broken off, it is not rare for its faithfulness to be imperiled and its quality of fruitfulness ruined" (51). However, the primary criticism is not the fact that there is no reference to any particular scriptural text, but the underlying understanding that the natural law is something totally integral in itself to which the evangelical or supernatural law is added.

Christian ethics cannot absolutize the realm of the natural

8. A wire release of N. C. News Service with a Vatican City dateline published in Catholic papers in this country during the week of August 4.
9. Bernard Häring, "The Encyclical Crisis," *Commonweal*, 88 (September 6, 1968), pp. 588–594.

as something completely self-contained and unaffected by any relationships to the evangelical or supernatural. Christian theology derives its perspective from the Christian faith commitment. The Christian views reality in the light of the total horizon of the Christian faith commitment—creation, sin, incarnation, redemption, and parousia. Natural law itself is thus Christocentric.[10] The doctrine of creation forms the theological basis for natural law, and Christ as *logos* is the one in whom all things are created and through whom all things are to be returned to the Father. Natural law theory has taken seriously the implications of the incarnation through which God has joined himself to the human, the worldly, and the historical. However, nature and creation form only a part of the total Christian view. The reality of "the natural" must always be seen in the light of sin, redemption, and the parousia. Nature and creation are relativized by the transforming Christian themes of redemption and final resurrection destiny of all creation. The natural law theory is theologically based on the Christian truths of creation and incarnation, but these aspects are not independent and unrelated to the full horizon of the Christian view of reality. The Christian situates natural law in the context of the total history of salvation which transforms and criticizes what is only "the natural." Thus in the total Christian perspective there is a place for the "natural," but the natural remains provisional and relativized by the entire history of salvation.

The full Christian view of reality also takes account of the existence of sin and its effects on human existence. However, the natural law theory as illustrated in *Humanae Vitae* does not seem to give sufficient importance to the reality and effect of human sinfulness. In section III under "Pastoral Directives" the papal letter speaks about the compassion of Christ and the Church for sinners. "But she [the Church]

10. Joseph Fuchs, *Natural Law*, tr. Helmut Reckter and John Dowling (New York, 1965).

cannot renounce the teaching of the law which is, in reality, that law proper to a human life restored to its original truth and conducted by the Spirit of God" (*H.V.* 19). The implication remains that the disruptive force of sin has already been overcome by the grace of God. Such an approach has definite affinities with a simplistic view of sin as depriving man of the supernatural gift of grace, but not affecting the substratum of nature. However, in the total Christian horizon the disrupting influence of sin colors all human reality.

Humanae Vitae does recognize some effects of sin in man. Sin affects the will of man, but the help of God will strengthen the good will of man (*H.V.* 20). Sin affects the instincts of man, but ascetical practices will enable the reason and will of man to achieve self-mastery (*H.V.* 21). Sinfulness also makes itself felt in some aspects of the social environment, "which leads to sense excitation and unbridled customs, as well as every form of pornography and licentious performances" (*H.V.* 22). But no mention is made of the fact that sin affects reason itself and the very nature on which natural law theory is based. Sin relativizes and affects all reality. How often has reason been used to justify human prejudice and arrogance! Natural law has been appealed to in the denial of human dignity and of religious liberty. The just war theory has been employed to justify wars in which one's own nation was involved.[11] History shows the effect of sin in the very abuses which have accompanied natural law thinking.

Recently, I have proposed the need for a theory of compromise in moral theology precisely because of the existence of sin in the world.[12] The surd brought about by human sinfulness is so oppressive that occasionally man cannot overcome

11. Christian Duquoc, *L'Eglise et le progrès* (Paris, 1964), pp. 68–117. The author considers the past teaching in the Church on slavery, the freedom of nations, the dignity of women, Church and State, torture, and questions of war and peace.

12. "Dialogue with Joseph Fletcher," *Homiletic and Pastoral Review,* 67 (1967), pp. 828, 829.

it immediately. The presence of sin may force a person to do something he would not do if there were no sin present. Thus in sin-filled situations (notice all the examples of such situations in the current literature) the Christian may be forced to adopt a line of action which he would abhor if sin were not present. A theory of compromise does not give man a blank check to shirk his Christian responsibilities. However, there are situations in which the value sacrificed is not proportionate to the demand asked of the Christian. Protestant theology has often adopted a similar approach by saying that in some circumstances the Christian is forced to do something sinful. The sinner reluctantly performs the deed and asks God for mercy and forgiveness.[13] At times Protestant theology has overemphasized the reality of sin, but Catholic theology at times has not paid enough attention to the reality of sin.

The recent papal encyclical presupposes a natural law concept that fails to indicate the relative and provisional character of natural law in the total Christian perspective. Critics have rightly objected to a theory which tends to absolutize what is only relative and provisional. Take, for example, the teaching in Catholic theology on the right of private property. The modern popes have approached the question of private property in a much more absolute way than Thomas Aquinas. The differences of approach are instructive for the moral theologian. The popes, especially Leo XIII, stressed private property as the right of every man stemming from the dignity of the human person, his rational nature, his labor, his need to provide for himself and his family, and his need to overcome the uncertainties of life.[14] Thomas gave greater importance to the social function of all property and the reality of human sinfulness. Perhaps Thomas was influenced by the often-cited opinion of Isidore of Seville that according to the natural law

13. Helmet Thielicke, *Theological Ethics I: Foundations,* ed. William Lazerath (Philadelphia, 1966), pp. 622ff.
14. Pope Leo XIII, *Rerum Novarum,* n. 7–14; Pope Pius XI, *Quadragesimo Anno,* n. 44–52.

all things should be held in common.[15] Thomas ultimately sees the sin of man as the reason for the existence of private property. Society would not have peace and order unless everyone possessed his own goods. Likewise, Thomas pointed out that earthly goods are not properly cared for if they are held in common.[16] Thomas maintained there would be no need for private property in the world of original justice.

There are other indications that private property is not as absolute a right of man as proposed in some papal encyclicals. With his understanding of a more absolute right of private property, Leo XIII spoke of the obligation of the rich to share their goods with the poor as an obligation of charity and not justice.[17] However, a very respectable and long tradition in the medieval Church maintained that the rich had an obligation in justice to share their goods with the poor.[18] Even in our own day one can ask if private property is the best way to protect the dignity and freedom of the human person. The great inequalities existing in society today at the very least must modify and limit the concept of the right of private property. In our historical circumstances man is much more conscious of the social aspect of property than was Leo XIII.[19] The teaching on private property well illustrates the dangers of a

15. Thomas explicitly cites Isidore in I–II, q. 94, a. 2, ob. 1. In II–II, q. 66, a. 2, Thomas gives the opinion proposed by Isidore without a direct reference. Thomas explains that reason has called for the right of private property not as something against natural law, but as something added to natural law.

16. The reasons adduced by Thomas in II–II, q. 66, a. 2, indicate that human sinfulness is a very important factor in the argument for the right of private property.

17. *Rerum Novarum*, n. 22.

18. Hermenegildus Lio, "Estne obligatio justitiae subvenire pauperibus?" *Apollinaris*, 29 (1956), pp. 124–231; 30 (1957), pp. 99–201.

19. Leo XIII was conscious of the social aspect of property (*Rerum Novarum*, n. 22), but he did not emphasize it. The subsequent Popes down to Paul VI have put increasingly more emphasis on the social aspects of property. The concentration on such social aspects explains the many discussions about the notion of socialization in the encyclicals of Pope John XXIII.

natural law approach that is not relativized by the whole reality of salvation history.

The natural law theory suggested in, and employed by, the encyclical *Humanae Vitae* has the advantage of affirming the existence of a source of ethical wisdom apart from the explicit revelation of God in Christ in the Scriptures. However, such a concept of natural law tends to absolutize what the full Christian vision sees as relative and provisional in the light of the entire history of salvation.

2. *"Physicalism" in the Encyclical*

The encyclical on the regulation of birth employs a natural law methodology which tends to identify the moral action with the physical and biological structure of the act. (Note that I am not denying the fact that the moral aspect of the act may correspond with the physical structure of the act.) The core practical conclusion of the letter states, "We must once again declare that the direct interruption of the generative process already begun, and above all directly willed and procured abortion, even if for therapeutic reasons, are to be absolutely excluded as licit means of regulating birth" (*H.V.* 14). "Equally to be excluded . . . is direct sterilization. . . . Similarly excluded is every action which, either in anticipation of the conjugal act, or in its accomplishment, or in the development of its natural consequences, proposes, whether as an end or as a means, to render procreation impossible" (*H.V.* 14). The footnotes in this particular paragraph refer to the Roman Catechism and the utterances of more recent popes. Reference is made to the Address of Pius XII to the Italian Catholic Union of Midwives in which direct sterilization is defined as "that which aims at making procreation impossible as both means and end" (13; *AAS* 43 [1951], 838). The concept of direct is thus described in terms of the physical structure and casuality of the act itself.

The moral conclusion of the encyclical forbidding any interference with the conjugal act is based on the intimate structure of the conjugal act (*H.V.* 12). The "design of God" is written into the very nature of the conjugal act; man is merely "the minister of the design established by the Creator" (*H.V.* 13). The encyclical acknowledges that "it is licit to take into account the natural rhythms immanent in the generative functions." Recourse to the infecund periods is licit, whereas artificial contraception "as the use of means directly contrary to fecundation" is condemned as being always illicit (*H.V.* 16). "In reality there are essential differences between the two cases; in the former, the married couple make legitimate use of a natural disposition; in the latter, they impede the development of natural processes" (*H.V.* 16). The natural law theory employed in the encyclical thus identifies the moral and human action with the physical structure of the conjugal act itself.

3. The Primary Area of Contemporary Debate: The Moral Act Described in Physical Terms

In the last few years moral theology and Christian ethics have been immersed in a controversy over situation ethics. The controversy tends to polarize opinions and fails to show the huge areas of agreement existing among Christian moralists. There are, nevertheless, many real differences in approaches and in some practical conclusions. The principal areas of practical differences between some situationists and the teaching found in the manuals of moral theology are the following: medical ethics, particularly in the area of reproduction; conflict situations solved by the principle of the indirect voluntary, especially conflicts involving life and death—for example, killing, abortion; sexuality; euthanasia; and divorce.

These major points of disagreement have one thing in common. In these cases, the manuals of Catholic moral theology have tended to define the moral action in terms of the physical structure of the act considered in itself apart from the person placing the act and the community of persons within which he lives. A certain action defined in terms of its physical structure or consequences (for example, euthanasia as the positive interference in the life of the person; masturbation as the ejaculation of semen) is considered to be always wrong. I have used the term "negative, moral absolutes" to refer to such actions described in their physical structures which are always wrong from a moral viewpoint. Thus the central point of disagreement in moral theology today centers on these prohibited actions which are described primarily in terms of their physical structure.

In the area of medical ethics certain actions described in terms of the physical structure of the act are never permitted or other such actions are always required. Artificial insemination with the husband's semen is never permitted because insemination cannot occur except through the act of sexual intercourse.[20] Contraception as direct interference with the act of sexual intercourse is wrong. Direct sterilization is always wrong. Masturbation as the ejaculation of semen is always wrong even as a way of procuring semen for semen analysis.[21] Frequently in such literature the axion is cited that the end does not justify the means. However, in all these cases the means is defined in terms of the physical structure of the act. I believe in all the areas mentioned above there are

20. Pope Pius XII, Address to the Fourth World Congress of Catholic Doctors, Rome, September 29, 1949, *AAS*, 41 (1949), 560; Pope Pius XII, Address to the Italian Catholic Union of Midwives, October 29, 1951, *AAS*, 43 (1951), 850; Pope Pius XII, Address to the Second World Congress of Fertility and Sterility, May 19, 1956, *AAS*, 48 (1956), 472.

21. Pope Pius XII, *AAS*, 48 (1956), 472; Pope Pius XII, Address to the Italian Urologists, October 8, 1953, *AAS*, 45 (1953), 678; Decree of the Holy Office, August 2, 1929, *AAS*, 21 (1929), 490.

circumstances in which such actions would be morally permissible and even necessary.

Catholic moral theology decides most conflict situations by an application of the principle of the indirect voluntary. Direct killing, direct taking of one's life, direct abortion, direct sterilization are always wrong. However, the manuals of theology usually define "direct" in terms of the physical structure of the act itself. Such a solution seems too facile and too easily be defined as the performance (or the omission of) an act, the primary and natural result of which is to bring about death." [22] According to the same author "direct abortion is the performance of an act, the primary and natural effect of which is to expel a non-viable fetus from its mother's womb." In these cases natural refers to the physical structure and consequences of the act itself. One exception in the manuals of theology to the solution of conflict situations in terms of the principle of the indirect voluntary is the case of unjust aggression. The physical structure of the act is not the determining factor in such a conflict situation.

In general a Christian ethicist might be somewhat suspicious of conflict situations solved in terms of the physical structure of the act itself. Such a solution seems too facile and too easily does away with the agonizing problems raised by the conflict. Likewise, such an approach has tended to minimize what is only an indirect effect. However, the Christian can never have an easy conscience about taking the life of another even if it is only an indirect effect.

The case of "assisted abortion" seems to illustrate the inherent difficulties in the manualistic concept of direct and indirect. For example, the best available medical knowledge indicates that the woman cannot bring a living child to term.

22. John McCarthy, *Problems in Theology II: The Commandments* (Westminster, 1960), pp. 159, 160. The author mentions other current definitions of direct killing (for example, an act which aims, *ex fine operis*, at the destruction of life) earlier on pp. 119–122.

If the doctor can abort the fetus now, he can avert very probable physical and psychological harm to the mother from the pregnancy which cannot eventually come to term. The manuals indicate that such an abortion would be direct and therefore immoral. However, in the total context of the situation, it does not seem that such an abortion would be immoral. The example of assisted abortion illustrates the impossibility of establishing an absolute moral norm based on the physical description of the action considered only in itself apart from the person placing the action and the entire community. It seems that the older notion of direct enshrines a pre-scientific worldview which is somewhat inadequate in our technological age. Why should the doctor sit back and wait for nature to take its course when by interfering now he can avoid great harm to the mother? In general, I do not think that conflict situations can be solved merely in terms of the physical structure and consequences of the act.

Perhaps the approach used in conflict situations of unjust aggression would serve as a better model for the solution of other conflict situations. In unjust aggression the various values at stake are weighed and the person is permitted to kill an unjust aggressor not only to save his life but also to protect other goods of comparable value.[23] Thus in the question of abortion there might be cases when it is moral to abort to save the life of the mother or to preserve other very important values.

The present discussion about the beginning of human life centers on the criteria for identifying human life. Are the physical criteria of genetics and embryology sufficient? Or must other criteria of a more psychological and personalistic nature be employed for discerning the existence of human life? What, then, would be the difference between the fetus in the womb and the newborn babe who is now existing out-

23. Marcellinus Zalba, *Theologia Moralis Summa II: Theologia Moralis Specialis* (Madrid, 1953), pp. 275–279.

side his mother's womb? There are many complicated problems in such a discussion. For many, the biological and genetic criteria are the only practical way of resolving the problem.[24] I am merely pointing out that the problem exists precisely because some people will not accept the biological and genetic criteria for establishing the beginning of human life.

Manualist moral theology has frequently distorted its teaching on sexuality by centering its entire approach around the physical structure of sexual actuation. Catholic theology has divided the sins against chastity into two categories—sins according to nature and sins against nature. Nature in that case means the physical structure of sexual actuation as the depositing of male semen in the vagina of the female.[25] The gravity attached to adolescent masturbation comes from a one-sided, physical approach to the problem. Catholic theology has paid too little attention to the psychological aspects of masturbation as also contributing to its objective meaning. The blanket gravity attached to all sins against sexuality indicates a crass and impersonal criterion which is not totally adequate.

The contemporary discussion about sexual relationships outside marriage centers on the precise question that the physical act of sexual intercourse might not always be identified with the moral act of marital relationship. Are there no circumstances outside marriage in which sexual relationships have a meaning? The problem is much too complex to even attempt a solution. However, the burden is increasingly upon the ethician to prove and not merely accept as a fact that sexual

24. Such an approach is adopted by Paul Ramsey who claims that at least from blastocyst the fetus must be considered as a human being. Ramsey's paper, which was delivered at the International Conference on Abortion sponsored by the Harvard Divinity School and the Joseph P. Kennedy Jr. Foundation, will be published as part of the proceedings of the conference by the Harvard University Press.

25. Zalba, pp. 349ff. In this section Zalba also explains the accepted teaching of the manuals that complete sins against sexuality always involve grave matter.

actuations have meaning only in terms of the marital act. Perhaps the ultimate reason for the traditional norm against extramarital and premarital sexual relations arises not primarily from the nature of the act itself but rather from the interpersonal and societal implications of such actions. There is a valid ethical argument for general norms based on the societal effect of human actions.

In the question of euthanasia, Catholic and other theistic ethicists generally approach the problem in terms of the limited dominion which man has over his own life. Today even the Christian claims a greater power over his own existence both because of scientific advances and because of better understanding of his participation in the Lordship of Jesus. However, in one important aspect in the area of euthanasia the question of dominion over one's life is not primary. Catholic thinking has maintained that the patient does not have to use extraordinary means to preserve his life. In more positive terms, there is a right to die. Many Catholic theologians remind doctors that they have no obligation to give intravenous feeding to a dying cancer patient. Likewise, a doctor may discontinue such feeding with the intent that the person will thus die. But the manuals of theology would condemn any positive action on the part of the doctor—for example, injection of air into the bloodstream—under the same circumstances.[26]

At the particular time when death is fast approaching, the primary moral question does not seem to revolve explicitly around the notion of man's dominion over his life. The problem centers on the difference between not giving something or the withdrawal of something necessary for life and the positive giving of something to bring about death. Is the difference between the two types of action enough to warrant the total condemnation of positively interfering? I think that

26. Gerald Kelly, *Medico-Moral Problems* (St. Louis, 1957), pp. 128–141.

Catholic theologians should explore the possibility of interfering to hasten the dying process, a notion similar to the concept of assisted abortion mentioned above. But the theologian would also have to consider the possibility of a general prohibition based on the societal effects of such interference.

The problem of describing moral reality in terms of the physical description of an act viewed in itself apart from the person also manifests itself in the question of divorce. According to Catholic teaching a consummated marriage between two baptized persons is indissoluble. But consummation is defined in solely physical terms. Thus the notion of consummation as found in the present law of the Church is inadequate.[27] Moreover, divorce in general qualifies as a negative, moral absolute in the sense described above. A particular action described in non-moral terms (remarriage after a valid first marriage) is always wrong. The entire question of divorce is too complex to be considered adequately in the present context since it involves biblical, historical, conciliar, and magisterial aspects. But the concept of "the bond of marriage" adds weight to the arguments against divorce. The bond becomes objectivized as a reality existing apart from the relationship of the persons which is brought into being by their marriage vows. All Christians, I believe, would hold some element transcending the two persons here and now. But can this bond always be considered apart from the ongoing relationship between the two who exchanged the marital promises?

Thus a quick overview shows that the critical practical areas of discussion in contemporary moral theology and Christian ethics center on the absolute moral prohibition of certain actions which are defined primarily in terms of the physical structure of the act. Moral meaning is not necessarily identical with the physical description of an act. Modern man

27. For a fuller critique of the notion of consummation, see Dennis Doherty, "Consummation and the Indissolubility of Marriage," *Absolutes in Moral Theology?*, pp. 211–231.

is in a much better position than medieval man to realize that fact. The underlying problem is common to every human science—the need clearly to differentiate the category of meaning as the specific data of any science involving human reality. Historians of ideas would be familiar with this problem from the nineteenth-century differentiation of Dilthey between the *Geisteswissenchaften* and *Naturwissenchaften*.[28] In the Anglo-American context, Matson has recently published an informative survey of the present status of this same differentiation involving the notion of human behavior.[29]

A word of caution is in order. It appears that some proponents of situation ethics have not given enough importance to the bodily, the material, the external, and the physical aspects of reality. On the other hand, contemporary man is less prone to accept the physical and the biological aspects of reality as morally normative. An analysis of the current scene in moral theology and Christian ethics in a broad ecumenical view indicates that the primary point of dispute centers on the existence of negative moral absolutes in which the moral action is described in physical terms. It would be unwarranted to conclude that the moral act is never identified with the physical structure and description of the act. However, one can conclude that an ethical theory which begins with the assumption that the moral act is identified with the physical structure and consequences of the act will find little acceptance by contemporary theologians.

4. Recent Catholic Critiques of Natural Law

In the context of the contemporary scene in moral theology, Catholic thinkers have been analyzing and criticizing the con-

28. Wilhelm Dilthey, *Pattern and Meaning in History* (New York, 1967).
29. Floyd W. Matson, *The Broken Image* (Garden City, 1966).

cept of natural law, especially understood as it is in *Humanae Vitae*. The next few paragraphs will summarize some of the recent considerations.[30] The natural law does not refer to a coherent philosophical theory with an agreed upon body of ethical content in existence from the beginning of time. Many thinkers in the course of history have employed the term "natural law," but frequently they defined natural law in different ways. Thinkers employing different natural law approaches have arrived at different conclusions on particular moral topics. Natural law in the history of thought does not refer to a monolithic theory, but tends to be a more generic term which includes a number of different approaches to moral problems.

Many erroneously believe that Catholic theology is committed to a particular natural law approach to moral problems. In practice, however, the vast majority of Catholic teaching on particular moral questions came into existenec even before Thomas Aquinas enunciated his theory. Likewise, contemporary Catholic theology recognizes the need for a pluralism of philosophical approaches in the Christian's quest for a better understanding of man and his reality. There is no longer "one Catholic philosophy."

In particular there has been much criticism of a natural law approach which defines the moral action in terms of the physical structure of the act itself. Thomas Aquinas in principle refutes such a theory. For Thomas the natural law is right reason. Thomas's own understanding of the absolute character of moral law is much less rigid than the exposition of the absolute character of the natural law found in many theology manuals.[31] The identification of the total human act with its physical and biological structure logically comes from the

30. See above, note 1; also essays by Curran, Häring, McCormick, and Milhaven in *Norm and Context in Christian Ethics*, ed. Gene H. Outka and Paul Ramsey (New York, 1968).

31. John G. Milhaven, "Moral Absolutes and Thomas Aquinas," *Absolutes in Moral Theology?*, pp. 154–158.

theory of the Roman lawyer Ulpian. Ulpian distinguished the natural law from the *ius gentium*. The natural law is that which is common to man and all the animals; whereas the *ius gentium* is that which is proper to man because of his reason.[32] The natural law thus was equated with physical, biological processes which man shares with all the animals. In general, Catholic theology avoids the identification of the human act with the physical structure of the act. Not every killing is murder; not every taking of something is theft; not every falsehood is a lie. However, especially in some of the areas mentioned above, Catholic moral theology has tended to describe the moral act in physical terms.

Such a theory of natural law seems conditioned by the pre-scientific circumstances in which it arose. In a pre-technological civilization, man found happiness by conforming himself to the rhythms of nature. But through science and technology contemporary man must interfere with the laws of nature to make human life more human. Perhaps the greatest reason for the insufficiency in the natural law theory found in the papal encyclical stems from the shift in horizon from a classicist world view to a more historically minded world view.[33] In a more historically conscious methodology things have a tendency to become "unstuck." [34] A classicist approach emphasizes the eternal, the immutable, and the unchanging. A more historically minded approach stresses the individual, the particular, the temporal, and the changing. The classicist view gives great importance to rationality, objectivity, order, and substances viewed in themselves. The historically conscious view sees rationality as only a part of man and appreci-

32. *The Digest* or *Pandects of Justinian*, Book 1, t.1, n. 1–4.
33. Bernard Lonergan, "The Transition from a Classicist World View to Historical Mindedness," in *Law for Liberty*, ed. James E. Biechler (Baltimore, 1967), pp. 126–133; John Courtney Murray, "The Declaration on Religious Freedom," *Concilium*, 2 (May 1966), pp. 3–10.
34. The phrase comes from Robert O. Johann, *Building the Human* (New York, 1968), p. 62. In this one volume Johann has gathered many of his articles expounding his relational approach to morality.

ates the importance of the subjective and the intersubjective in its understanding of man and his world. A classicist methodology tends to be more *a priori* and deductive; whereas the historically conscious methodology employs a more *a posteriori* and inductive approach. The different methodologies also have different understandings of truth and certitude which of necessity color one's understanding of the moral life.

Humanae Vitae in its methodology well illustrates a classicist approach. The papal letter admits that "changes which have taken place are in fact noteworthy and of varied kinds" (*H.V.* 2). These changes give rise to new questions. However, the changing historical circumstances have not affected the answer or the method employed in arriving at concrete conclusions on implementing responsible parenthood. The primary reason for rejecting the majority report of the papal commission was "because certain criteria of solutions had emerged which departed from the moral teaching on marriage proposed with constant firmness by the teaching authority of the Church" (*H.V.* 6).

The encyclical specifically acknowledges the fact that there are new signs of the times, but one wonders if sufficient attention has really been paid to such changes. The footnotes to the encyclical are significant even if the footnote references alone do not constitute a conclusive argument. The references are only to random scriptural texts, one citation of Thomas Aquinas, and references to earlier pronouncements of the hierarchical magisterium. A more inductive approach would have been inclined to give more importance and documentation to the signs of the times. The footnote references contain no indication of any type of dialogue with other Christians, non-Christians, and the modern sciences. When the letter does mention social consequences of the use of contraception, no documentation is given for what appear to be unproven assumptions. Since the methodology describes the human act in physical terms, the practical moral conclusion is the absolute condemnation of means of artificial birth control. The encyclical thus betrays an epistomology that has been rejected by many Catholic theologians and philosophers today.

5. Different Approaches with Different Conclusions

Natural law theory has traditionally upheld two values that are of great importance for moral theology: (1) the existence of a source of ethical wisdom and knowledge which the Christian shares with all mankind; (2) the fact that morality cannot be merely the subjective whim of an individual or group of individuals. However, one can defend these important values for moral theology without necessarily endorsing the particular understanding of natural law presupposed in the encyclical. In the last few years Catholic thinkers have been developing and employing different philosophical approaches to an understanding of morality. One could claim that such approaches are modifications of natural law theory because they retain the two important values mentioned above. Others would prefer to abandon the term "natural law" since such a concept is very ambiguous. There is no monolithic philosophical system called the natural law, and also the term has been somewhat discredited because of the tendency among some to understand natural in terms of the physical structure of acts. We can briefly describe three of the alternative approaches which have been advanced in the last few years— personalism, a more relational and communitarian approach, a transcendental methodology. All these approaches would deny the absolute conclusion of the papal encyclical in condemning all means of artificial birth control.

A more personalist approach has characterized much of contemporary ethics. For the Christian, the biblical revelation contributes to such an understanding of reality. A personalist approach cannot be something merely added on to another theory. A personalist perspective will definitely affect moral conclusions, especially when such conclusions have been based on the physical structure of the act itself. Personalism always sees the act in terms of the person placing the act. The *Pastoral Constitution on the Church in the Modern World* realized that objective standards in the matter of sexual morality are "based on the nature of the human person and his acts" (51). The essay by Bernard Häring shows how a personalist perspective would not condemn artificial contraception as being always immoral.

Classical ethical theory embraces two types or models of ethical method: the teleological and the deontological. H. Richard Niebuhr has added a third ethical model—the model of responsibility. Man is not primarily a maker or a citizen but a responder. There are various relationships within which the responsible self exists. "The responsible self is driven as it were by the movement of the social process to respond and be accountable in nothing less than a universal community." [35] Robert Johann in developing his understanding of man acknowledges a great debt to Niebuhr.[36]

A more relational understanding of morality stems from a different view of man. The natural law approach as found in the manuals of theology views nature as a principle of operation within every existing thing. Man thus should act according to the design of God inscribed in his very nature which should be unfolded in his life and actions. Note that the encyclical adopts such a view of man. However, many thinkers today view man not as a substantial entity existing in himself with his own nature as the guiding principle of his life embedded within him, but rather as a person existing as a being with others in a network of relationships. Man is not

35. H. Richard Niebuhr, *The Responsible Self* (New York, 1963), p. 88.
36. Johann, pp. 7–10.

a being totally programmed by the nature he has. Rather, man is characterized by openness, freedom, and the challenge to make himself and his world more human in and through his many relationships. The human person is actually constituted in and through these relationships. Relationality thus characterizes man and his existence. A philosophy of process is somewhat further along the same line of a more relational and historical approach to reality.

In the particular question of contraception, a more relational approach would not view the person or a particular faculty as something existing in itself. Each faculty exists in relationship with the total person and other persons within a universal community. Morality cannot merely be determined by examining a particular faculty and its physical structure or a particular act in itself. The changed ethical evaluation of lying illustrates the point. Manuals of moral theology have generally accepted the Augustinian definition of lying as speech against what is in the mind (*locutio contra mentem*). The malice of lying thus consists in violating the purpose of the faculty of speech. Recently Catholic theologians have proposed a different understanding of lying which actually corresponds more with the thinking of the earlier Augustine before he arrived at his famous definition of *locutio contra mentem*.[37] The malice of lying consists in the violation of my neighbor's right to truth. Falsehood is the physical act of speech which is contrary to what is in the mind; but lying as a moral act consists in the violation of my relationships with my neighbor and the community. Both Johann and van der Marck have employed a more relational approach to argue for the liceity of contraception in certain circumstances.[38]

37. J. A. Dorszynski, *Catholic Teaching About the Morality of Falsehood* (Washington, 1949).

38. Robert O. Johann, "Responsible Parenthood: A Philosophical View," *Proceedings of the Catholic Theological Society of America*, 20 (1965), pp. 115–128; William H. van der Marck, *Toward a Christian Ethic* (Westminster, 1967), pp. 48–60. Note that Germain G. Grisez, in

A third philosophical approach to man espoused by a growing number of Catholic thinkers today is a theory of transcendental method. Transcendental methodology owes much to Joseph Maréchal and is espoused today in different forms by Bernard Lonergan, Karl Rahner, and Emerich Coreth.[39]

In general, transcendental method goes beyond the object known to the structures of the human knowing process itself. According to Lonergan, "the intrinsic objectivity of human cognitional activity is its intentionality." [40] Lonergan's ethics is an extension of his theory of knowing. Moral value is not an intrinsic property of external acts or objects; it is an aspect of certain consciously free acts in relation to my knowledge of the world. Man must come to examine the structures of his knowing and deciding process.[41]

Lonergan uses as a tool the notion of horizon analysis. Basic horizon is the maxiumum field of vision from a determined standpoint. This basic horizon is open to development and even conversion. Lonergan posits four conversions which should transpire from the understanding of the structures of human knowing and deciding—the intellectual, the moral, the religious, and the Christian. Ethics must bring people to this Christian conversion so that they can become aware of their knowing and doing and flee from inauthenticity, unreasonableness, and the surd of sin. Thus Christian ethics is primarily

---

his *Contraception and the Natural Law* (Milwaukee, 1964), argues against artificial contraception although he explicitly denies the "perverted faculty" argument. However, Grisez seems to accept too uncritically his basic premise that the malice of contraception "is in the will's direct violation of the procreative good as a value in itself, as an ideal which never may be submerged."

39. For a succinct exposition of transcendental philosophy, see Kenneth Baker, *A Synopsis of the Transcendental Philosophy of Emerich Coreth and Karl Rahner* (Spokane, 1965).

40. Bernard Lonergan, *Collection* (New York, 1967), p. 278.

41. In addition to the bibliography of Lonergan's which has already been mentioned, see Bernard Lonergan, *Insight* (New York and London, 1964); also Donald H. Johnson, "Lonergan and the Redoing of Ethics," *Continuum*, 5 (1967), pp. 211–220.

concerned with the manner in which an authentic Christian person makes his ethical decisions and carries them out. However, such a meta-ethics must then enter into the realm of the normative, all the time realizing the provisional value of its precepts which are limited by the data at hand.[42] One commentator has said of Lonergan's ethic as applied to moral theology, "The distinct contribution of the moral theologian to philosophical ethics would consist in clarifying the attitudes which are involved in man's responding in faith to the initiative of a loving God who has redeemed man in Christ."[43] Thus a transcendental method would put greater stress on the knowing and deciding structures of the authentic Christian subject. Such a theory would also tend to reject the encyclical's view of man and his generative faculties.

There has been even among Catholic theologians a sharp, negative response to the practical conclusions of the papal encyclical on the regulation of birth. This essay has tried to explain the reason for the negative response. The concept of natural law employed in the encyclical tends to define the moral act merely in terms of the physical structure of the act. The problem of such negative moral absolutes defined in terms of the physical dimension of the act is perhaps *the* central area of dispute among Christian ethicists today. In contemporary theology such an understanding of natural law has been severely criticized. Newer philosophical approaches to the understanding of man have been accepted by many Catholic thinkers. Such approaches logically lead to the conclusion that artificial contraception can be a permissible and even necessary means for the regulation of birth within the context of responsible parenthood.

42. David W. Tracy, "Horizon Analysis and Eschatology," *Continuum*, 2 (1968).
43. Johnson, *loc. cit.*, pp. 219, 220.

BERNARD HÄRING THE INSEPARABILITY
OF THE UNITIVE-PROCREATIVE FUNCTIONS
OF THE MARITAL ACT

The encyclical *Humanae Vitae* rests chiefly on the assertion that the procreative and unitive elements of the conjugal act are inseparable, and evinces optimism and confidence that all men of good will can accept this proposition: "We believe that men of our day are particularly capable of seizing the deeply reasonable and human character of this fundamental principle" (*H.V.* 12). Our attention will therefore be given to that part of the encyclical.

1. *Openness of Each Marital Act to Procreation*

For centuries the Church shared the common belief that each conjugal act was, by its very "nature," procreative and could only accidentally fail to be so. It was not until the nineteenth century that medical scientists posited the ovule of the woman as a condition for procreation; closer scientific investigation revealed a certain rhythm in nature which set limits on fecundity. It was further found that natural rhythm, unreliable as it may be, tends to separate the procreative and unitive functions of the marital act by restricting biological fecundity to few conjugal acts only. It was then evident that the "procreative good," at least in the sense of an actual transmission of life, could not be truly obtained during infertile periods. Thus it was only with great reluctance that the Church accepted marital intercourse to be good when it was intentionally limited to the infecund periods.

Indeed, a long tradition in the Church had consistently maintained that conjugal intercourse was truly and fully good only when it intended procreation explicitly or implicitly. It followed logically that marital intercourse during a pregnancy was immoral. St. Ambrose reflected the thinking of many theologians over the centuries when he stated, "God does the marvels of creation in the secret sanctuary of the mother's womb, and you dare to desecrate it through passion! Either follow the example of the beasts or fear God." [1]

The marital intercourse of sterile persons was generally condoned by the bishops and theologians on the basis of the persons' desire for fecundity. The biblical stories of women who had been considered definitively sterile and who became blessed with offspring could be used as supportive arguments for the lawfulness of intercourse. However, where there was neither hope nor desire for fecundity, the general trend was to discourage intercourse; not only was it considered most imperfect behavior but it indicated a lack of self-control and mortification.

The encyclical *Humanae Vitae* reaffirms the positive value of the marital act as expressive of conjugal love; such valuation was not at all common before St. Alphonsus of Liguori, or even before Pius XII and Vatican II. Conjugal acts, the encyclical states, "do not cease to be lawful if, for causes independent of the will of husband and wife, they are foreseen to be infecund, since they remain ordained towards expressing and consolidating their union. In fact, as experience bears witness, not every conjugal act is followed by new life. God has wisely disposed natural laws and rhythms which, of themselves, cause a separation in the succession of births" (11). Thus the simplistic alternative, "either the spouses have the

1. Saint Ambrose, *Expositio Evangelii secundum Lucam*, liber I, Migne PL 15, 1552.

explicit or at least implicit intention to transmit life or they are indulging in lustful desires," is finally eliminated. On this point, *Humanae Vitae* marks a tremendous progress over *Casti Connubii*. The question is raised, however, as to whether *Humanae Vitae* is as consistent as was *Casti Connubii* in its own way since such an important presupposition has now been eliminated.

Paul VI follows an ancient tradition when he asserts that each individual marital act must manifest readiness to transmit life: "The Church, calling men back to the observance of the norms of the natural law, as interpreted by her constant doctrine, teaches that each and every marriage act must remain open to the transmission of life" (*H.V.* 11). This main thesis of the new encyclical is rightly introduced by the word "nonetheless." Attention is called to the fact that apparently the same conclusion is reached in spite of the changed general premises. Moreover, the thesis not only stands on different premises but has a very different and most limited meaning. In the older tradition, the thesis was taken literally and absolutely; therefore, according to many Church Fathers, intercourse during a pregnancy was considered a kind of sacrilege. The majority of theologians before St. Alphonsus maintained the necessary intent to transmit life; if, somehow, they approved the lawfulness of a marital act when chiefly motivated by the "remedy to concupiscence," they insisted on the inclusion of the intention to procreate.

The expression "open to the transmission of life" has much less meaning now. The marital act during pregnancy is acknowledged as being "open to new life," and so is the conjugal act in the infecund periods despite the fact that scientific calculations might practically eliminate the probability of any transmission of life. It is unfortunate that Pope Paul uses the same phrase in referring to the "constant doctrine" of the Church when historically the expression originated at a time when scientific theories on infecund periods were unknown.

178

Today the same expression refers to a totally different reality. According to *Humanae Vitae*, the calculated use of infecund periods is not contraceptive; rhythm keeps the marital act open for procreation but in a totally new sense, namely, it follows "the natural laws and rhythms of fecundity which, of themselves, cause a separation in the succession of births" (*H.V.* 11). The openness is still asserted relative to "each and every marital act," but the openness remains as long and only as long as the "laws of the generative process" (*H.V.* 13), "the natural laws and rhythms of fecundity" (*H.V.* 12), are observed, although this is done to avoid a new pregnancy.

In the past it was generally asserted that the conjugal act could not be free from sinfulness unless it truly sought the transmission of life. The same teaching is emphatically maintained now but with a different wording: "An act of marital love, which is detrimental to the faculty of propagating life . . . is in contradiction to both the divine plan according to whose norm matrimony is instituted, and the will of the Author of life. To use this divine gift destroying, even if only partially, its meaning and its purpose is to contradict the nature both of man and woman and of their most intimate relationship" (*H.V.* 13). But in context, the malice is not in the unwillingness to propagate life while engaging in the conjugal act; rather it now lies in intercourse without absolute respect for "the laws of the generative process" (*H.V.* 13), namely, the "natural laws and rhythms of fecundity which, of themselves, cause a separation in the succession of births" (*H.V.* 11). For good reasons or motives, those natural laws and rhythms can lawfully be exploited for the unitive meaning of the marriage act while assuring that the procreative meaning is respected only by eliminating it through the use of calendar, temperature charts, or other means. It is evident that "openness to the transmission of life" is not necessarily synonymous with "readiness to transmit life" through intercourse; rather it lies in the observance of the "natural laws and rhythms of fecundity" in order to exclude transmitting new life as effectively as possible through the use of "natural rhythms" and by no other means.

2. Respect for Biological Laws

Humanae Vitae confines the procreative meaning of the marital act to the faithful observance of biological laws and rhythms. It implied therein that God's wise and divine plan is revealed to the spouses through these absolutely sacred physiological laws. This is undoubtedly the philosophy underpinning the argumentation of the whole encyclical. It goes so far as to declare biological laws as absolutely binding on the conscience of men.

"In relation to the biological processes, responsible parenthood means the knowledge and respect of their functions; human intellect discovers in the power of giving life biological laws which are part of the human person" (*H.V.* 10). Does it follow that God governs the human person through the same biological laws as animals? The answer is: No! In animals, the biological laws are linked to instinct. As for man, the encyclical cautions strongly, "In relation to the tendencies of instinct and passion, responsible parenthood means the necessary dominion which reason and will must exercise over them" (*H.V.* 10). Instinct is not a natural law in man; rather it is a questionable theory that has been superseded by motivation theories of drive or passion. The absoluteness of biological laws can apply to the human person to the extent that he knows them; he then has to observe them, even against the proddings of passion.

Some of the questions which arise spontaneously are: How did God govern man during the thousands of years when the biological laws relative to the separate unitive and procreative functions of the marital act were unknown? How does he govern those for whom the "natural laws and rhythms" do not function properly? And what about the less educated people who are incapable of acquiring and using the modern knowledge of these rhythmic tendencies? How absolute can "natural laws and rhythms" be if we can prove that over long periods of history they are undergoing slow but deep changes? How can one ascribe absoluteness to biological laws if they are "inscribed in the very being of man and woman" (*H.V.* 12) not as absolute laws but as changing and unreliable trends? The fundamental question remains: Is man to be absolutely subjected to biological laws and rhythms or is he and should he be their wise administrator?

The response of *Humanae Vitae* is apodictic: "In fact, just as man does not have unlimited dominion over his body in general, so also, with particular reason, he has no such dominion over his generative faculties as such, because of their intrinsic ordination towards raising up life, of which God is the principle" (13).

The premise "man does not have unlimited dominion over his body" cannot be denied. Modern medicine is based on a *reasonable, limited* dominion over the organism. Good medical art rejects any *arbitrary* interference with the biological functions, but it does intervene whenever it is to benefit not only the biological organism but *the whole person*. It would have seemed logical to pursue the thought to its proper conclusion: ". . . so also, with particular reason, he has *no unlimited dominion* over his generative faculties . . ." Man must be a wise—never an unwise or arbitrary—steward of his generative faculties as such; this would mean that any *arbitrary* interference is against the moral natural law. But *Humanae Vitae* seems to say: Although man has a real but limited dominion over his body, he has *no* dominion over the biological functions related to the transmission of life. In my opinion, this total difference between "limited dominion" and "no such dominion" demands a special proof. The quote from

Pope John's encyclical *Mater et Magistra* seems intended for this purpose: "Human life is sacred; from its very inception it reveals the creating hand of God" (*H.V.* 13). Here again we encounter unequal members in the comparison: the absolute sacredness of the *biological laws and rhythms* is compared and equated with the sacredness of *human life*. The difference is as great as between "no dominion" and "limited dominion." Biological functions, including the human sperm and ovule, are not human life nor the inception of human life.

In spite of the unreliability of biological laws and rhythms, the encyclical seems to consider them as a part of the human person. It seems to go so far as thoroughly to subordinate the whole human person and the marriage itself to the absolute sacredness of biological laws which have only recently become better known. It has, in fact, been learned that they are not "unchangeable" but are constantly subject to change. We know, for example, that certain animals capable of begetting offspring two or three times a year adjust rapidly when transferred from tropical or subtropical regions to northern areas with a long winter. By a change in their biological "laws and rhythms" they adjust the process of begetting to once a year. Man's biological nature differs from that of lower animals; it is slower in its changes. However, man survives precisely because he can make use of such artificial means as clothing, modern technology, and, most importantly, medicine in adjusting in a typically human way.

3. Minister of the Creator's Design (H.V. 13)

The expression "minister of the design established by the Creator" has or can have a deep meaning. All can agree that man must act in wisdom as a faithful steward in submission to the loving will of God. Man must not be the "arbiter of the sources of human life." In our interpretation, it becomes: man must never act arbitrarily; he must make the best possible use of all the gifts of God; he must administer his biological and psychological heritage in generous responsibility to the best of the whole person, of himself, and of his closest neighbor, especially of the marriage as a community of persons. However, *Humanae Vitae* intends an entirely different meaning: it seems to say that any effort of man to be the steward of biological reality is arbitrary; man is expected to be simply and absolutely submitted to biological "laws and rhythms," at least insofar as "each and every marriage act must remain open to the transmission of life." Human biology, not human reason, determines whether a conjugal act is to become fruitful or not, even at times and in situations when a new pregnancy or total continence would destroy persons or the marriage itself. There is no doubt left that respect for biological laws must be absolute: "It is not licit, even for the gravest reasons, to do evil so that good may follow therefrom . . . even when the intention is to safeguard or promote individual, family, or social well being" (*H.V.* 14).

Humanae Vitae seems to allow only one exception to the absolutely binding power of "natural laws and rhythms of fecundity" and it refers to the correction of the biological functions themselves. It appears to be the intended meaning of the principle: "The Church does not at all consider illicit the use of those therapeutic means truly necessary to cure diseases of the *organism*, even if an impediment to procreation, which may be foreseen, should result therefrom, provided such impediment is not, for whatever motive, directly willed" (*H.V.* 15). Medicine is generally based on the principle that biological functions may be interfered with and even destroyed if it is necessary for the well being of the *person*. It is evident that the final perspective of an anthropologically grounded medicine is not the mere restoration of the *organism* but the wholeness of a *person* in community. Medical practices of the last century often tended to focus on the

183

organism instead of the person as a person; today, however, the trend has been reversed and corrected by the best of medical thought.

Let us consider the case of a postpartum psychosis or of a psychotic fear of pregnancy. How else can a woman in either instance be helped and her capacity to render the marital due be restored if not by an interference into her biological "laws and rhythms" so as to ascertain avoidance of a pregnancy? A literal interpretation of *Humanae Vitae,* and this in the whole context, condemns such an interference because it seeks directly to impede procreation; the intervention is not intended to cure a disease of the organism but to help the whole person. While the cure of organic ailments is allowed, the wholeness of the person does not seem to justify the treatment.

It is quite clear that in *Humanae Vitae* "the natural laws and rhythms" are considered as "the established order of the Creator"; therefore, the only way to regulate births is to follow "the natural rhythms immanent in the procreative functions" by "the use of marriage in the infecund periods only" (*H.V.* 16). The text is emphatic in elaborating the difference between "recourse to infecund periods" and "the use of means directly contrary to fecundation": "In reality, there are essential differences between the two cases: in the former, the married couple make use of a natural disposition; in the latter, they impede the development of natural processes" (H.V. 16).

The only solution for the difficulties, according to *Humanae Vitae,* is to bring rhythm to perfect functioning and to let married people determine their infecund days. This frame of reference truly suggests a place for a "catholic pill," namely, one that would ascertain or fix the time of ovulation; such regulation would respect "the established order of the Creator" and "the natural laws and rhythms," while a pill that postpones ovulation would be intrinsically evil and immoral since it does not respect these laws.

I think that modern man is particularly incapable of grasping the total difference in the moral import of these two means of interference. Today man thinks much more in terms of the good of the whole person than in terms of absolutely sacred but often dysfunctional "natural laws and rhythms." I must humbly confess that for me it is impossible to come to an understanding of

(1) how and in what realistic sense the marriage act can truly remain "open to the transmission of life" when a perfectly calculated use of rhythm—and, if needed, an artificial correction of the improperly functioning "natural laws and rhythms"—guarantees no new life in the marriage act;

(2) why such a difference in the morality of

   (a) interference in the organism for the restoration of the organism or the correction of improperly functioning "natural rhythm";

   (b) the responsible use of other means of birth regulation with even less interference into the biological functions.

Why should a pill that fixes the date of ovulation and guarantees the loss of the ovule be more "catholic" than a pill that preserves the ovule which, here and now, is not needed because procreation would be irresponsible? One point emerges clearly: in the first case the treatment respects the "law" of rhythm, while in the other it does not respect the absolute validity of the natural rhythm. Yet it is common knowledge today that in millions of cases "the natural law of rhythm" by itself is not functioning or is at least unreliable.

Should the salvation of a marriage or even the eternal salvation of a person depend so greatly on whether or not the "natural rhythm" is functional? Should heavy and very dangerous burdens be shouldered by couples who simply cannot rely on natural rhythm while others go justified because they can operate "safely" within such bounds and thereby avoid pregnancy?

4. Disregard for Biological Functions and Destruction of Marital Love

The encyclical *Humanae Vitae* marks an advance over earlier teaching by its acknowledgment of the true meaningfulness of the marriage act even when childbirth is not desired, but it remains adamant in the assertion that a marriage act bespeaks genuine love only when the biological laws and rhythms are fully observed and respected. It argues that "the dignity of man and wife" must be defended in this way; where man relies on technical means he is no longer a responsible being: the Church "engages man not to abdicate from his own responsibility in order to rely on technical means" (*H.V.* 18). I agree: if man were to *rely* on technical means *alone* without discernment in the proper use of technical means, mankind would be degraded. But the argument runs differently: any use of technical means relative to "natural processes" would necessarily destroy the integrity of conjugal love. Such a thesis finds no basis in experience; it assumes that biological laws and rhythms best protect man's dignity and capacity to love if dutifully followed, if observed with absolute respect and submission. How can such an assumption stand without proof?

The encyclical attempts to prove the unavoidably destructive character of all artificial means of birth control by signaling the "necessary" consequences: "Let men consider, first of all, how wide and easy a road would thus be opened up towards conjugal infidelity and the general lowering of morality. Not much experience is needed in order to know human weakness. . . ." (*H.V.* 17). Pope Paul VI is convinced that nothing can better express the unitive and procreative meaning of marriage, can better check immorality, infidelity, and promiscuity, than the absolute sacredness of biological processes: "Consequently, if the mission of generating life is not to be exposed to the arbitrary will of men, one must necessarily recognize insurmountable limits of the possibility of man's domination over his own body and its functions. . . . Such limits cannot be determined otherwise than by the respect due to the integrity of the human organism and its functions" (*H.V.* 17).

Somehow, a strange counter-argument could run something like this: Unmarried couples who, by an accurate observance of the natural rhythm, let their intercourse be open to transmitting life while being, at the same time, absolutely sure that they do so only in infecund periods, can express mutual love while respecting "the integrity of the human organism and its functions." This argument cannot be disregarded if the "natural laws and rhythms" are the chief cornerstone of sex morality. Such argumentation, however, is immediately seen as fallacious if we come to a deeper understanding of the need to preserve the unitive and procreative meaning of the marital life; application of the principle of totality encompasses the nature of the *person* and the *personal* acts.

5. A Personalistic Approach to the Unitive-Procreative Meaning of Marriage

There is need for a thorough study of the problem raised by the encyclical *Humanae Vitae*, namely, that of the relationship between the unitive and the procreative meaning of the marriage act. The encyclical could have been worded very differently had this problem received adequate attention in Catholic moral theology of the past decades. There is and

187

must be a close linkage of the two meanings, and great care must be exercised never to separate them unduly or totally in any aspect of sex morality.

Moralists of the past did touch upon the problem, however, when they declared that extra-marital intercourse was immoral because it did not respect the "*bonum prolis*," the good of procreation; if a child should result, it would not be born into a family. This argument could be developed along the following lines of thought: the unitive meaning of marriage is also disregarded because the partners do not look upon one another as a spouse or a possible parent of his/her children; they do not want to unite as spouses nor in view of the parental vocation. However, the old argument emphasizing only responsibility towards possible offspring when partners are unmarried does not go far enough; these two people do not want to be now and forever "two in one flesh." Their union is casual and superficial, not truly sincere; they lie in becoming "one flesh" while remaining separated.

Adulterers who use the rhythm method with the greatest skill and certainty observe the biological laws and relate the unitive and procreative meaning in the unrealistic and tenuous sense of "openness to the transmission of life" as emphasized in *Humanae Vitae*. From the personalistic point of view, they have totally divorced the two meanings because they do not bind themselves in a covenant uniting the conjugal and parental vocation. Indeed, they have fully neglected both meanings while respecting the biological laws and rhythms.

It is not easy to explain the relationship of the procreative to the unitive good in the marriage of proven sterile partners. Their marriage can fulfill the unitive meaning while it cannot truly and really fulfill a procreative role. However, I think the combined functions are not totally excluded in such marriages, in which the partners truly consider each other as spouses, and love each other in a way that would keep them open for the parental vocation were such within the range of possibility. One who sincerely loves his spouse as spouse would not refuse to have him or her as parent of his or her child if the choice were given.

Homosexuality is by no means a union of two *persons* "in one flesh," not only because sex activity of this kind is totally and absolutely opposed to any kind of parental vocation, but also because the sexual behavior of the partners fails to convey that love which is the gift of God for married people. The unitive semblance of homosexual behavior has nothing in common with the covenant of loves between man and woman. Not only is there lacking the biological basis for the unitive-procreative functions, but also the basic criteria of true love which are taken from an understanding of married love and union.

Premarital intercourse is another instance where the unitive and procreative functions of marriage are separated; it is a case of seeking the unitive meaning before uniting themselves in a lasting covenant of love, before a marriage that would assure a family setting for expected offspring. The two meanings are separated in spite of the fact that the partners could be observing the "natural laws and rhythms."

A husband who imposes a new pregnancy every year on his sick and nervous wife, doing so at the expense of proper family care, also separates the unitive from the procreative meaning of marriage. While the conjugal act may observe "the integrity of the human organism and its functions" (*H.V.* 17), it totally disregards genuine love for the wife and responsibility for the family. The unitive function is destroyed by this lack of love and responsibility while the procreative function is used irresponsibly.

6. Pastoral Considerations

Both the communicative-unitive good of the marriage and the good of the children impose constant sacrifices on the spouses who strive incessantly to do their best for the family.

These sacrifices cannot be determined and motivated by a biological understanding of natural law or by mere respect for badly functioning rhythm. There are higher, more demanding but less frustrating criteria of "natural law." I am referring to the very nature of the persons as persons and the meaning of the acts of persons.

Vatican II was explicit in setting the direction for all future research relative to preserving the genuine human connection between the unitive and procreative meanings of marriage: "The objective standards, based on the nature of the human person and the acts of the person, preserve the full sense of mutual self-giving and human procreation in the context of true love" (*Pastoral Constitution on the Church in the Modern World*, 51). The Latin text emphasizes "*personae eiusdemque actuum natura . . .*" The genuine relationship is broken whenever the conjugal act becomes sexual exploitation. It does not matter, then, whether such exploitation is done in conformity with biological laws and rhythms or against them; an irresponsible act of procreation can destroy the unitive meaning of marriage as well as the irresponsible use of contraceptive means.

It can positively be said that when a couple strives in the best possible way to grow in mutual affection, to promote the unity and stability of the marriage so as better to fulfill the parental vocation as regards good education and readiness to desire as many children as they can responsibly accept, then they preserve the human connection between the two meanings. Total continence can undermine a whole marriage. The *Pastoral Constitution* points to a dangerous disregard for the psychological and moral connection between the communicative-unitive good and the procreative good. It states: "Where the intimacy of married life is broken off, it is not rare for its faithfulness to be imperiled and its quality of fruitfulness ruined. For then the upbringing of the children and the courage to accept new ones are both endangered" (51).

When an absolute respect for improperly functioning, changing, or unknown biological laws and rhythms imposes total continence or an anguished, anxiety-arousing periodic continence, the unitive-procreative meanings of marriage can be severed. The procreative good is not obtained by a procreation which is against genuine human responsibility. The unitive good of the conjugal acts is not observed when total continence does, in fact, separate what God has joined together. Much human experience and, above all, shared experience is necessary in order to determine how, in the totally new situation of this day and age, the closely related unitive and procreative goods can remain effectively welded together. The encyclical seems to say that in this matter that "not much experience is needed" (17). It should be a matter of factual truth, a question of shared experience whether or not total continence imposed on the other spouse out of absolute respect for the natural biological functions and rhythms carries greater risks for conjugal fidelity and generous fecundity than a moderate and responsible use of some artificial means of birth regulation.

There is one point of the encyclical that should not be overlooked: "It is also to be feared that the man, growing used to the employment of anti-contraceptive practices, may finally lose respect for the woman and, no longer caring for her physical and psychological equilibrium, may come to the point of considering her a mere instrument of selfish enjoyment, and no longer his beloved companion" (17). I would not dare deny that this danger can arise. Everyone should be fully aware, however, that the danger cannot be dismissed by teaching the meaning of natural law, in a biological frame of thought, but the risk can at least be reduced by a better understanding of the nature of the person and his actions as a person. Countless spouses and marriage counselors testify to the fact that users of artificial means of birth regulation can be most attentive to the feelings of the spouse, caring in a very special way for the physical and psychological equilibrium of the spouse. There lurks the danger that they will not care or not enough; therefore, the moral teaching must alert them. I do not think that the doctrine of the absolute sacredness of the biological laws provides sufficient help in this direction. The close relationship between the unitive and procreative good of the marriage and of the conjugal act must be explained at a much higher, more demanding, and less frustrating level than that of an absolute respect for biological "laws and rhythms" which are anything but absolute.

ROBERT MCAFEE BROWN "HUMANAE VITAE":
A PROTESTANT REACTION

In recent years it has been the rule of ecumenical encounter not to engage in vigorous criticism of the "other" side. The proper ecumenical stance has been to concentrate on the failings of our own confessional family and to appreciate the good qualities of our ecumenical counterparts. On the whole, this is a good principle. But to assume in relation to *Humanae Vitae* a judicious silence, when so much is at stake, not only for ecumenism but for the whole family of man, is no way to contribute to the ecumenical future. If my own denomination, or the World Council of Churches, made a mistake as monumental as I feel *Humanae Vitae* to be, I would want every Catholic who could to join the chorus of criticism, so that we might collectively forestall the repetition of such an error in the future. So the ecumenically responsible thing to do is not to say, "Wasn't *Populorum Progressio* forward looking?", but to ask, "How can the harm of *Humanae Vitae* be undone?"

Ecumenical responsibility demands personal honesty, and it is therefore only fair to forewarn readers at the start that the underlying presupposition of the following pages is that *Humanae Vitae* is a tragedy for the Catholic Church and for the contemporary world. It is not only its content that upsets me, although I think it objectively wrong on almost every score, from its lack of contact with the modern world to its limited understanding of the psychology of marriage and its faulty understanding of the place of sexual intercourse in that relationship. It is also the manner of its issuance that upsets me; it not only fails to produce convincing arguments to support its thesis and to go counter to the overwhelming majority opinion of the papal commission that was presumably to guide its final content, but it also flies in the face of the collegial principle that I thought had been established by Vatican II and implies, possibly by intent, that papal authority is once again to be understood along the most reactionary lines of nineteenth-century Catholic thought.

It grieves me to write such words, for I know that to many Catholics they will seem shrill and lacking in the ecumenical charity all of us have been trying to establish. But if our goal is to speak the truth in love, we must remember that sometimes in the name of love we are forced to speak in terms that initially hurt. And if out of hurt can come healing, then perhaps out of the total episode of *Humanae Vitae*—both its presentation and reception—some good may yet come.

1. *"Humanae Vitae" as a Non-Protestant Problem*

Is *Humanae Vitae* really a matter on which Protestants should comment? Is it not after all an internal Roman Catholic problem concerning which Protestants should remain silent, anguishing for Catholic friends caught in the curial vise, and yet inwardly relieved that they do not face the same dilemma?

(1) There is a sense, of course, in which this is true. Protestants, not believing that Christ gave all authority to the see of Peter, are not bound by the pronouncements of the incumbent of that see. We examine papal statements for their historical, theological, and pastoral value and often learn from them. But where we find a papal teaching inadequate or incorrect, anything from *Unam Sanctam* to the *Syllabus of Errors*, we can accept this fact with considerably less existential anguish than we can our Roman Catholic friends, since repudiation does not create a crisis in our understanding of teaching au-

thority. In that sense, *Humanae Vitae* does not vitally concern us.

(2) Furthermore, we can respond (a mite too self-righteously) that in the face of burning human problems—Vietnam, social revolution, urban blight, racial discrimination—we do not intend to let our energies get sidetracked on an issue that for most of us was settled long ago. To spend time debating whether or not married couples can use contraceptives without risking damnation seems a frivolous, if not morally suspect, waste of time, and we are grieved that some of the best theological minds of our age must now give inordinate amounts of time and energy to a question that seems to us as diversionary from real problems as would be a reopening of the question of whether or not we can square Genesis with evolution. In this sense also, *Humanae Vitae* does not vitally concern us.

(3) Finally, what is going to be done to repair the harm of *Humanae Vitae* is going to be done largely by Catholics. The curia knew in advance that Protestants, Jews, and secularists would dissent from this particular piece of papal teaching, and nothing we can say or do is going to have much impact. If the teaching of the encyclical is to be challenged, the challenge to be effective will have to come from within. It will therefore be up to the priests, theologians, and laity of the Roman Catholic Church to register the kind of responsible dissent that may finally lead to a reconsideration of what one of them has called "a fallible document, written by a fallible man in the fallible exercise of his office." [1] So in this sense, too, *Humanae Vitae* does not vitally concern us.

1. John T. Noonan, "Historical Precedents for Fallible Statements," *The National Catholic Reporter* (August 7, 1968), p. 9.

2. "Humanae Vitae" as a Protestant Problem

But, fortunately or unfortunately, the matter is not quite that simple. For in at least two ways, *Humanae Vitae* does concern us deeply.

(1) It concerns us first of all *as Christians*, since it affects part of the Christian family with whom we have felt increasing *rapport*. We have all discovered that whatever happens in one part of the Christian family affects all of the members, whoever and wherever they are. A Roman Catholic problem is no longer merely that; it is also a Christian problem. That Catholics face a crisis in teaching authority makes it necessary for Protestants to rethink their own understanding of teaching authority, and—since a reunited church will presumably contain the bishop of Rome—to rethink the possible relationship of Protestants to the Roman Catholic magisterium.

The encyclical and the response it has gotten are also important to Protestants for what they tell us about Roman Catholicism, and the way they correct our misapprehensions of it. The content of the encyclical, for example, came as a surprise to me. It had seemed inconceivable, in the light of the openness of Vatican II, the overwhelming vote of the papal advisory commission for a change in the teaching, and the state of theological discussion in Roman Catholicism, that the Pope would turn the clock back as unequivocally and definitively as he did. The Catholic response also came as a surprise to me. Upon first reading the encyclical I anticipated that there would be anguish, a few quiet defections, and a feeling of increased *malaise* on the part of twentieth-century Catholics. It did not occur to me that hundreds of Catholic theologians (whose names read like a *Who's Who* of important contemporary theologians) would take such unequivocal issue with the Pope's conclusions. Thus I erred (a) in underestimating the intransigency of a papacy that in many other respects has been so open and creative, and (b) in underestimating the degree of creative dissent within the modern church, even in the face of an encyclical whose binding authority is presumed to be very high. *Humanae Vitae* thus gives me a more accurate picture than I had of the state of contemporary Catholicism.

(2) The encyclical also concerns us *as members of the human family*, whether we are Protestants or not. No one could presume that the consequences of this teaching are limited to Roman Catholics or to Christians. As the New York *Times* correctly editorialized, "When the Church presumes to speak for one-sixth of mankind, on an issue that could affect the very survival of the human race, others cannot remain indifferent. The papal encyclical is bound to retard recently promising efforts to check a population explosion that threatens in the next few decades to plunge the world into hopeless poverty and chaos." [2]

And when the Pope exhorts heads of state, "Do not allow the morality of your peoples to be degraded; do not permit that by legal means practices contrary to the natural and divine law [for example, artificial means of contraception] be introduced into that fundamental cell, the family" (paragraph 23), it is clear that an issue of moment for *all* people has been raised. Are heads of state to subject themselves to the bishop of Rome and outlaw contraception? Are foreign aid programs to be forbidden if they include contraceptive information or devices? Can governments, in this day and age, let their policy decisions by made in Vatican City?

Finally, since the encyclical does not claim to be based on divine revelation but is dealing with conclusions based on natural law and reason (which in principle are available to all men whether Catholic or not), the arguments of the encyclical are a fair subject of debate for all concerned about the

2. "Of Human Life," The New York *Times* (July 30, 1968), p. 38.

meaning of sex, marriage, population control, and the future welfare and happiness of men.

3. The Minor Problem: Birth Control

The encyclical poses two problems for all of us, one minor and one major. The more disposable issue is the substantive issue of the encyclical, birth control. I do not mean to suggest that birth control is itself a minor problem, but rather that the encyclical adds nothing substantively new to a discussion that has been going on for some years. If anything, it regresses from the teaching of Vatican II, and the great bulk of recent Catholic theology, back to the intransigency of *Casti Connubii*. Its sole importance for a theology of birth control is that it is enunciated on papal authority and for that reason demands the assent of the faithful. Thus the real issue posed by the encyclical is not its teaching about birth control but its claim that its teaching now has authoritative status.

Before turning to the issue of authority, however, I will comment briefly, from a Protestant perspective, on some of the substantive claims about birth control contained in the encyclical.

I was among those most heartened by Vatican II's treatment of birth control in the *Pastoral Constitution on the Church in the Modern World*, for the constitution left the door for change fully open; had the progressives tried to force a vote at that time they would have been outnumbered and the matter foreclosed. The very fact that the issue was left open suggested that there was dissatisfaction with the traditional teaching. Had there not been such dissatisfaction, the traditional teaching would have been unambiguously reaffirmed.

The pastoral constitution also seemed to provide a theological breakthrough by giving a high place to conjugal love in marriage as a good in and of itself. There was a recognition by the bishops (explicitly stated in speeches by such leaders as Cardinal Suenens, Cardinal Alfrink, Cardinal Léger, and Patriarch Maximos) that sex in marriage was intrinsically good, whether or not a child was conceived by the union.

But *Humanae Vitae* cancels all that potential gain. It does not take advantage of Vatican II's recognition of the good of sex in marriage apart from procreation. Indeed, the encyclical denies it, and the question can be raised, quite apart from my competence to determine, whether *Humanae Vitae* can therefore be held to be consistent with the teaching of Vatican II.[3]

It is the major assumption, "the fundamental principle," of the encyclical (quite apart from the question of its consistency or lack of consistency with Vatican II) that raises the most serious question about the encyclical's substantive content. For Pope Paul states unambiguously that every sexual act must remain open to the possibility of procreation. The "fundamental principle" is that sexual intercourse must not only be an expression of human love but must also allow for the creation of new life if such should result. The Pope enunciates an "inseparable connection, willed by God and unable to be broken by man on his own initiative, between the two meanings of the conjugal act: the unitive meaning and the procreative meaning" (12). If this is true, then all else follows.

But it is far from clear that this "fundamental principle" *is* true. It has been widely questioned in the past, and the encyclical advances no *new* reasons to accept it as true save that the Pope now says it is—an argument that lacks compelling force not only to non-Catholics, but also, as the response to the encyclical has so dramatically demonstrated, to extraordinarily devoted and intelligent Catholics.

It is luminously clear to me, both as a Protestant and a married man, that the "fundamental principle" of the en-

3. See Häring, "The Encyclical Crisis," *Commonweal* (September 6, 1968), p. 694.

cyclical is false, and grievously so. There is abundant evidence from countless marriages that at times the "procreative principle" gives deep richness to sexual intercourse in marriage, but that on many more occasions the "unitive principle," *in and of itself*, is the very deepest gift God can give to a man and a woman, and that to separate it from the procreative principle, by whatever means the couple agrees upon, is the way to enrich and deepen and sanctify that particular marriage relationship before God. To state that sex under such circumstances is "intrinsically dishonest," as the encyclical states, is simply to forfeit the credentials of credibility. And to imply, as the encyclical implies, that sex so experienced is evil, sinful, cheap, or dirty—which are the only implications one can draw from *Humanae Vitae*—is to increase the credibility gap almost beyond repair. Nothing in the entire encyclical carries more unrealism and pathos than the concluding sentence of the crucial paragraph 12; "We believe that the men of our day are particularly capable of seizing the deeply reasonable and human character of this fundamental principle."

Since the "fundamental principle" of the encyclical is incorrect, many conclusions that are drawn from it are incorrect. Let me call attention to only two. In paragraph 17, the Pope states that the use of contraceptives will lead "towards conjugal infidelity and the general lowering of morality." Later in the same paragraph he states that "the man, growing used to the employment of anticonceptive practices, may finally lose respect for the woman and . . . may come to the point of considering her as a mere instrument of selfish enjoyment."

Even the most superficial study of the psychology of marriage, particularly of good and happy marriages where contraceptives have been employed, would reveal the wildly improbable nature of the conclusions drawn in the quotations above. On the contrary, it must be insisted that the place of sex in marriage, *apart* from the intent to procreate, intensifies rather than destroys "conjugal fidelity," and that "respect for the woman," rather than being diminished (as it could be if she were looked upon merely as a producer of children), can be enhanced when only the "unitive principle" is the aim of a particular act of intercourse. I would be appalled to discover such statements as those of paragraph 17 in any responsible book on marriage, and I am the more appalled when I read them in a document purporting to set forth definitive Christian teaching.

4. The Major Problem: Authority

These comments indicate that the substantive teaching of the encyclical cannot be separated from the obedience one is asked to give to its teaching. If an individual believes that the teaching of the encyclical is false, then the authority of the promulgator of the encyclical, who says that its teaching is true, is clearly called into question. It is to this deeply vexing problem of authority that we now turn.

Protestants have taken rather strict views of what they believe papal authority means, and tend to be fundamentalists in their reading of papal documents or documents about papal power. Modern Catholics have demythologized many past utterances about papal power, but until *Humanae Vitae* they gave the general impression that on important matters it was still true that when Rome had spoken the case was closed. Papal sayings might be ignored (as was Pope John's *Veterum Sapientiae* which insisted that all seminary instruction be in Latin), and, more importantly, they might be "interpreted" (as was *Munificentissimus Deus* dealing with the assumption of the virgin), but they were hardly to be publicly disputed and disavowed. An article in *Osservatore Romano*, that bastion of orthodoxy, appearing in late August 1968, suggested that Catholics should accept the teaching of *Humanae Vitae* unquestioningly, since the Pope knows best, just as a patient unquestioningly accepts the diagnosis of a doctor because of the doctor's superior wisdom, or a foot soldier unhesitatingly carries out the command of his superior officer because of the officer's greater knowledge of military tactics. Even on the basis of these very dubious analogies it could be argued that a doctor might diagnose wrongly, and a military tactician make an unwise decision. So too, pressing the analogy, might a pope be incorrect. Conservatives as well as progressives have conceded that the encyclical is not infallible. Since the opposite of infallibility is fallibility, it might be presumed that one could question the conclusions of a fallible document, and that, of course, is precisely what the dissenters have done.

But the ecclesiastical authorities have questioned this right. They have demanded ecclesiastical loyalty oaths from those who dared to differ, and have begun engaging in punitive measures against those who do not fall into line. This, I assume, is because papal encyclicals up to now have enjoyed a kind of "practical infallibility," so that although one might have inward doubts, he did not voice them, lest scandal be caused to the faithful.

At all events, earlier papal encyclicals have been accorded a high degree of authority. But this has not been true of *Humanae Vitae*. From the moment of its release it has been the object of strong dissent by many of the most able Catholic theologians of our time, as well as priests and laymen. The authority of the pope, in other words, has been seriously questioned.

The type of questioning, I believe, is of an order different from past questioning. When the dogma of the assumption was promulgated in 1950, for example, many Catholics said that they questioned the "opportuneness" of the definition, but not that they questioned its substantive truth. Today, the disaffection over *Humanae Vitae* is not merely with the "opportuneness" but with the substantive claims. The Pope, so say the Catholic dissenters, is wrong. Rome has spoken, but the case is *not* closed. On the contrary, it remains open, and hundreds of theologians have said in effect that although the Pope has denied to Catholics the right to use contraceptives, Catholics can for good and sufficient reasons use them anyhow.

What does this do to the notion of papal authority? It obviously compromises it in very serious terms, and means that drastic overhauling of traditional views of authority is urgent, with no guarantee provided that the overhauling will be rapid enough to overtake the disintegrating process.

Let me indicate how I think the problem of authority has been developing in recent Catholic thought, and how I think it could continue to develop. As a result of Vatican I, there was a period in which papal authority was magnified all out of proportion, so that in practice what the pope said enjoyed the kind of "practical infallibility" referred to above, even though the actual prerogative of infallible pronouncement was exercised only once. But a view developed that the teaching of Vatican I was one-sided, since its unfinished agenda, having dealt only with the teaching authority of the bishop of Rome had not gone on to deal with the teaching authority of the other bishops. Thus Vatican II "completed" Vatican I by defining authority in collegial terms, indicating that the bishop of Rome speaks as head of, and in the name of, the college of bishops. By this action the conception of authority in Roman Catholicism was both broadened and deepened.

But *Humanae Vitae* is not a product of these collegial procedures. Its topic was specifically removed from the agenda of Vatican II, it was not permitted on the agenda of the later Synod of Bishops in the fall of 1967, and although an advisory papal commission made specific recommendations to the Pope, those recommendations were disregarded. We thus face the remarkable and unprecedented situation that there is a significant rift not only between the bishop of Rome and most of the reputable Catholic theologians, but between the bishop of Rome and the bishops of many national episcopal conferences. National groups elsewhere have not given the pope the kind of support the American bishops gave him in their November pastoral letter, "Human Life in Our Day." On the contrary, however tactfully they may have worded it, they have said, in instance after instance, that they will respect and honor the decision in conscience that a Catholic couple makes about contraception, even when such decision goes contrary to the explicit prohibitions of *Humanae Vitae*. I see no other way to read the pastoral letters on this topic by the French, Belgian, German, Dutch, and Canadian hierarchies. It is one thing when a theologian of the church like Karl Rahner comes to such a decision. It is quite another thing, full of the gravest implications, when the bishops themselves do. The result is that there is now a real crisis of authority, as the pope and curia say one thing, and teaching authorities in the rest of the church say something contrary—a crisis far too deep to be dismissed by saying that it is only the work of a handful of dissidents who were always a little kooky anyhow.

Instead, the dissenters are making an appeal, across the rift, to truth and to conscience. Where the question of truth is involved, they are unwilling to accept a thing as true just because someone says it is true. They are asking for reasons, and they are stating that the reasons the encyclical gives are not compelling. And since the encyclical makes no attempt to base its truth on Scripture or revelation, there is eminent justice in their demand that its conclusions be rationally compelling. And since the reiterated reasons it offers were not rationally compelling *before* the issuance of the encyclical, there are legitimate rational grounds for dissent from its mere reiteration of those reasons.

The appeal to conscience is a subtler and trickier appeal,

for it is easier to be led astray by appeals to conscience than by appeals to truth. If I say that something is not true, it can be demanded that I produce my evidence, and the matter can then be argued on the basis of criteria objectively available to all. But if I say that something goes contrary to my conscience, I am finally the sole arbiter of such a claim. Furthermore, my conscience may be ill-informed, or I may be using it as a device for giving moral sanction to something I want on other grounds.

Even so, the church in the past has always accorded a high place to the rights of conscience and has acknowledged that the criterion of conscience can be profoundly related to the criterion of truth, since conscience at its best strives to be true to what is ultimately true. Vatican II, for example, went on record officially as respecting the conscience of the man who says that he cannot participate in war, even though the majority of his fellow churchmen may feel that under identical circumstances such participation by them is justified. In an extension of this principle of conscience, many Catholic couples, and many priests and theologians, now believe that contraception is not only morally defensible, but that in certain cases it may be morally preferable to abstinence or the insecurities of rhythm, both of which can wreak untold psychic havoc on a marriage. And now they are not willing to give this belief up, simply because the pope says they must. To do so would be to deny their integrity, their rationality, and their humanity, and to deny also their devotion to a church which, when it is in error, must be corrected.

I see no way in which this crisis of authority can be resolved without great damage to the Roman Catholic Church. The priests, theologians, and lay people are not going to accept *Humanae Vitae* with the dutiful docility the curia expects, and the Pope is not about to admit that he was wrong. (A papacy that cannot yet be quite sure if a mistake was made about Galileo will be in no hurry to acknowledge that a mistake has been made about birth control.) In the past, of course, such an *impasse* was solved by time. Catholics can now look at *Unam Sanctam* and dismiss it as time-bound, and they can employ the same procedure with the *Syllabus of Errors* or Pius IX's characterization of the notion of religious liberty as a "nightmare." In these and dozens of other instances, there has been time for the church to adjust. With *Humanae Vitae* there is not. For not only does it appear in an age of instant communication, but it appears in an age where, if its teachings were widely followed, many well-informed people believe that the consequences in terms of population explosion could well destroy man's future.

Can one then do no more than throw up his hands in dismay? I believe there are other options and that the most important one centers around the pressing of the very principle the encyclical appears to have bypassed, the principle of collegiality. Heiko Oberman, a Protestant observer at Vatican II, stated that while it had affirmed the collegiality of the bishops, it might take Vatican III to affirm the collegiality of the pope. The crisis of authority in the church today indicates that even more than this will be needed, and that it will be needed considerably sooner than Vatican IV. What will be needed is an extension of the principle of collegiality to include the collegiality of the whole people of God, for example the drawing into the highest councils and decisions of the church of the priests, theologians, and laity. Such an extension could be justified on the controversy over birth control alone, for it is clear that the wisdom of the laity in this matter has exceeded the wisdom of the bishops, the bishop of Rome included. (Joseph Noonan has a cartoon in the *National Catholic Reporter*, August 21, 1968, p. 4, which shows a woman saying, "I keep asking myself 'Do I really have a better understanding of the matter than the Pope?' And I keep answering 'Yes.' ")

The church could learn from the experience of the reception of *Humanae Vitae* that the full exercise of teaching authority cannot rest with the bishop of Rome alone, nor even with the college of bishops alone, but must include the priests, theologians, and laity as well. Informally, the principle has long been acknowledged: the teaching of the church must correspond to the *sensus fidelium*. But the *sensus fidelium* in recent years has been highly elusive, particularly to inhabitants of Vatican City, to be intuited perhaps but never validated by a head court. Surely now, however, some kind of structure must emerge by means of which subsequent articulations of the Catholic faith can take account of the charisms that Vatican II insisted were not the exclusive prerogative of the hierarchy. The reception of *Humane Vitae* is a grim reminder that when the hierarchy speaks without "consulting the faithful in matters of doctrine," it paints itself into awkward corners.

Unfortunately, institutions being what they are, the extension of the collegial principle will not come overnight. In the meantime, papal authority has suffered a serious, possibly a fatal, blow. From the long perspective of history, men will look back on *Humanae Vitae* as a mistake subsequently corrected, just as earlier papal mistakes were subsequently corrected. But in the interval we can predict that men will look elsewhere for their moral insights, or at least that they will treat with respect only those future papal insights in which it is clear that the collegial principle has been employed, and that the faithful have been consulted.

It is that interval that is troubling, for during it so many lives will continue to be scarred, and having examined the institutional toll the encyclical will exact, we must now turn to the human toll.

5. The Immediate Victims

As I look at what the encyclical is doing to Catholics I both admire and care for deeply, I see a number of groups being hurt in ways that will leave permanent scars no matter how the controversy is finally resolved.

(1) Near the top of the list are the Roman Catholic couples who during or even before the years of papal indecision decided to follow their mutually agreed upon decisions about contraceptives and even found priests sympathetic enough to understand them. Such couples must now feel betrayed. The Pope demands something they cannot in conscience accept. They know better. They know that their use of contraceptives has not degraded the wife or led to sexual promiscuity or made their relationship "intrinsically dishonest," no matter how much the Pope may now insist on these things. They have been participating in the sacramental life of the church, and have been sustained by it. And now they face hard choices. They must either (a) forsake the sacraments because of their convictions, or (b) forsake their convictions at what may bring deep harm to their marriage relationship, or (c) walk the disturbing tightrope of giving formal allegiance to the teaching office of the church but failing to apply its specific teachings to their own lives. I imagine many will quietly drift away from the church. Those who stay will increasingly wonder about the integrity of a situation in which church membership necessitates a disregard of church teaching. Whatever they do, their anguish will be great.

(2) Even more deeply, perhaps, do I feel for almost all the priests I know. Most of them, sensing the mood of Vatican II, of contemporary theology and of the tenor of the papal commission's recommendations, had been confident that *some* change in teaching would come, and that in the interim, since the teaching of the church was in a state of doubt, it was right to counsel couples to follow the dictates of conscience. Now they face an agonizing dilemma: either give public assent to papal teaching, both in pulpit and confessional as the encyclical abjures them to do, at the cost of injuring the lives of people who have come to trust them; or dissent as the

price of maintaining personal integrity, and place their entire priesthood in jeopardy.[4] Even if no public action against them is taken, they will be left with the uncomfortable realization that there is a deep conflict between what they believe as individuals and what the church demands that they publicly affirm and impose upon the lives of others. A terrible dilemma will have been forced upon them—a realization that loyalty to Christ may demand disloyalty (as it will be interpreted) to his vicar on earth. A church that forces such a problem upon its ordained sons is in serious trouble. But I am even more concerned with what this does to the individuals than to the church, to those who have given their lives, with remarkable selflessness, to the service of the church, and now discover that common integrity jeopardizes the continuation of that service.

(3) A particularly poignant group of victims of the encyclical are Roman Catholics living in the underdeveloped nations of South America, Africa, and Asia. Sophisticated Roman Catholics in Europe and North America may find ways to square contraception and conscience, and even in the event of unexpected pregnancies, they will have the financial resources to cope with large families. But what of the illiterate and unsophisticated Catholics in the "third world," who, retaining a simplistic view of papal authority, will feel bound by the encyclical? Not only will they have increasingly large families they cannot support, but they will thereby contribute to the population explosion the demographers tell us has the human race already on the brink of disaster, and will do so precisely in those areas of the world most devoid of technological resources for development.

4. I find it hard to believe that the hierarchy is going to remove every priest who does not unquestioningly accept the encyclical, since to do so would decimate the leadership of the church. Nevertheless, at the time of writing the bishop of Buffalo had already removed seven priests from his seminary faculty and the archbishop of Washington had taken severe disciplinary actions.

It is simply not enough for defenders of the encyclical to urge us to produce more food and to increase technical assistance to underdeveloped areas of the world as a sufficient answer to this problem. Those things are drastically necessary *in their own right*, but as sufficient answers to the population explosion they are trivial. For population increases are geometrical, and there is simply not time to "perfect the rhythm method" and teach millions of unlettered persons all the subtleties of time-and-temperature charts. The encyclical, if enforced in the third world, can only leave a wake of personal and social tragedy, multiplying human misery, poverty, squalor, and despair. It may be a high responsibility of Protestant missions in these areas to make contraceptive information and devices available to all who desire them, however ecumenically divisive such a step might seem. Here is a place where concern for Christ's children must outweigh concern for Christ's institution.

6. The Long-Range Gains, or, Bringing Good out of Evil [5]

But all is not lost. In my years of ecumenical involvement I have always been impressed with the resiliancy of individual Catholics in the fact of ecclesiastical disappointment. Again and again at the Vatican Council, for example, setbacks that first plunged individuals into despair could be reinterpreted in a matter of days or even hours into modest triumphs. "It's really better that it happened this way," would be the beginning of a new appraisal. French theologians did the same thing after *Humani Generis* tried to clip their wings back in 1950. Either a theologian said, "I was not named, and my beliefs were not being proscribed, so I feel vindicated," or

5. In what follows I draw in part from "*Humanae Vitae:* An Ecumenical Boon?", *Commonweal* (September 6, 1968), pp. 595–596.

groups of them said, "The strictures were so mild that we interpret the encyclical as giving us a green light."

At the council I found this procedure initially impressive, then rather amusing in its predictability, and finally made the interesting discovery that I was joining in the game myself. And while I shall not now pretend that the Pope deliberately intended to do other than exactly what he did, namely, reiterate the traditional teaching on birth control in unequivocal fashion, I shall suggest that in fact the unintended consequence of his action may be to open the ecumenical doors wider than we could have dared to hope in the pre-*Humanae Vitae* era of ecumanical relations.

Before the appearance of *Humanae Vitae* Protestants looked upon papacy as the ultimate stumbling block to reunion. We feared that we would be required to submit our individual judgments of conscience to the voice of authority emanating from Vatican City, and subordinate our personal convictions to whatever was definitively spoken by that voice. We believed that our Catholic brethren would insist on this as a precondition of reunion, and that they were always prepared, at the end of the day of free discussion, to subordinate their own convictions and doubts, conforming them to authoritative papal teaching. We foresaw perhaps a half century of Faith and Order discussions with Catholics on the meaning of papal authority, with little assurance that the logjam could be broken.

But now, most of that tedious theological maneuvering has been rendered unnecessary. For if we Protestants were not able to submit our consciences to papal decrees in the past, it is now clear that we need not expect to do so in the future either. All we need insist upon is that our response to papal directives have the same degree of freedom presently being expressed by Catholics in their response to *Humanae Vitae*. Papal teaching, as many Catholic commentators on the encyclical have been pointing out, is *one* factor in the decision an individual Catholic makes, but it is not the only factor, and it may not even be the decisive factor. To paraphrase a line of reasoning I have encountered a dozen times over in recent weeks: just as the Pope went through great anguish in reaching *his* decision and consulted many authorities, so Catholic couples make *their* decision by (a) careful evaluation of all the facts, (b) conscientious reflection, (c) prayer, (d) examining the opinions of a variety of theologians, (e) reflecting on what the bishop of Rome thinks, (f) studying problems of population control, and (g) acquainting themselves with the psychology of marriage. After these and other factors have been fully weighed, a responsible personal decision must be made. The decision may be contrary to the pope's decision, but since he does not speak infallibly on such matters, one can responsibly disagree with him and act contrary to his instruction.

What more could a Protestant ask? What Protestant would be unwilling to consider what the pope says as one item in terms of which he reaches his own decision? In this sense, *Humanae Vitae* may inadvertently be the greatest gift to the ecumenical movement since the election of Pope John, for its reception shows conclusively that many traditional views of papal authority are no longer being taken seriously, and that loyal and committed Catholics feel no greater sense of being bound to questionable doctrine than do Protestants.

Curiously enough, anything less unequivocal than *Humanae Vitae* would have failed to produce such a result. (a) A statement leaving the decision about contraception up to individual couples would have been eminently credible, and the teaching authority of the papal office would have been buttressed by such a statement, so that earlier ecumenical hangups about papacy would have remained unchanged. (b) A statement advocating a "change" in Catholic teaching would also have been eminently credible. It would have been such a creative breakthrough that many Protestants would

212

have been forced to develop a new theology about an authoritative teaching office as a visible symbol of Christian unity, and the resultant controversy within Protestantism would have been divisive to the uttermost. (c) The encyclical, however, takes neither course, with the result that it cannot be described as credible, let alone "eminently credible." It is so out of touch with the modern world, so oblivious to the breakthroughs prepared for by Vatican II, so lacking in comprehension of the psychology of marriage, and so rigid and reactionary in its theological understanding of all of these matters, that it is impossible to accept it as a statement of Catholic teaching that exemplifies the claims traditionally associated with the solemn teaching authority of the papal office. Conservatives argue that the authority of the papacy would have been "compromised" by a change in Catholic teaching about birth control. How much more drastically it has been "compromised" by this refusal to change.

What, then, of the future of the papacy in the "coming great church"? The reception of *Humanae Vitae* makes clear that there will be great changes in the papacy of the future. I fully believe Pope Paul when he says that he reached his decision only after great personal anguish, and I can sympathize with how uncomfortable it must make even a pope to discover, in the storm of criticism, that the force of world opinion is ranged against him. But the very nature of the decision indicates how isolated the pope has become from the world around him, and how much indeed he is "the prisoner of the Vatican," in regular contact only with people who are at least as out of touch, if not more so, than he. Furthermore, the encyclical boxes him in and he is almost irretrievably harmed by his decision, no matter what he does subsequently. To hold the line without deviating can only alienate him further from the rest of the world and cause his teaching office to be taken less seriously. To change his position would win him the sympathetic appreciation of millions and yet would compromise even further the notion that his teaching office is based on divine authority.

The problem thus moves beyond the papal person to the papal office, and the credibility of the teaching office has been, if not destroyed, at least dramatically disturbed. For the vicar of Christ to be so wrong on a basic issue affecting millions of human beings can only suggest that he could be wrong on other issues as well. So when we conjecture about the future of the papacy, we can anticipate that it will surely be "there," and that it will not wither away, at least not for a long time. But it will be "there" more as a symbol of what once was a great power in determining the affairs of the church, than as the supremely effective power in directly the church in the future. It will be accorded the kind of veneration we extend to other offices and practices that once compelled the total allegiances of men but do so no more. It will remain formally true that the pope can speak in ways that bind the consciences of his followers, and that he could, if he chose, make an infallible pronouncement, but we will all know that his utterances will not, in fact, bind the consciences of his followers if they go contrary to those consciences, and that he will not attempt anything so foolhardy as an infallible utterance. It may be awhile before the college of bishops is all that it should be, and even longer before the full collegiality of all the people of God has become effective, but the bright future of both instrumentalities as the effective functioning forms of the future church was ensured on the day that *Humanae Vitae* was signed. And even though the bishop of Rome may still be called the supreme pontiff, he will *de facto*, I believe, gradually become *primus inter pares* with his fellow bishops, who, in turn, will become *primus inter pares* with all the faithful.

7. *Conclusion*

Whatever long-range good may thus come out of it, I must sadly conclude that the encyclical itself seems to me to be based on an inadequate theology of sex, embroidered with a deficient sociology of modern man and a faulty psychology of marriage. As such, it is far from the best of which Roman Catholic theology is capable. Therefore, I would like to believe that the encyclical could be buried and forgotten as soon as possible, but I realize that that is an exceedingly difficult thing to do with encyclicals. The next step, therefore, must be for all of us, Catholic and Protestant together, to develop a theology of contraception that will not only meet the needs of the times but be persuasive even to those presently persuaded by the encyclical. Until that has been done, following the example of those Roman Catholics whose integrity and convictions I admire most, I will refuse to believe that *Humanae Vitae* represents Rome's final and definitive word.

ANDRÉ E. HELLEGERS A SCIENTIST'S ANALYSIS

It is the function of the academician to analyze documents of importance to the area of his academic interest. This includes documents emanating from the Church. I hasten to add that it causes me no great difficulty to acknowledge that my analysis of the encyclical, and of what it entails, may be totally erroneous. It is one of the advantages of scientific training that one knows how common it is for scientists to make errors.

For the scientist the encyclical presents a number of puzzling aspects: in the first place comes the absence of scientific evidence for, or indeed of scientific thought in reaching, the conclusions which the encyclical draws. Secondly, the scientist is struck by the absence of biological considerations in the entire encyclical. It is striking that the first section which deals with "New Aspects," and which alludes to demographic, sociological, and educational problems, nowhere acknowledges that there might have been new biological facts of importance discovered since the encyclical *Casti Connubii*. Thus paragraphs 2 and 3 of the encyclical are written as if no biologist had ever been appointed to the Papal Commission. Equally interesting, but more ominous in this context, is paragraph 6. Here it is made clear that nothing that a present or future scientist could possibly contribute in terms of scientific data could have any pertinence to the subject, if certain criteria of solutions would emerge which departed from the moral teaching of marriage proposed with constant firmness by the teaching authority of the Church. To the scientist it is difficult to see why the Papal Commission should have been called at all. The teaching proposed with constant firmness by the Church was well known before the Commission was appointed, and it did not require the energy and financial expenditures involved in bringing several dozen consultants to Rome to gather information if, *a priori*, such information was to be eliminated if it led to different conclusions than in the past.

The implications of this paragraph extend far beyond the subject of contraception. The wording of the paragraph is of cardinal importance for the relationship between science and theology. The paragraph implies that theology need not take into account scientific data, but shall reach its conclusions regardless of present or future facts. Had the encyclical stated that the data, advanced by the commission, were wrong or irrelevant, or were insufficient to warrant a change in teaching, that would have been one thing. It is quite another thing to imply that agreement with past conclusions is the *sine qua non* for acceptance of a study. Such wording pronounces the scientific method of inquiry irrelevant to Roman Catholic theology.

The scientific paradox is, perhaps, compounded in paragraph 24 where the scientist is asked to "contribute to demonstrate in actual fact that, as the Church teaches, a true contradiction cannot exist between the divine laws pertaining to the transmission of life and those pertaining to the fostering of authentic conjugal love." Yet if the scientist must still contribute to this demonstration in actual fact, it would seem to follow that the matter has not as yet been demonstrated. The implication is therefore rather clear: that the encyclical is based on undemonstrated fact and that the function of the scientist is restricted to bringing forward such data as confirm the teaching of the past, but to reject such data as might be in opposition to its conclusions. This is, of course, the antithesis of scientific procedure.

I should make it crystal clear that I am not among those

who believe that the only course open to the Pope would be to accept the data and recommendations of a study commission. The Pope is obviously correct when he states that the conclusions which the commission arrived at could not dispense him from a personal examination of this serious question. Moreover, it is clear that if he found the data and conclusions, proferred by the commission, erroneous, he should disagree with them. The problem of the scientist is rather that the Pope nowhere disagrees with the data, but in essence pronounces them irrelevant *since they lead to conclusions different from those of the past.* It is therefore because of the *reasoning* of paragraphs 6 and 24 that the scientist will have particular difficulty in seeing where the scientific method has any relevance to the Roman Catholic Church.

The absence of scientific method comes out also in paragraph 17, in which the dire consequences of the use of contraception are described. I would not wish to confirm or to deny that these consequences may in fact exist, but I am not aware of any evidence to support the conclusion. It is therefore remarkable that it is implied that the conclusion might be arrived at by "upright men" who "care to reflect." The phraseology is all the more unfortunate in that it stamps many individuals on the Commission, including several bishops and cardinals, as either not "upright" or else as not caring to reflect. Again it is the assertion, in the absence of data, which is depressing to the scientist. It is equally unscientific to conclude that a dangerous weapon would be placed in the hands of public authorities "who take no heed of moral exigencies." Such governments are not dependent on fostering any particular method of birth control to reach their goals. They could just as easily "apply to the solutions of the problems of the community" the accepted rhythm method. They could leave the method of birth regulation entirely in the hands of individuals and simply exact fiscal and other restrictive penalties on those who fail. Moreover, it is exceedingly difficult to see how use of a method like *coitus interruptus* could be in any way prohibited or imposed.

Most of the remainder of this chapter, then, will be devoted to giving the biological data, from which many questions arise.

Biological Background to the Debate

The major cause of present family difficulties (as it is of the present population explosion) stems from the fact that not too long ago 50% of children born to a couple were buried before the age of five, but now they survive. In the past they were mourned for some time, but they did not contribute to the pressures which the modern family undergoes.

In addition to this decrease in the perinatal and infant mortality rate there are other factors which have increased man's ability to reproduce. One of these is the earlier occurrence of the menarche. For the United States it occurs, on the average, shortly after the age of twelve, that is, even before the recognized Canon Law age for marriage. It is known that the trend in the past century has been for the menarche to occur earlier than in previous centuries at a rate of four months per decade.[1] As a consequence sexual pressures which did not exist in the past are now present.

Other recent data [2] show that menstrual periods are recurring earlier after childbirth than before, regardless of whether mothers breast feed their children or not. This makes the spacing of children obviously more difficult than in the past.

Finally, just as the menarche is occurring earlier, so the menopause is being delayed and now occurs by and large at

1. J. M. Tanner, "The Trend Towards Earlier Physical Maturation," in *Biological Aspects of Social Problems*, ed. J. E. Meade and A. S. Parkes (New York, 1965).
2. E. Salber, M. Feinleib, and B. MacMahon, "The Duration of Post Partum Amenorrhea," in *Am. J. Epidem*, 82, 347 (1965).

the age of fifty.[3] With the delay in the menopause has come the ability to reproduce children at a later age, and since this is accompanied by an increased incidence in the birth of infants with congenital anomalies, a problem of quality of reproduction has been added to that of quantity.[4] Moreover, men and women who previously would have died in childhood from congenital diseases (like blue babies) or from acquired diseases (like diabetes) now survive to adulthood and present reproduction problems unlike those seen in previous generations.

At the level of the individual family all these facts mean that previously an average achieved family size, without any form of family planning, was about seven children. This number is now from twelve to fifteen. Sociological and educational difficulties involved in managing such a family will not be commented on in this chapter; they are too obvious to anyone.

From the population expansion point of view it is worth remembering that from 2.2 to 2.4 children per family would keep the population stable. The fact that this is not 2.0 children is due to non-marriage by a fraction of the population, and to the fact that approximately 10% of married couples have sterility problems. It is obvious then that an average of 3.0 children per generation causes an increase in population size of 0.6 children per family per generation. A simple expansion from an average of 3.0 to 4.0 children increases the surplus two and one-half fold from 0.6 to 1.6 per generation per family. Now it should be obvious to anyone who is acquainted with the average family size in the world today, that a 12-15 child family is a statistical aberration. In other words, something is being done about family planning. From the point of view of the teaching in the encyclical it would

3. "Age at Menopause, United States 1960–1962," National Center for Health Statistics, Series 11, Number 19 (Washington, October 1966).

4. T. McKeown, *Congenital Malformations*, ed. M. Fishbein (Philadelphia, 1961).

be nice if this could be ascribed to rhythm, but this is obviously nonsense. In the Western world marked decreases in family size long preceded the discovery of the notoriously inaccurate Ogino-Knaus method, and since the temperature-rhythm method was not properly developed until 1945 it will be obvious to anyone that rhythm was not the cause of this decrease in population size. It will be remembered that in France and Switzerland the transition from the large to small family occurred as early as the late eighteenth and early nineteenth century. From Table 1, giving data preceding the IUD and pills, and excluding sterilization and abortion, it is rather obvious—as is known to many Catholic priests with pre-1960 confessional experience—that *coitus interruptus* was the major method used for restricting family size. (When the ban on artificial contraception contained in the encyclical was first made public, it was my immediate reaction to think that the ban would simply entail a return to the method of *coitus interruptus* among Catholic populations.)

It is interesting to note that a recent post-encyclical booklet, issued by the archdiocese of Washington,[5] asks the following question (q. 25): "Can a Catholic who practices contraception continue to receive the sacraments?" The first paragraph of the answer goes as follows: "Not if they have made up their minds to go on practicing contraception. *One clear sign of such a frame of mind would be keeping contraceptives on hand.*" The next phrase in the answer is as follows: "But a couple who honestly tried to stop using contraception and fall into sin should not despair even if it happens over and over." A less subtle recognition of the role of *coitus interruptus* in a Catholic environment could hardly be imagined.

Elsewhere (q. 21) this same document states that "Unless methods like abortion and mass sterilization are used, population growth does not seem to level off until people have

5. P. O'Boyle, *Sex in Marriage; Love-giving, Life-giving*, Archdiocese of Washington (September 8, 1968), p. 22.

achieved, through education and economic development, the skill and motivation to control the size of their families. Stressing contraception as the answer to the population problems is putting the cart before the horse. Economic and educational development must come first." This indeed has been the experience in the Western world. What is obviously not stated, is that socio-economic development has led people directly to the use of contraception, not to the use of rhythm. The question arises whether the consistent support of papal social encyclicals like *Populorum Progressio* and others will not lead directly to practices condemned as intrinsically immoral in *Humanae Vitae*. Some indication of this interrelationship between socio-economic development and contraception can be seen in Figure 1 which compares the percentage of illiteracy in all countries with their birth rate.[6] A rapid perusal of the figure will show that, of the 50 countries with illiteracy rates of more than half the population, not a single country has a birth rate below 35. On the other hand, of the 30 countries with illiteracy rates below 10% only one (Mongolia) has a birth rate *above* 35 per thousand, and most birth rates are below 20 per thousand. In the intermediate group, one-half of the countries have birth rates below 35 and one-half above 35. It should be rather clear that the best method of avoiding the intrinsic evil of contraception on an international scale would be to keep countries in a state of illiteracy and poverty.

It might next be well to raise some questions about problems inherent in the rhythm method itself, since this is now clearly the only licit method available to Catholics, and since it is so much a source of confusion in Catholic circles.

Looking at the problem first at the population level, we may consider the logistics task facing the Church in getting the method diffused to the Roman Catholic population.

In 1966 there were approximately 233,000,000 Catholics be-

6. *World Population Data Sheet 1968*, Population Reference Bureau, Washington, D.C. (1968).

tween the ages of 15 and 45. Their geographic distribution was as follows: 104,000,000 in Europe, 82,000,000 in Latin America, 20,000,000 in North America, 15,000,000 in Asia, 1,000,000 in Africa, and 1,400,000 in Oceania.

It will be obvious that the physician force required to teach the rather complicated method would have to be present in proportions precisely opposite to the ones existing geographically in the world at present. This simply is to say that there where the need would be the greatest, the physicians would be the fewest.

The practicalities of the matter are that this leaves two options open to the Church: (1) disregarding the problem of population; (2) tolerating the provision of artificial contraceptives where there is an inability to do anything constructive within established guidelines of the encyclical. It is to be remembered that the above figures involve the Catholic population alone. One must multiply them by five or six to cover the entire world's population. It makes the present teaching, regardless of whether it is correct, irrelevant in practice. For demographic problems, recognized in Section 1 of the encyclical, rhythm is therefore not a solution at all. Thus also paragraph 23 of the encyclical, while lofty in intent, faces peculiar difficulties that not only disregard the implications of the data contained in Figure 1, but which offer solutions that are only pertinent to an economically developed élite who have access to the physicians required for the program. It is of some interest to note that the relatively most successful rhythm programs have been in France, Britain, Canada, and the United States, but even these have reached only a minuscule fraction of their own Catholic population. (A concerted effort on the island of Mauritius has added a further drop in the ocean.) It is obvious that these facts leave up in the air the question of how public authorities are to tackle the population problem, even if they agree with the conclusions of the encyclical.

The average person is not immediately faced with problems

on an international scale, and therefore it may be well to focus on the problem of the individual. If nothing else is done immediately, it would be beneficial for the Church's communications media to begin to point out that what is commonly called the rhythm method among Catholics is hopelessly out of date. The average Catholic here refers to the method of Ogino-Knaus (calendar rhythm), in which the individual woman hopes that she ovulates on the same day of her menstrual cycle as the statistical average of a large number of other women. Individual variations in time of ovulation and menstruation are so large that a recent study has come to the conclusion that 70% of women cannot effectively use this method.[7] Since this is the method of rhythm so commonly attacked by the popular press, and rightly so, we might do well to add our voice to its condemnation as useless. It might indeed be well if the word "rhythm" was never used in Church circles again, since it has come to be associated with this calendar method.

Medically well-informed people realize that the only periodic continence method which might be of benefit to couples is that in which the woman determines the time of *her own* ovulation, regardless of what is occurring in other women. This is done by taking a daily temperature and noting when a temperature increase of 0.5°F. occurs and *is maintained for three straight days*. A sufficient body of evidence is at hand to demonstrate that if intercourse is restricted to the days following these three days of temperature rise, the pregnancy rate will be negligible. It should be realized that in following this method about 60% of potential intercourse days are lost. It can, however, be confidently said that if the logistics problem could be overcome, the majority of couples should be able to use this method at *some* time in their life. It should also be frankly recognized that the majority of women

7. F. T. Brayer, L. Chiazze Jr., and B. J. Duffy, "Calendar Rhythm and Menstrual Cycle Range," in *Fertility and Sterility* (in press).

cannot use this method at *other* times in their life. The method is particularly poor at precisely those times when it is most needed, namely, in the post-partum period and in the several years preceding the menopause. Failure at these times leads to the particularly vexing problems of (1) non-spacing of children, (2) the birth of children at high maternal age, with the consequent risks of abnormal pregnancy outcome. There are, of course, in the modern world a number of other couples who will also not be able to use this method at all, due to the fact that husbands have itinerant jobs, so that their presence at home cannot be correlated with the vagaries of the thermometer. One may, however, expect that the encyclical will not alter the recent medical practice of "reinforcing nature," or "correcting defects of nature," which consists in suppressing "abnormal" ovulations which occur post-partum and before the menopause. That such ovulations should only be treated in Roman Catholics, and then only in married Roman Catholics with more children than they want, seems to have led to little serious questioning regarding the scientific justification for the "treatment." The "disease" can be simply described by saying that the ovulation is "abnormal" in that it prevents Roman Catholics from having intercourse without production of children.

In conjunction with the temperature method many physicians will also permit intercourse to take place *prior* to ovulation. This period of time is called the pre-ovulatory phase of the menstrual cycle. It is obvious that if intercourse is had closer and closer to the time of ovulation the chances of pregnancy increase. As a consequence it may be said that the *pre*-ovulatory phase of the menstrual is not really safe, while the *post*-ovulatory phase is exceedingly safe. Reference to Figure 2 will explain which parts of the menstrual cycle are being referred to. With increasing study, pregnancies have been observed with intercourse occurring as long as nine or ten days before the time of ovulation. For those women whose cycles are rather short the pre-ovulatory phase of the menstrual cycle is therefore hardly available for intercourse with real safety.

Again prescinding from a judgment on the logistics problem of rhythm, one would be hard put to describe the fraction of the female population to which the method is biologically inapplicable at times additional to the post-partum period and the time close to menopause. The figure 20% might be a first approximation.

It is likely, then, that scientists and many couples will continue their criticism of the rhythm method in terms of its efficacy and applicability.

Even more so, and probably progressively more so, they will be increasingly puzzled by the liceity of the rhythm system, and the illiceity of artificial contraception. It is here in particular that the scientist has difficulty. When the scientist considers the process of reproduction, or the "transmission of life," he analyzes it in terms of *all* the biological phenomena which bring about its occurrence. The Church's teaching on the difference between rhythm and artificial contraception views the biological process of life transmission only at the genital level. Not long ago Professor Thomas Hayes attempted a first analysis of some of the underlying scientific concepts [8] which draw into question the analysis of rhythm at the genital level alone. For a proper understanding of the difference between the scientist's and the theologians' analysis of rhythm we should rapidly review the process of human reproduction.

Fertilization can occur only once during a menstrual cycle. In the normal course of marital life the likelihood exists that a series of acts of intercourse occur which are rather randomly distributed around the time of ovulation. That is to say that some acts of intercourse may take place before, some during, and some after the time of ovulation. The acts of intercourse

8. T. L. Hayes, "The Biology of the Reproductive Act; its Application to Various Methods of Birth Control," in *Cross Currents*, 393 (Fall 1965).

are the result of a natural biological phenomenon—libido. The first point to be noted is that, in its considerations, the encyclical really disregards libido as an event based on biological nature. The biological nature of intercourse is treated at the genital level, as if there were no people attached to these genital organs. It would, in fact, be correct to state that the interruption of a randomly occurring set of acts of intercourse as is much an interference with the nature of reproduction as is interference with the act of intercourse itself. This is not to espouse the cause that libido should never be interfered with; it is simply to state that, if it is interfered with, man does in fact interfere with the biological nature of reproduction. Some physicians, more particularly in Europe, have spoken of the establishment of a "time barrier" to reproduction in rhythm, rather than the interposition of a physical barrier. To many theologians this has seemed to be quibbling with words. But to scientists, acquainted as they are with the importance of the randomness or non-randomness of processes, this is not so. Particularly is this not so when it is remembered that sperm have a more prolonged survival time than the ovum. It means, in short, that if the ovum should be fertilized by sperm deposited sometime before ovulation, there is inbuilt into the system the fact that such sperm shall be old by comparison to sperm which would have been more recently ejaculated. As a result the ovum may be fertilized by what has been called "aged sperm." It has in recent years been shown, in a variety of mammals, that such a disturbance in the timing of mating has serious consequences. It is not just that pregnancy occurs, but among the fertilized eggs there is a significant increase in spontaneous abortions and in abnormal offspring. This has been shown in the chick,[9] sheep, cow, and rabbit.[10] Although there may be an initial inclination

9. A. F. Nalbandov, and L. E. Card, "Effect of Sperm on Fertility and Hatchability of Chicken Eggs," in *Poultry Science*, 22, 218 (1943).

10. C. Thibault, "Analyse Comparée de la Fecondation et de ses Anomalies chez la Brebis, la Vache et la Lapine," in *Ann. Biol. Anim. Bioch. Biophys.* 7, 5 (1967).

to say: "Well those are animals and not humans," it would be imprudent to do so in the biological realm, since fundamental biological processes observed in animals have so frequently been duplicated in man. Until the present, few such studies have been carried out in man. They could hardly be done except by gathering data on the precise effects which various time intervals between intercourse and fertilization have on pregnancy outcome. Such data can be obtained in two groups of cases: (1) those impregnated by artificial insemination, (2) those impregnated in the course of using the temperature method.

It is therefore of some interest that a recent first study, which obviously must be confirmed by other investigators before its full impact can be accepted, showed that the sex ratio of infants born as a result of this sperm aging is altered.[11] When children were born following intercourse which preceded ovulation by more than five days, 65% of the children were boys and 35% were girls. The difference was statistically highly significant. The result, if confirmed, would suggest that those sperm leading to the birth of females die before those leading to the birth of males. It is already known that among spontaneous abortions in the human there is an excessive number of male fetuses.[12] This would not be surprising in the light of animal data. If "aged sperm" lead to an excess of male children, one might also expect there to be an excessive number of *male* spontaneous abortions. With respect to the production of infants with congenital anomalies, there are absolutely no data available at this time, nor are there likely to be for quite some time in the future. The incidence of congenital anomalies is too small to permit the drawing of

11. R. Guerrero, "Time of Insemination in the Menstrual Cycle and its Effects on the Sex Ratio," Harvard thesis (January 1968).

12. A. C. Stevenson, "Observations on the Results of Pregnancies in Women Resident in Belfast. III. Sex Ratio with Particular Reference to Nuclear Sexing of Chorionic Villi of Abortions," in *Ann. Hum. Genet.* 23, 415 (1959).

conclusions on the basis of the study of small samples. The question of a *possible* relationship between the phenomenon of sperm aging and the production of congenital anomalies, such as mongolism, has already been raised in the literature, amongst others by the author.[13] While this should therefore not at present be a cause of worry in practice, it should certainly be so at the theoretical level.

The animal studies, and this first human one, are raised because of the implications they have for a concept of rhythm as simply the avoiding of intercourse. In paragraph 3 of the encyclical it is stated, "It is also asked whether, in view of the sense of responsibility of modern man, the moment has not come for him to entrust to his reason and his will, rather than to the biological rhythms of his organism, the task of regulating birth." To the scientist the paragraph represents a paradox. The paradox is not new. Rhythm is presumably a practice considered as entrusting responsible parenthood to "the biological rhythms of his organism." The result, however, is that intercourse is had at times precisely opposed to the biological rhythms of the organism, that is, intercourse is had when there is no ovum. It seems to the scientist rather illogical to indulge in the practice of avoiding ova in the name of conforming to the natural law.

If the production of optimum offspring is best produced by a random set of acts of intercourse around a single point of ovulation, the question is in how far the positive interference with this randomness can be described as the *absence* of a reproductive act (even though there is absence of a genital act), when optimum pregnancy outcome may be precisely related to not interfering with the randomness of intercourse. It raises the entire question of man's responsibility not just for the quantity of children produced, but also

13. A. E. Hellegers, "Medical and Public Health Aspects," in *World Population and U.S. Government Policy and Programs*, ed. F. T. Brayer (Washington, 1968).

for their quality and biological fate. In brief, quite apart from the matter of logistics, or that of efficacy in the prevention of pregnancy, the biological implications of the rhythm method for the quality of reproduction have as yet been insufficiently thought through. This is, of course, only a biologist's view and may have absolutely no implications for the moral order.

It will have been noted that I have not attempted a psychological analysis of rhythm. Since psychology and psychiatry are areas outside of my competence it would be unwise for me to attempt to do so. Two problems are so commonly brought up, however, that they are worth a comment.

The first is the commonly stated assertion that rhythm is unnatural in that it deprives couples of intercourse at precisely the time of maximum libido. I am firmly convinced that there are no scientifically valid data which would confirm that there is a significant increase in libido at the time of ovulation, except perhaps in those practicing rhythm.[14]

More common, however, is the observation that rhythm leads to acts of intercourse which are not strictly related to libido, but which result from the exigencies of the thermometer or calendar. It is interesting that in paragraph 13 of the encyclical it is stated, "It is a fact justly observed that a conjugal act imposed upon one's partner without regard for his or her condition and lawful desires is not a true act of love and therefore denies an exigency of right moral order in the relationship between husband and wife." All would agree with this statement if it referred to forcible rape. It is my personal opinion, however, that many Catholics who practice rhythm feel that the rhythm system leads to acts of intercourse which come close to the description in this paragraph —with the calendar or thermometer being the external "im-

14. L. A. G. J. Timmermans, *Huwelyksbeleving van Katholieke Jong-gehuwden, Deel III. Mens en Gezin* (Utrecht-Nymegen, 1964).

posing" agent. To my knowledge no adequate scientific data exist which would confirm or deny my opinion.

There also remains, with the acceptance of rhythm, a problem of language. In several places in the encyclical the term "open to the transmission of life" is used in connection with the act of intercourse. I think it is agreed after the encyclical, even if it might not have been so by all before, that rhythm is a licit method of conception control. Indeed, for the second time a pope has urged the scientific community to improve the method. Precisely what is meant by making the method "sufficiently secure" is not known, but this term is generally interpreted as perfecting the method. At this juncture it might be well to consider for a moment the consequences of such "perfect rhythm." It seems to me that one of the first difficulties is the fact that then, in spite of knowing with 100% assurance that a given act of intercourse will not lead to the birth of a child, the act of intercourse will nevertheless be "open to the transmission of life." The Catholic Church has previously used the terminology *"actus per se aptus ad prolis generationem."* The rhythm system has made this term almost ununderstandable in lay circles. On the one hand one is taught that it is *the act* which is *per se* apt; we have then established rhythm clinics where, by means of a thermometer, we teach that the act need not be apt at all but that it all depends on whether the stage of the menstrual cycle is such that the *woman* is apt to conceive. A language problem therefore arises. The concept of "open" and "closed" to the transmission of life clearly has nothing to do with the biological consequences, nor does it deal with the intent, since with the perfection of rhythm, both at the level of intent and at the level of fact, no transmission of life can occur. It will therefore be of some importance to develop a terminology which will make this concept of "openness" to the transmission of life understandable even when scientifically it will be 100% closed. Some physicians have already had difficulty in this concept. In women who have passed the natural menopause, or in whom the menopause has occurred through a surgical operation, it occurs not infrequently that with the changed balance of hormones they develop a particular kind of vaginal infection. The difficulty in its treatment is that, if intercourse is continued, the particular organism causing the infection (*Candida albicans*) can be transmitted to the male, who can then retransmit it to the female at the next intercourse, even though she may have been in the meantime successfully treated. Thus the infection is perpetuated. Two options are open to the physicians: (1) advising the patient not to have intercourse during the time of therapy, or (2) advising the husband to use a condom during intercourse.

I have on several occasions explained these options to patients. While the term "condomistic intercourse" has a particularly odious connotation in Catholic circles, it had somehow never entered my mind that in this particular case any moral significance could be attached to the wearing of a condom. Since the patients were past the menopause it seemed in my naïveté that "openness to the transmission of life" could not possibly be involved. I have been fascinated since then to learn that the wearing of a condom in such cases might, by some, be considered an interference with "openness of the act to the transmission of life." It will be particularly difficult to explain to the modern lay mind that such acts of postmenopausal intercourse can be open to the transmission of life at all.

The consequences of perfect rhythm will also require some further explanation. When absolute assurance of nonreproduction in an act of intercourse exists with the perfect rhythm method, why will the same dire consequences, predicted in paragraph 17 of the encyclical, not befall those who practice perfect rhythm? The privileged aspect of perfect rhythm, as a method, should be explained with some clarity in the light of paragraph 17.

232

Is its acceptance based on the presence of a given failure rate? This hardly seems likely since other contraceptive methods also have failure rates.

Is the acceptance based on the abstinence involved? Does it in fact only open a "narrow and difficult" road towards conjugal infidelity in contrast to the "wide and easy road" predicted for artificial contraception? If abstinence is the crux of it, the matter could of course have been dealt with by an encyclical advocating abstinence for all, including the users of artificial contraception, as indeed some physicians advise.

While I grant the value of abstinence, is it thought that the dangers of artificial contraception lie in the possibility of unlimited intercourse? This seems unlikely since our forefathers, by burying half their children, were indeed not restricted in their intercourse. Moreover, in the 10% of couples who presently have sterility problems this speculation regarding effects of unlimited intercourse does not seem to arise. I am not acquainted with any data which would suggest that the husbands of sterile women, or the wives of sterile husbands, come to the point of considering their spouses mere instruments of selfish enjoyment and no longer as their respected and beloved companions. If indeed our forefathers did so consider their wives, then it would seem to me that the introduction of contraception in the modern age has not yet yielded evidence that modern women are less respected and beloved companions than their predecessors. In short, some consideration should be given as to how to explain the essential difference in morality between perfect contraception and perfect rhythm, when both totally divorce intercourse from procreation. It will have to be explained why the one constitutes "openness to the transmission of life" and the other not.

These, then, are a variety of problems which result from the Church's rejection of contraception and its acceptance of perfect rhythm. Whatever can be said for the matter one fact can be agreed to by all. It is clear that through the ages the

Church has protected the "good of procreation." Whether this good is an invariable good is another matter. More problematical will be how the Church will protect "the good of procreation" when perfect rhythm is developed. It would seem to me that although the present tendency is to worry about excessive procreation, one might begin to think about what the implications of perfect rhythm would be. Already those who have worked in temperature clinics have encountered the totally and absolutely successful temperature method user, who, after a while, comes to realize that the moral problem is no longer one of whether to use effective contraception or effective rhythm, but rather the one of whether to reproduce or not to reproduce. It is precisely here that the major moral problems will occur for mankind in the future regardless of what the perfect method of fertility control will be. Whether births are regulated through perfect contraception or perfect rhythm the question arises: what are the objective criteria by which a judgment is to be made as to whether to reproduce or not. Frequently, it is thought that the acceptance of artificial contraception would lead to an absence of objective criteria by which it might be judged whether the contraceptives could be used. The problem already exists with the present day effective rhythm user, and would obviously exist for all if rhythm were to be perfected. This is a question then which is independent of methodology, and it is in this matter that perhaps the greatest moral leadership could have been expected from the Catholic Church. The fact of the matter is that no other organization is at present effectively addressing itself to this fundamental question. It had been my hope that the Catholic Church might have taken over the leadership in this entire area, but, by its differentiation between perfect rhythm and perfect contraception, this is not the moral question to which the present encyclical has addressed itself. It looks, therefore, as though in the foreseeable future we shall rather return to the types of legal analyses by which answers to practical problems, connected with the present stage of the rhythm method, will be sought in looking for loopholes and in casuistry. It is a depressing thought. It is a little wonder that some of the loudest reactions to the encyclical have come from priests and doctors who have had several years of experience in practicing an exquisite form of intellectual dishonesty in passing patients to each other for the purpose of legitimizing the "treatment" of "diseases," which exist only in married Catholics. One question will be whether, after the encyclical, the moral courage will exist among both priests and doctors simply to state outright to patients that they have no disease, and that the only honest answer to their problem is to refrain from intercourse altogether. Such advice would involve virtually all post-partum women, and most women between the ages of forty and fifty, as well as perhaps a quarter of all other women. This is too depressing a thought for the present. It is therefore perhaps more realistic to expect that the morally devastating games of the past years will be continued until such time as the rhythm method is really perfected, and the fundamental problem regarding the duties to procreate can finally emerge. It may then be realized fully that the method of fertility control was not the primary moral problem at all.

In the meanwhile, those who would hasten that moment would do well to be realistic. From all sides research in reproductive biology is verbally encouraged. Popes and prelates have urged it. But it remains a simple fact of life that not one single Roman Catholic organization has ever donated a research chair in reproductive biology at a Roman Catholic university, or the research space, or the research support, with the exemplary exception of the Christian Family Movement, which recently took the initiative in supporting a research laboratory at one Catholic university. Recriminations as to who are good Catholics and who are bad Catholics will fly back and forth in archdiocesan newspapers, but until such time as Catholics individually, and in concert, support the necessary research it is doubtful that the present encyclical will carry much practical force at the level of the individual family. Forced into a choice between the welfare of their family and a teaching which does not even claim adherence on the basis of the quality of the arguments advanced the numbers using contraception are likely to increase. This is likely to be so regardless of the *verbal* adherence given to the encyclical.

Perhaps some of the problems in the encyclical will be clarified by further papal statements. This would be particularly desirable in the matter of the relationship between theology and science.

15. J. Sutter and S. Siebert, "Attitudes devant la Maternité," in *Population* 18, 655 (1963).

16. V. G. Valaoras, A. Polychronopoulou, and D. Trichopoulos, "Control of Family Size in Greece," *Pop. Studies* 18, 265 (1965).

17. L. Andolsek, quoted by K. Mehlan, in "The Socialist Countries of Europe," in *Family Planning and Population Programs*, ed. B. Berelson *et al.* (Chicago and London, 1965).

18. D. V. Glass, in *Research in Family Planning*, ed. C. V. Kiser (Princeton, 1962).

19. *Kotzponti Statisztikai Hivatal*, Budapest, 7 (1963).

20. B. Berelson, *Turkish Seminar on Population*, Istanbul (April, 1964).

21. Timmermans, *op. cit.*

22. C. A. Mira, "Some Misconceptions Disproved: A Program of Comparative Fertility Surveys in Latin America," in *Family Planning and Population Programs*, *op. cit.*

23. L. T. Badenhorst, "Family Limitation and Methods of Contraception in an Urban Population," in *Pop. Studies* 16, 294 (1963).

24. "Sixth Opinion Survey on Family Planning and Birth Control in Japan," Tokyo, Mainichi Newspapers, 29 (1961).

25. R. M. Pierce and G. Rowntree, "Birth Control in Britain," in *Pop. Studies* (July and November, 1961).

26. C. F. Westoff, R. G. Potter, P. C. Sagi, and E. G. Mishler, *Family Growth in Metropolitan America* (Princeton, 1961).

TABLE 1

Frequency Ranking of *Coitus Interruptus* among Contraceptive Methods (Excluding Douching) and Most Used Method, by Country, for Given Year

Country	C.I. Ranking	1st Ranked Method	Year of Study or Publication	Footnote Reference
France (Grenoble)	1	—	1961-1962	15
Greece	1	—	1965	16
Yugoslavia	1	—	1963	17
Czechoslovakia	1	—	1961	18
Hungary	1	—	1959	19
Turkey	1	—	1964	20
Netherlands (R.C.)	2	Rhythm	1964	21
Netherlands (non-NVSH)*	2	Rhythm	1963	21
Netherlands (NVSH)*	4	Condom	1963	21
Colombia (Bogota)	2	Rhythm	1963-1964	22
Venezuela (Caracas)	2	Condom	1963-1964	22
Costa Rica (San Jose)	2	Condom	1963-1964	22
Mexico (Mexico City)	3	Rhythm	1963-1964	22
Brazil (Rio de Janeiro)	3	Rhythm	1963-1964	22
South Africa	2	Condom	1963	23
Japan	3	Condom	1965	24
Britain	2	Condom	1961	25
U.S.A.	4	Condom	1961	26

Note: 1) Table excludes pills, IUD's, abortion, sterilization.
2) The frequency of rhythm preceding *coitus interruptus* in ranking is high. The use in combination is frequently not given.

* NVSH—Netherlands Society for Sexual Reform

FIGURE 1

THE RELATIONSHIP BETWEEN BIRTH RATE AND LITERACY 1968

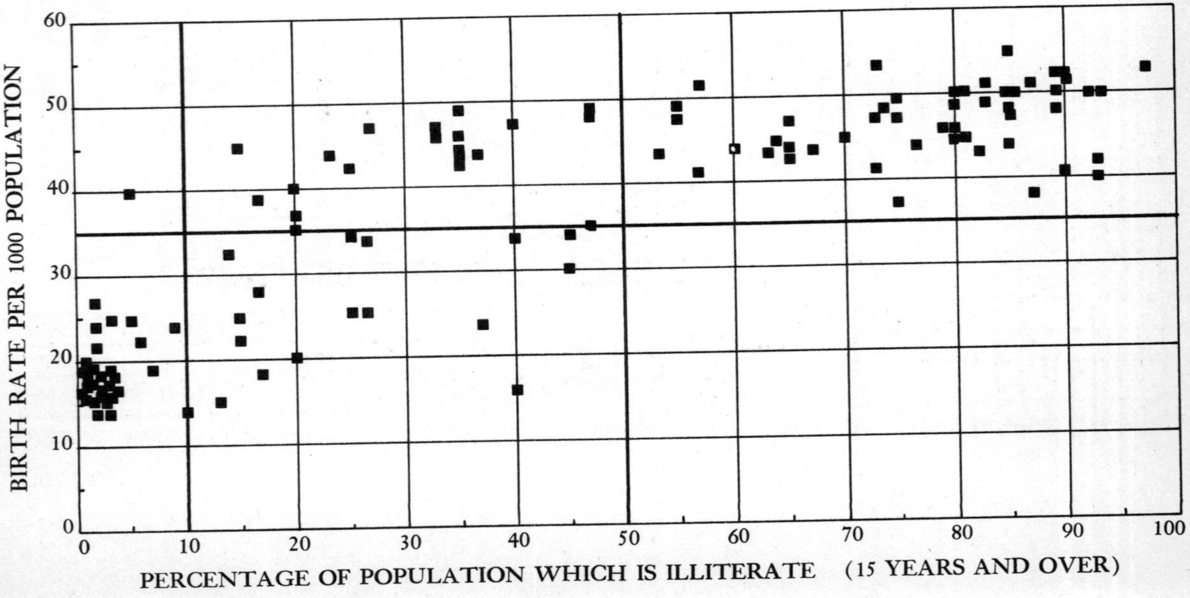
BIRTH RATE PER 1000 POPULATION
60
50
40
30
20
10
0
0
10
20
30
40
50
60
70
80
90
100
PERCENTAGE OF POPULATION WHICH IS ILLITERATE (15 YEARS AND OVER)

FIGURE 2

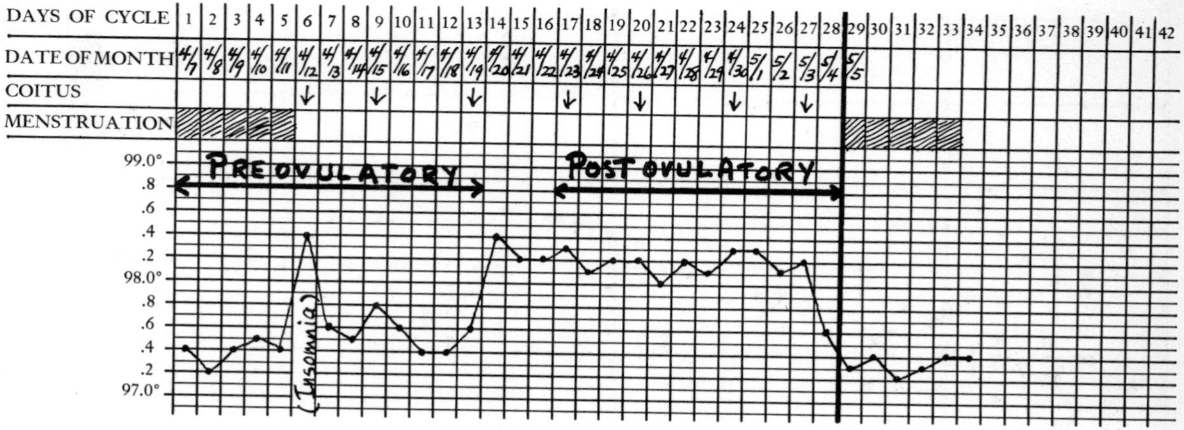
DAYS OF CYCLE
1 2 3 4 5 6 7 8 9 10 11 12 13 14 15 16 17 18 19 20 21 22 23 24 25 26 27 28 29 30 31 32 33 34 35 36 37 38 39 40 41 42
DATE OF MONTH
4/7 4/8 4/9 4/10 4/11 4/12 4/13 4/14 4/15 4/16 4/17 4/18 4/19 4/20 4/21 4/22 4/23 4/24 4/25 4/26 4/27 4/28 4/29 4/30 5/1 5/2 5/3 5/4 5/5
COITUS
MENSTRUATION
99.0°
.8
.6
.4
.2
98.0°
.8
.6
.4
.2
97.0°
PREOVULATORY
POSTOVULATORY
(Insomnia)